GYMNASTIC EXERCISES FOR
HORSES

"Build up your horse with simple exercises."
Nuno Oliveira

First published 1995

(Originally published as
Gymnastic Exercises for Horses
1985, 1987, 1989)

Equine Educational
(R.H. & M.A. Kerrigan)
"Marooan"
Lochinvar
NSW 2321
AUSTRALIA 1995

E and E RUSSELL
©E and E RUSSELL 1995

Typeset by Right Pc's Singleton, N.S.W
Printed By Alken Press Smithfield, N.S.W

ISBN 1 875381 14 7

THE CONTENTS OF THIS BOOK ARE SUBJECT TO COPYRIGHT
All right reserved. NO part of this publication may be reproduced in any manner, stored in any retrieval system, or transmitted in any form or by any means, electronic, mechanical, photocopying, recording or otherwise, without the prior permission in writing of the publishers.

INTRODUCTION

This note book is a collection of exercises to assist the physical and mental development of the horse's body.

Dressage to me has always been the physical and mental development of the horse's body to make him more pleasant to ride and to prolong his useful life. Horses that are gymnastically fit and supple are far less likely to break down when asked for a major effort, than a stiff and nervous horse whether they be showjumpers or dressage horses.

Since Franz Mairinger died, there have been quite a variety and number of trainers giving schools in this country. As most of them had exercises for horses, also a great variety, and it is so hard to remember all of them, it seemed to me that as they were all a variation on the same theme (Classical Training) it might be a good idea to collect them into a notebook.

It is difficult to know how many exercises to include; friends have said too many will confuse! Also, someone said, if you cannot get your horse correctly on the bit, the exercises are of no benefit, and if you can, you will not need the exercises. This seemed a bit defeatist to me. So what follows includes brief notes on getting your horse on the bit, on lungeing, and on aids when mounted.

But, primarily it is a collection of exercises (up to medium level) to help develop your horse's muscles to give him more strength. The repetition and design of the exercises teach him greater obedience, all combined to give him confidence in doing what you request, and so the resultant relaxed and happy combination becomes just that.

Eleanor Russell 1995

CONTENTS

Brief Do's & Don'ts When Lungeing	1
To Assist to Bring a Green Horse or Young Horse on the Bit	3
Warming Up Exercises	6
Shoulder-In Exercises	8
Serpentines	14
Loosening the Horse's Shoulders	16
And so: to Downward Transitions	18
Another Exercise for Loosening the Horse's Back	20
Exercises to Improve the Horse's Canter	22
Exercises Using Hindquarters-In	24
Half-Pass	30
Another Exercise to Help with Half-Pass	32
Notes & Exercises on Developing Collection	35
Counter-Canter	38
Exercise to Help the Horse Bend his Hind Legs	40
Extended Trot Exercises	42
Preparation for Flying Changes	45
An Exercise to Teach Your Horse a Single Flying Change	46
Another Exercise to Teach a Young Horse His First Flying Change	48
Exercises to Improve Single Flying Changes	50
Another Exercise to Improve Flying Changes	51
Exercise to Relax and Stretch	52
Active Regular Walk	54
Exercises with Cavalettis	55
The Rider's Balance	57
Starting of You and Your Horse	58
The Use of the Cavaletti as a Jumping Foundation	59
"InOuts"	66
To Lengthen the "InOuts"	68
To Shorten the "InOuts"	70
Trot and Pop	72
Extra Exercises	75
Exercises for an Enthusiastic Horse	78
Variation on Cavalettis:1	81
Variation on Cavalettis:2	83
Variation on Cavalettis:3	84
Exercises for Turning	86

Brief Do's & Don'ts When Lungeing

Do Vary your voice to command and reward.

Do Allow your horse to develop his natural cadence, even if it appears in the beginning a little slow. As he gains his balance, and more strength, he will be able to maintain his cadence with a stronger tempo.

Do Vary the size of the circle

Do Make 1001 transitions.

Do Have light contact when the horse is doing what you ask - strong contact will encourage him to tilt his ears (poll) out and twist his head and to sometimes lean on the forehand

Do Lengthen and shorten the strides in each gait.

Do Watch for rhythm, that is, regular, even, balanced, cadenced strides.

Do Look at his back muscles flexing and relaxing.

Do Sometimes bring the horse's forehand in towards a smaller circle for a few strides in his own balance, then let him enlarge the circle again at the same time encourage him to stretch down with his head and neck - reward him with your voice and repeat a few times.

Do Sometimes include a small jump as a gymnastic exercise (NO side reins).

Do Watch for "Tracking Up", that is, whether the horse's hind feet are landing in front of the front hoof print. For lengthened strides the hind feet should overstep more.

Don't Use short side reins - this teaches your horse evasions, such as to hollow his back.

Don't Make your horse go too fast. Momentum is **NOT** impulsion!

Don't Let your horse become bored.

Don't Lunge in too small an area. A few small circles during the lungeing are good gymnastically, but the circle should be large enough for a young horse to canter forward comfortably.

Don't Forget, lungeing may improve your horse, but it can be physically exhausting on the animal so take care. Lungeing doesn't improve your riding position or your physical fitness.

To Assist to Bring a Green Horse or Young horse on the Bit

Everybody has ways of getting the horse to come on the bit. The way I find easiest is by getting the horse to accept your inside leg. This can be achieved by two or three ways, but somehow he has to learn to move 'sideways forward'.

You can teach him the beginnings of the turn on the forehand with you on the ground.

Face your horse to the wall or a fence, stand beside him and gently tap with the handle of a whip just behind but close to the girth, help him by a small vibration on the rein on the same side. If he steps one step sideways with his hindlegs, stop, and pat him! If he doesn't, you should tap increasingly harder and perhaps also on the hindquarters until he does get the message. The important thing is to **stop** and reward him as soon as he takes **one** step with his hindlegs sideways.

Begin again with the lightest of taps and if necessary increase the tap until he steps away again (only with his hindlegs). Always, always, begin again with the lightest of taps.

When he has got the message, repeat on the other side. Do not forget, to pat and reward him immediately he steps sideways with his hindlegs.

After a couple of days try it mounted, for preference with someone on the ground to give the same taps and you gently give your leg aid at the same time, all just, behind but close to, the girth.

Do make much of him whenever he does what you ask. And, stop before he gets bored, a little well done is not just enough - **it is wonderful!**

A day or two later, advance to thinking 'turn on the forehand walking forward' and before you know where you are, you are doing 'sideways forward', 'leg yielding', 'beginnings of shoulder-in', whatever you want to call it, and even better your horse has dropped his head and appears to be accepting the bit.

The very instant he gives in his poll (relaxes his jaw) you must 'give', that is lightening the weight in the reins. You must have some contact in the reins so that when he gives, you have something to give also.

You can now walk in a circle and enlarge the circle by pushing the horse out onto a larger circle using your inside leg. Alternate two to three steps sideways with walking forward and another two to three steps sideways on the circle. Don't push with your inside leg, give a clean aid of squeeze and relax, if no reaction, follow quickly with a kick and then relax

Next try the same at a trot, not fast, remembering to give with the reins as soon as your horse drops his head - relaxes in the jaw and poll - and begins to accept the bit.

You can now use this beginning of training to help with warming up exercises.

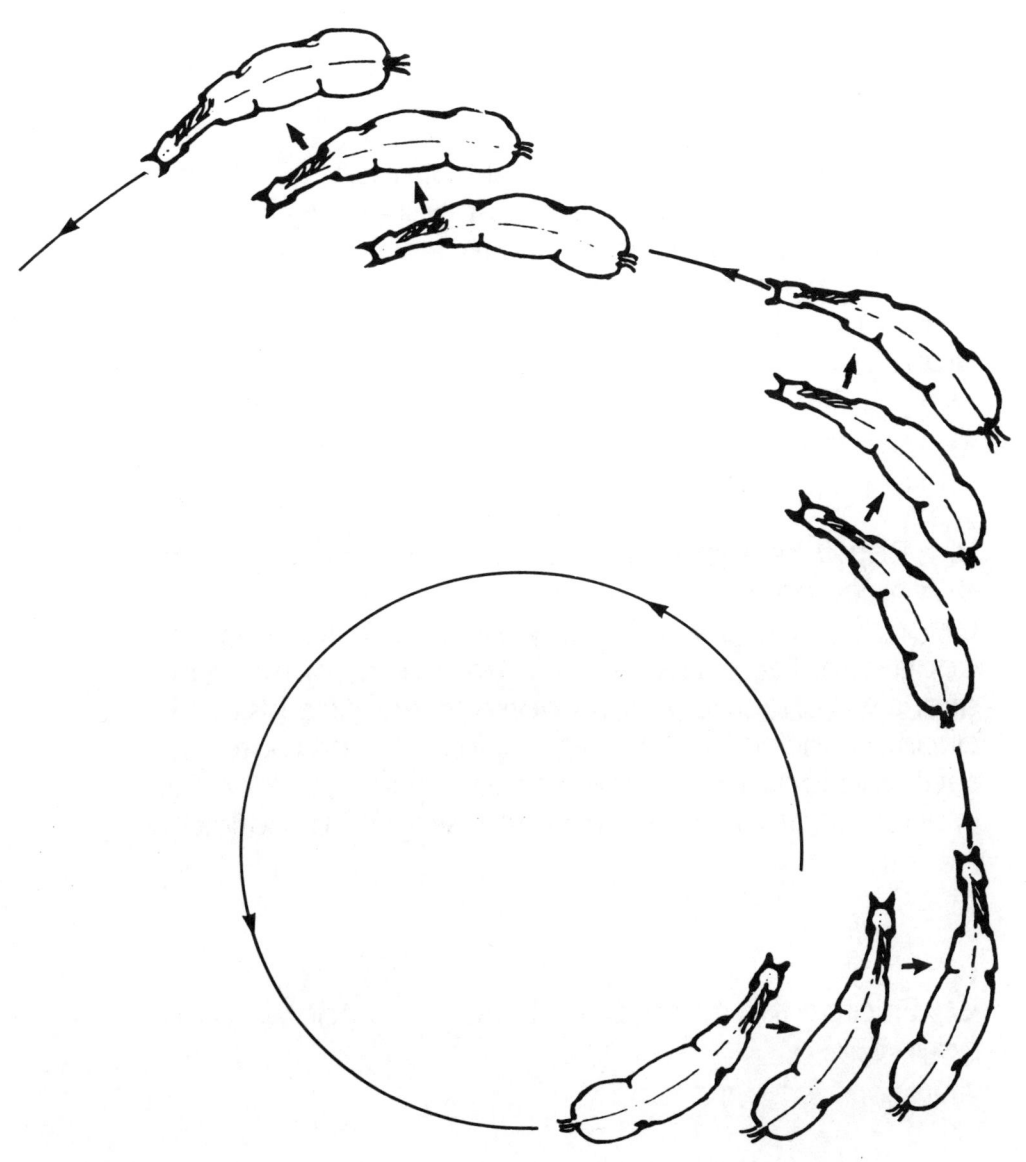

DIAGRAM 1

Warming Up Exercises

1. At walk or trot on a long rein with light contact, move away from the wall, in response to your new inside leg (e.g. on right rein apply left leg to move away from wall), then back to the wall using the other leg as the inside leg and repeat. (see Diagram 2)

2. Rapid sequences of transitions, anywhere, for example, on a circle, on the long side, across the diagonal, doing whatever your horse's training will cope with. The quickness and frequency of the transitions will encourage your horse to engage his hindquarters and so become lighter in front. The more the seat and leg aids are used, and the less the hand is used, is what will make the exercise most beneficial.

3. Enlarge the circle at walk, trot, and canter as on page 58

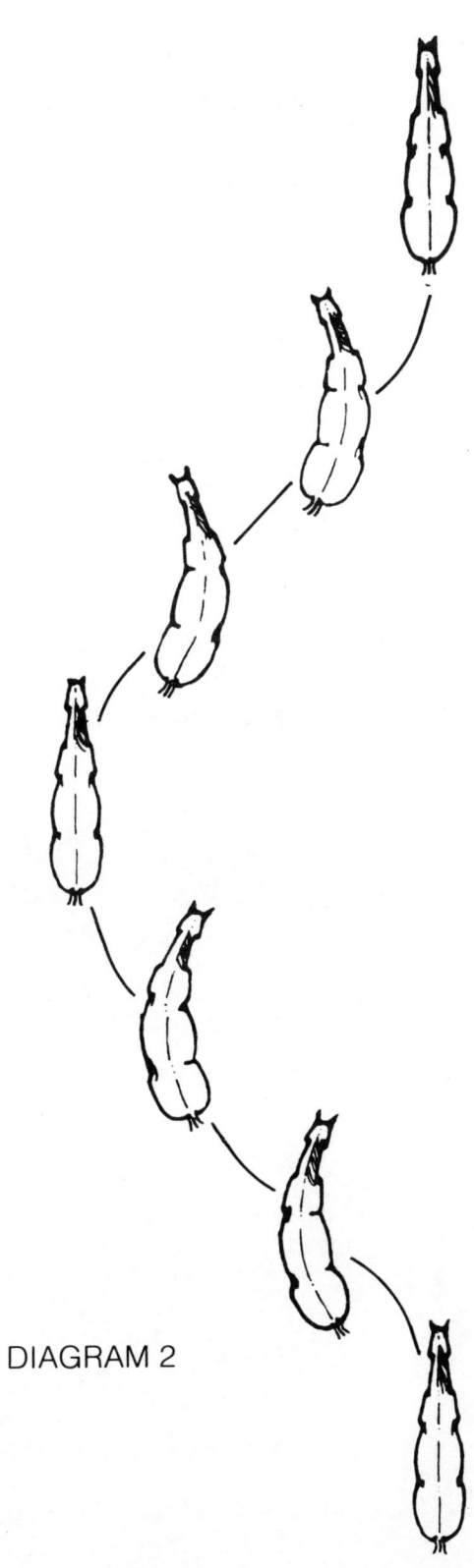

DIAGRAM 2

Shoulder-In Exercises

1. Walk along the short side of the school, try to walk correctly around the corner - if necessary taking the inside rein a little away from the inside neck to lead the horse around the corner (as on page 86), then bring your hand back to the neck. Now very carefully bring the horse's forehand and shoulders a little off the track, as if to begin a small circle. At the same time use the inside leg on the girth and push the shoulders sideways. The hands will, very lightly, now take and give a little to allow the shoulders to move sideways away from the inside leg.

After two to three little steps of shoulder-in, stop and pat him, and allow him to walk forward in the direction he was facing. (see diagram 3).

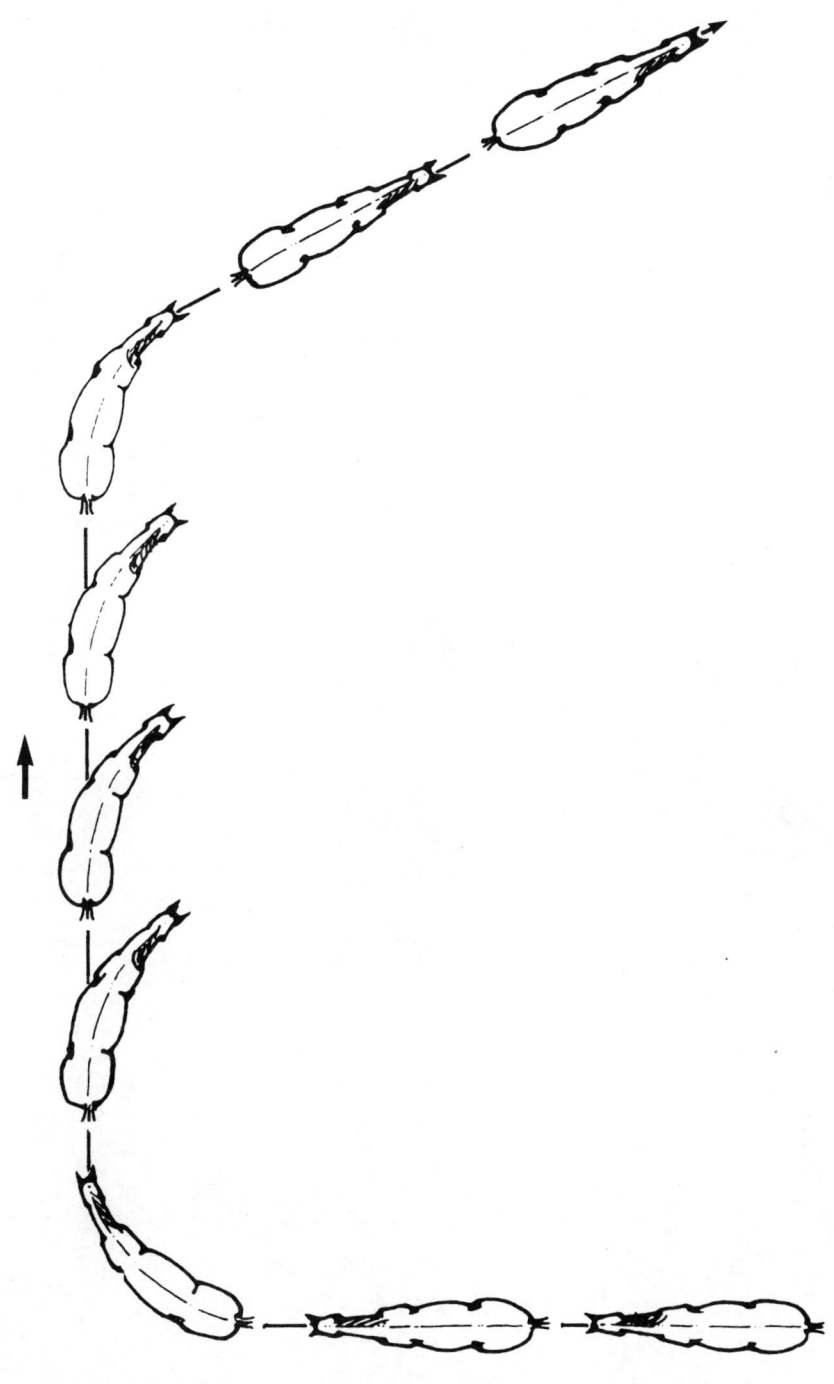

DIAGRAM 3

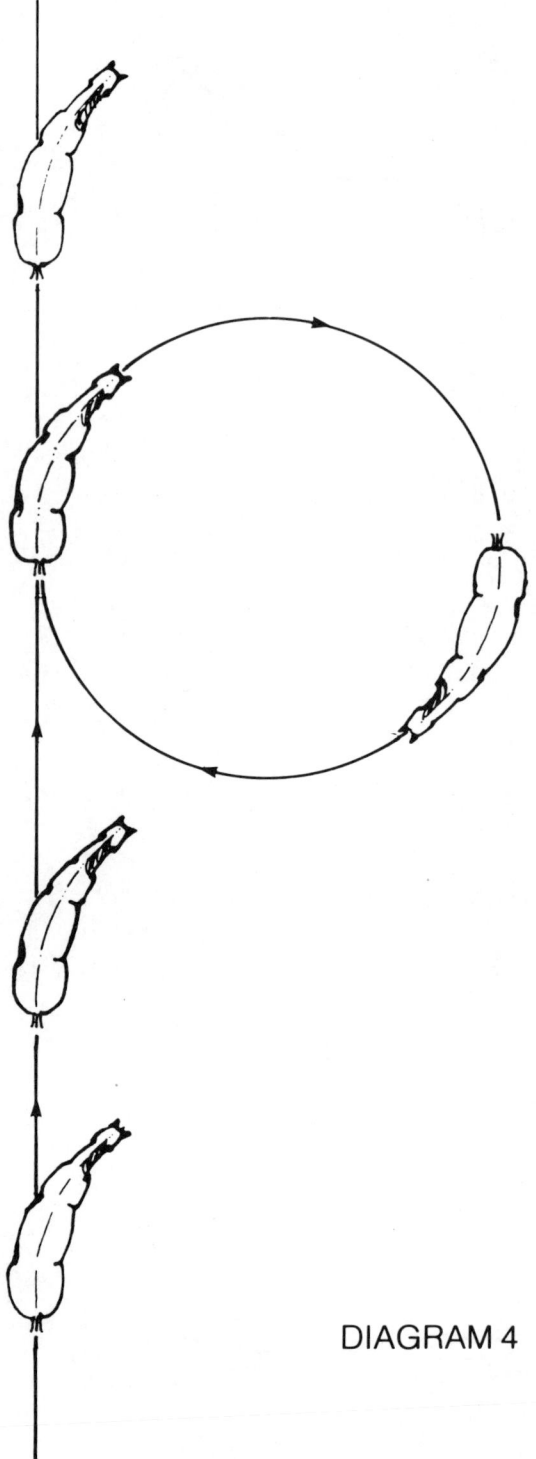

2. When your horse will do three to four steps shoulder-in at walk either to the right of left, then include the small circles as in diagram 4. This enables you to make more use of the outside rein, your horse is also accepting your aids to a greater degree. This exercise can be repeated often.

DIAGRAM 4

3. Walk along the short side and out of the corner and begin your shoulder-in. When your horse has done three to four balanced and cadenced steps then, through the use of the outside rein, walk forward straight across the school to the other side, turn to the opposite direction and begin the other shoulder-in. After two to four steps that are again balanced and feel good, walk straight forward again and begin the exercise again.

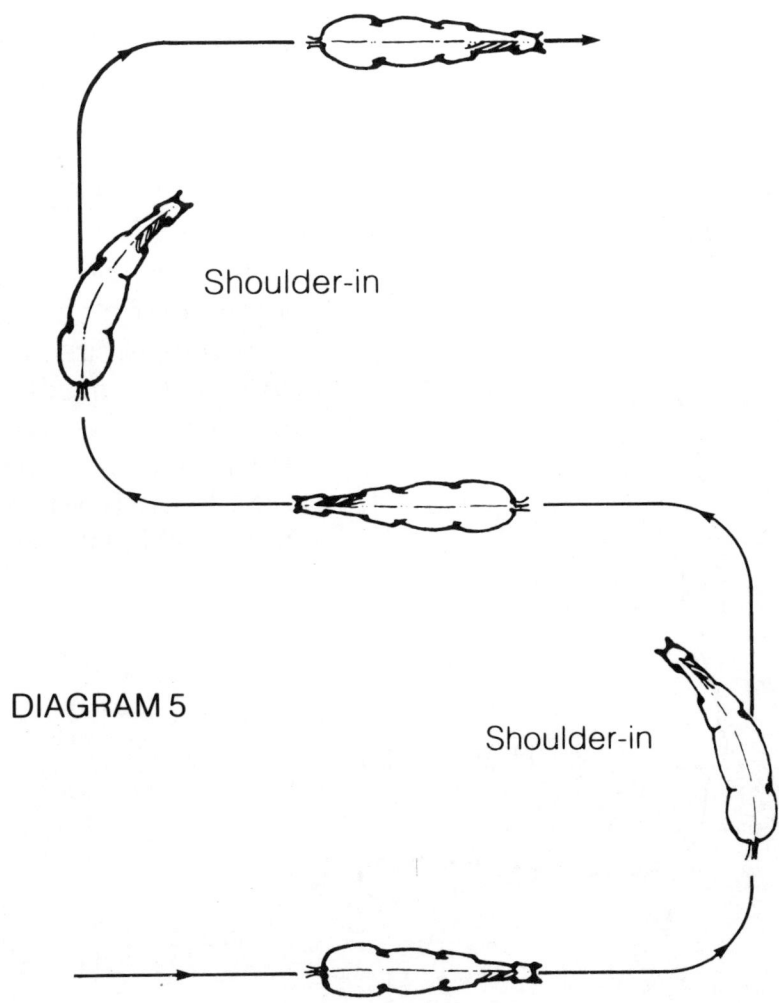

DIAGRAM 5

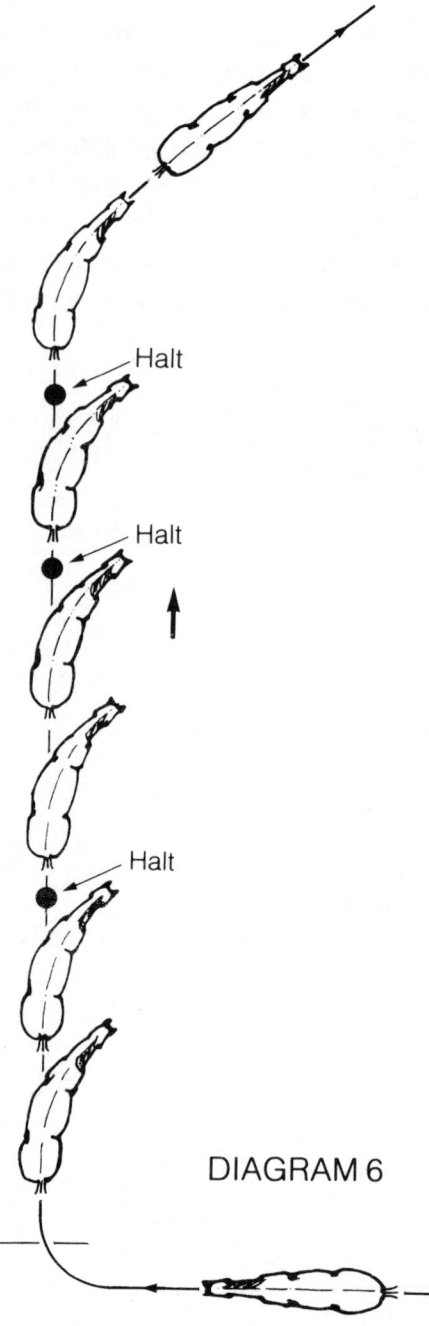

DIAGRAM 6

4. At walk with any horse, it is very good to ask him to halt, completely quiet, in the position of shoulder-in. Wait in the halt a few seconds and then quietly and carefully begin again the shoulder-in without losing either your track or the previous position (angle off the track) of shoulder-in.

Then repeat in the opposite direction.

Later in the horse's training when he can do the above exercise happily, then do it at collected trot being sure to use the seat aids and minimal hands, and relaxing the reins a little at the halt.

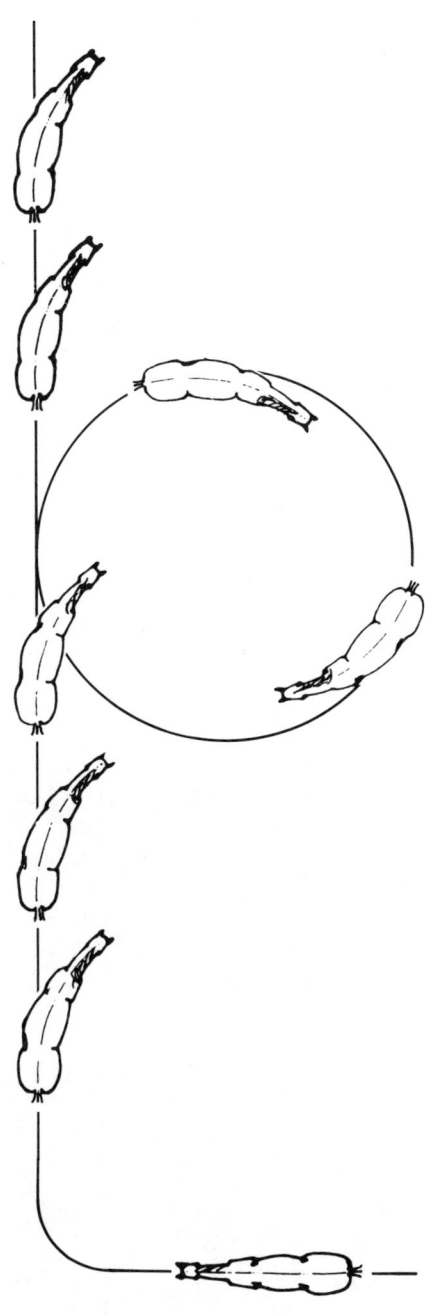

5. Shoulder-in on a circle. Commence shoulder-in on the long side, begin a circle but maintain your shoulder-in on that circle. The circle should be large, about 10 metres (33 feet).. On completing the circle continue the shoulder-in again before walking forward in a very straight line.

6. Shoulder-in through the corner - commence shoulder-in along the wall, continue shoulder-in through the corner. This is done by slowing down the shoulders a little and making the hindquarters 'walk more' through the corner. The horse then continues the shoulder-in at the same angle off the track as he was prior to the corner.

When your horse has to use his hindlegs and step more in the corner you can feel it very clearly.

DIAGRAM 7

14

Serpentines

Serpentines are a geometric fact of life! The easiest way to get them correct is to measure them correctly on your menage and place markers, or draw lines, for you to learn your line.

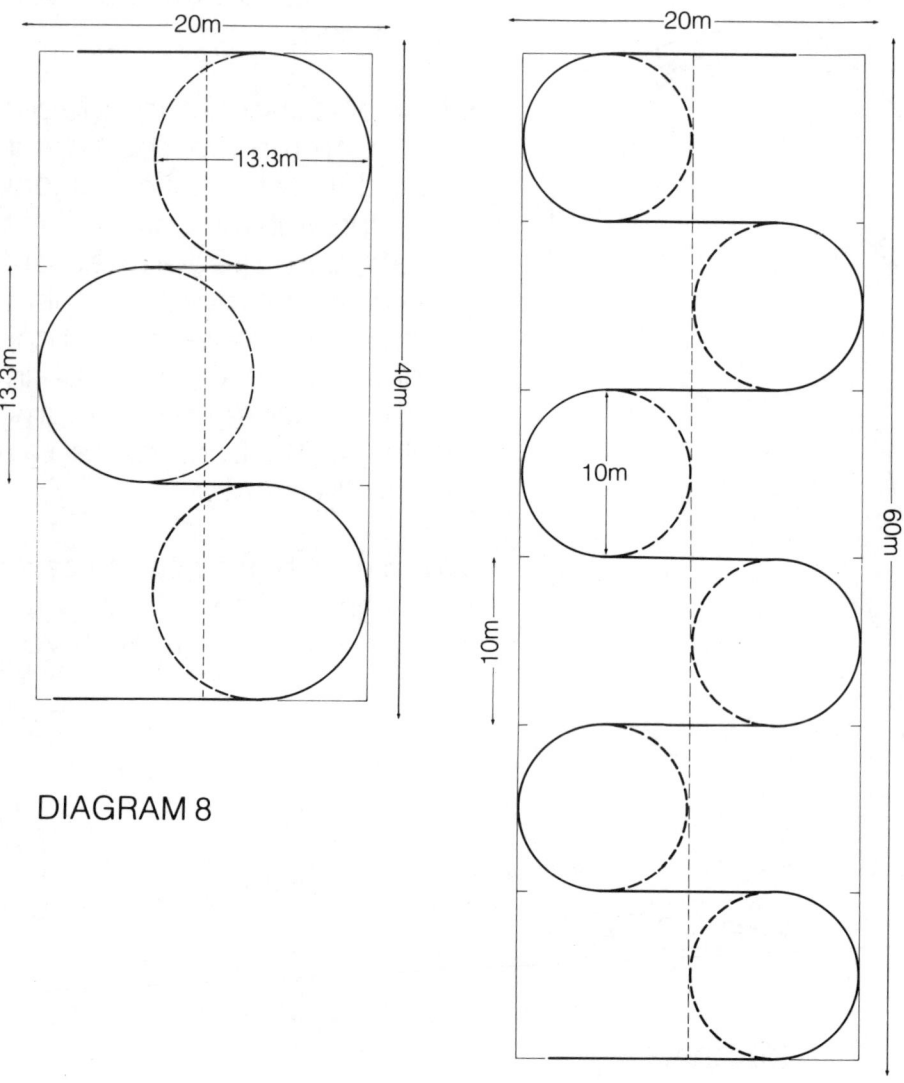

DIAGRAM 8

DIAGRAM 9

Variation for riding a serpentine.

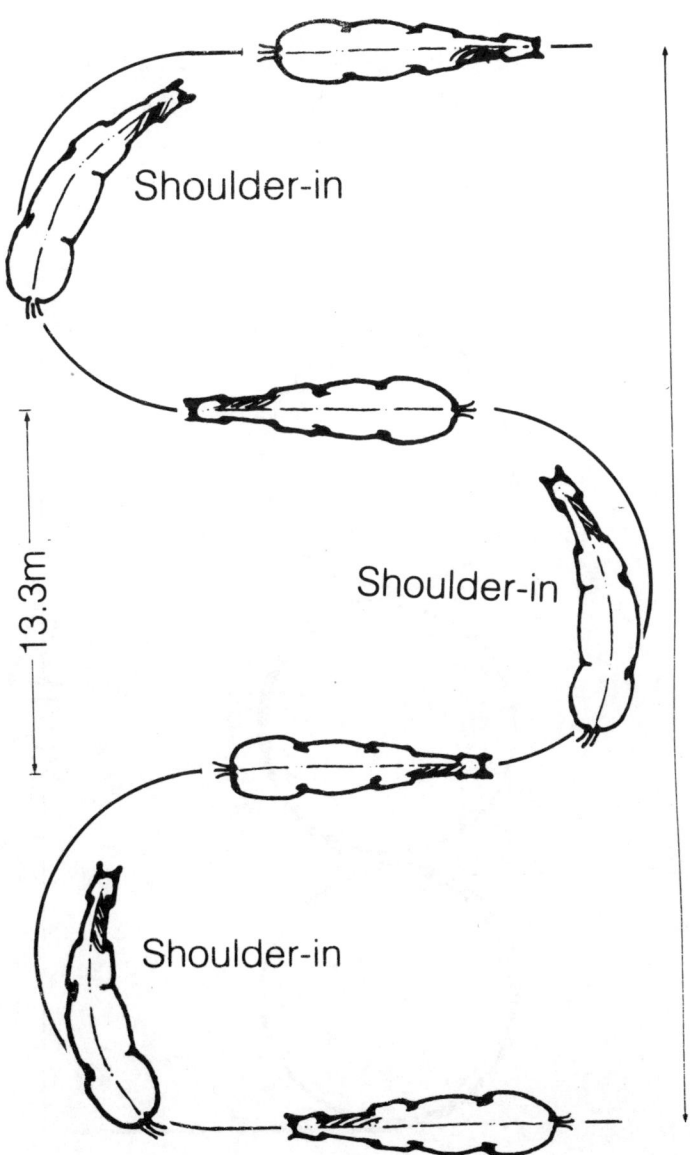

DIAGRAM 10

Loosening the Horse's Shoulders

1. At trot ride three 6 $^1/_2$ metre (21 foot 6 inches) circles, each circle has to be ridden one and a half times.

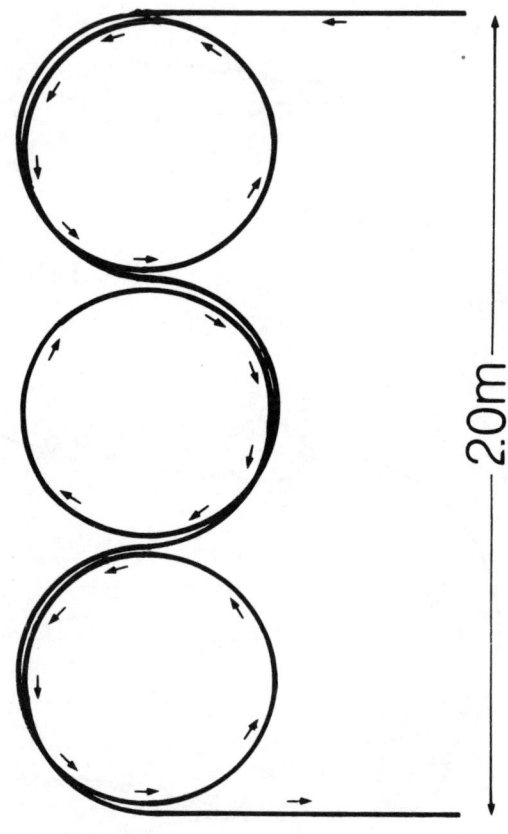

DIAGRAM 11

17

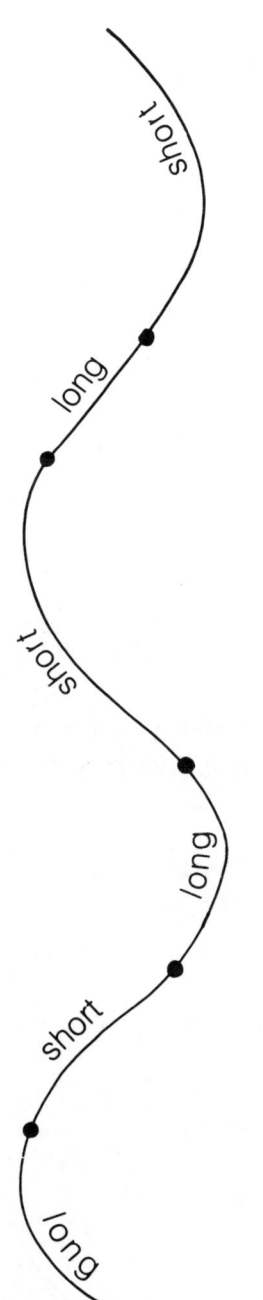

2. At walk and trot 'slalom' down the long side of the menage, varying the length of the stride, carefully not going faster or slower.

3. See also 'Two Way Stretch' page 84 and for the more advanced horse, the exercises including hindquarters-in, renvers, and trot pirouettes.

DIAGRAM 12

Downward Transitions

1. On a twenty metre circle (66 feet) at sitting trot, horse lightly on the bit, incorporate four transitions, to walk or halt on the circle. Do not always do the same thing at the same place.

Sometimes do two or three 'trot to halt', next time, trot, walk, trot, halt, rein back, and trot forward.

Aids for the downward transitions are: back, seat, legs, and then your hand which is minimal, and if always the last aid given, very quickly your horse will learn to respond to your back and leg aids and your hand will hardly be needed at all!

Not much later you will find your horse starting to lower his hindquarters a little to halt, and his hindlegs will be under him.

Always trot forward without any walk steps - it does not matter if sometimes the trot is too fast the first few steps, or even if he canters once or twice, at least he is trying to do what you ask - going forward!

Not only does this help your downward transitions, but also your move off from a halt and salute in a dressage test, which are so frequently ragged and wandering.

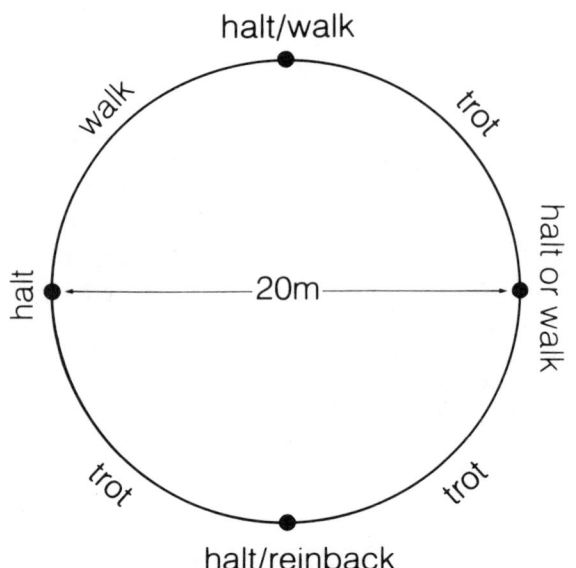

DIAGRAM 13

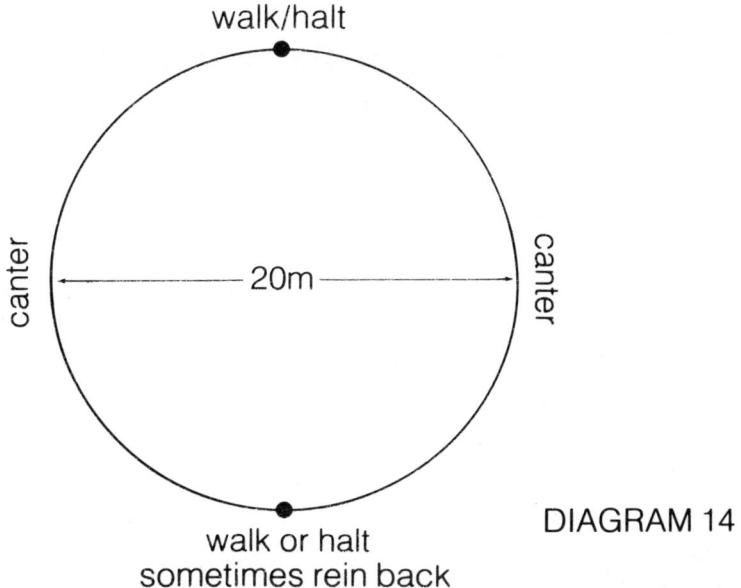

DIAGRAM 14

2. Do the same exercise at a canter, alternating the walk and halt and occasionally a few steps rein back.

Try to canter forward without any walk or trot steps!

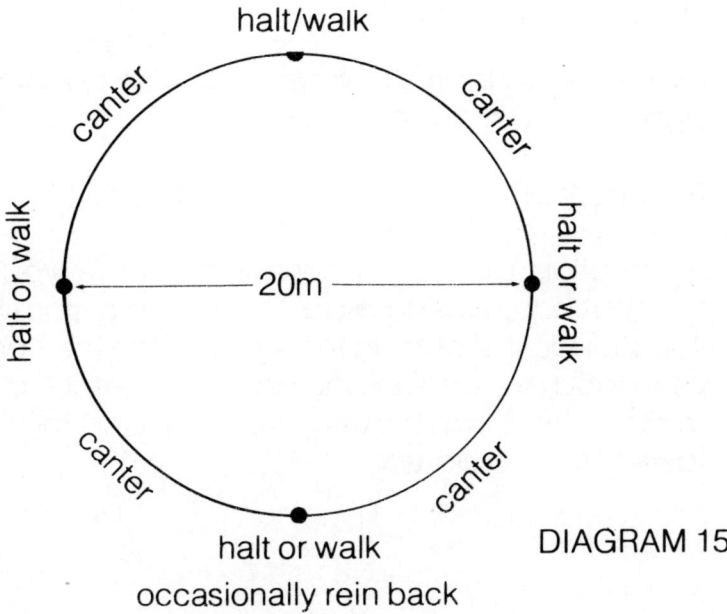

DIAGRAM 15

Another Exercise for Loosening the Horse's Back

This exercise should start on a very slight slope to begin with.

On a 20 metre circle (66 feet) with a long, low head carriage - not a collected one - carefully do rising trot on the circle.

The uphill strengthens the horse's back muscles, the downhill loosens his back and here the rider should lean back a little to allow the horse to balance himself (if you lean forward you will encourage him onto his forehand).

On the two level sections of the circle the horse has time to recover himself.

Try to establish a very rhythmical trot so that you do not run down the slope and then slow down going up the hill.

As your horse learns to cope, you can advance to a slightly steeper slope.

This also builds up the horse's neck.

A variation of this exercise is to lunge your horse (without side reins) in a paddock with a dam bank. If you include the bank in the lunge circle the horse gets very good exercise up and down. Do not do too much to start with, it can be very strenuous and the muscles take time to build up.

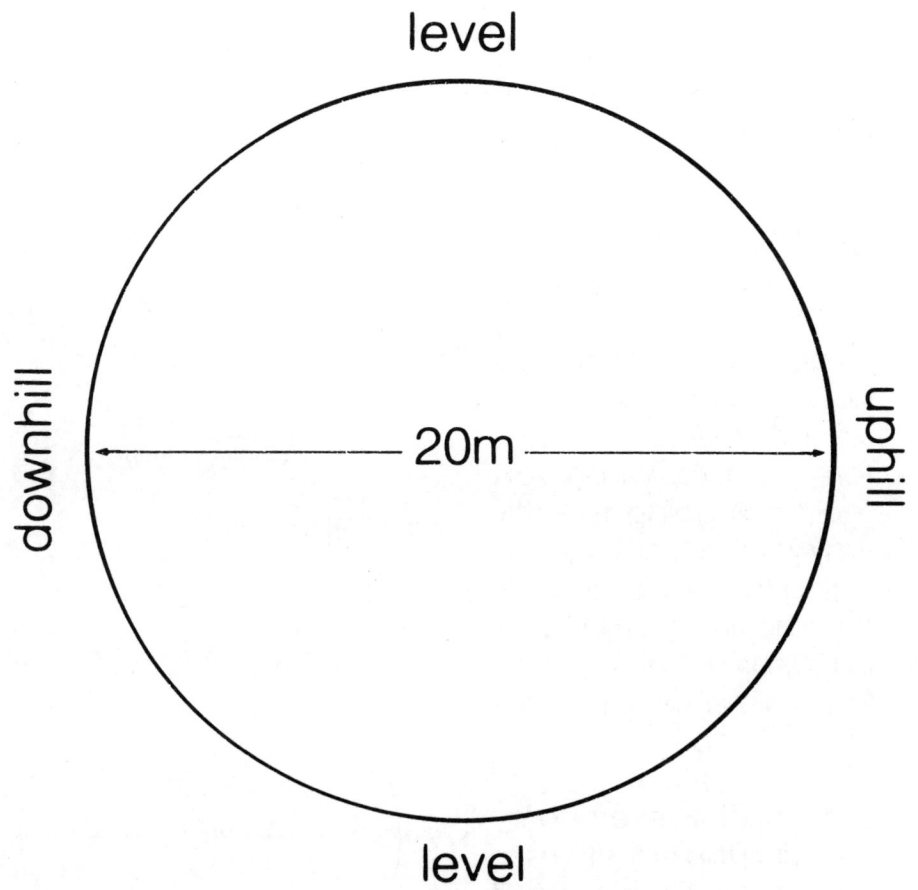

DIAGRAM 16

Exercises to Improve the Horse's Canter

Start with a twenty metre circle (66 feet), do working trot (sitting) for half the circle and working canter for the other half. This develops the horse's inside hindleg.

When giving your aids from canter to trot - which are: sit down, inside leg, and then take and give the outside rein - try to give the rein immediately the horse starts to begin the trot, that is, he has understood what you have asked. You may sometimes even give before he trots, when you feel he is going to - this way your aids are encouraging the horse to act in the hindquarters and your hands are again becoming minimal and the transition is clearly forward

Develop this exercise increasing the transitions to 3 per circle, then later to 4 transitions as in DIAGRAM 18.

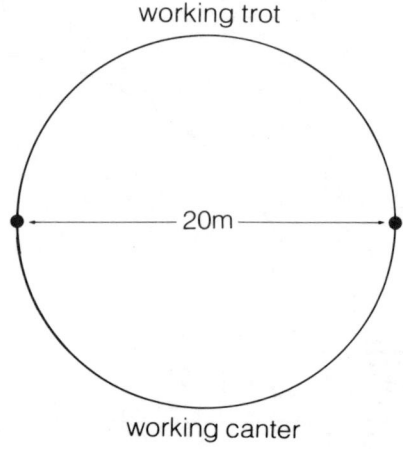

DIAGRAM 17

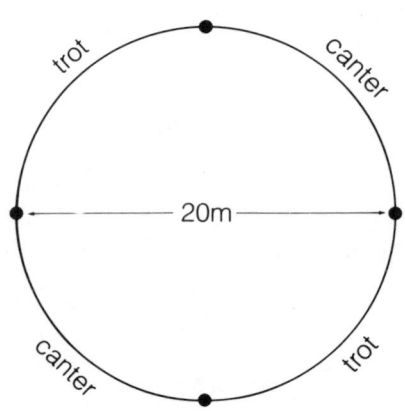

DIAGRAM 18

And later reduce the diameter of the circles.

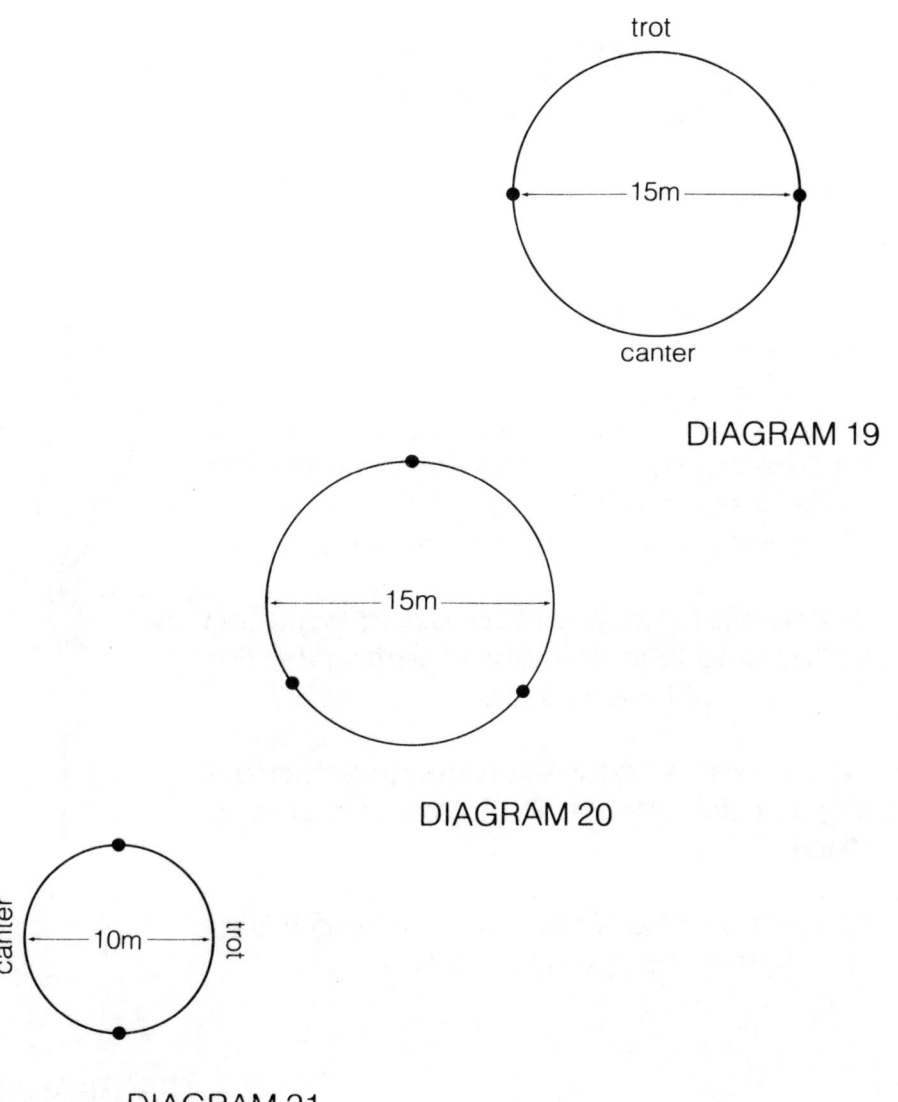

DIAGRAM 19

DIAGRAM 20

DIAGRAM 21

Exercises Using Hindquarters-In

To begin hindquarters-in, walk along the short side, bend correctly through the corner, and as you start down the long side, move your outside leg back behind the girth and push the hindquarters towards the inside. Keep the forehand on the track and the horse looking forward down the track.

It can help to have someone on the ground with a long whip to assist in getting the first few steps of hindquarters-in.

When beginning this exercise, do only a few steps hindquarters-in. Don't ask for too many steps.

When the horse is capable of doing this at a walk then progress to a trot.

DIAGRAM 22

The following exercises are good suppling exercises and loosen the back.

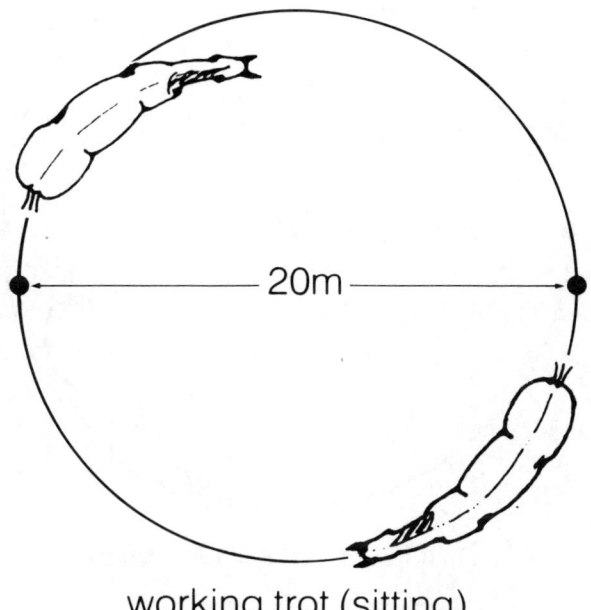

DIAGRAM 23

When the horse can cope with hindquarters-in in a relaxed and happy way, begin the following exercise first at walk, and later progressing to doing the exercise at trot.

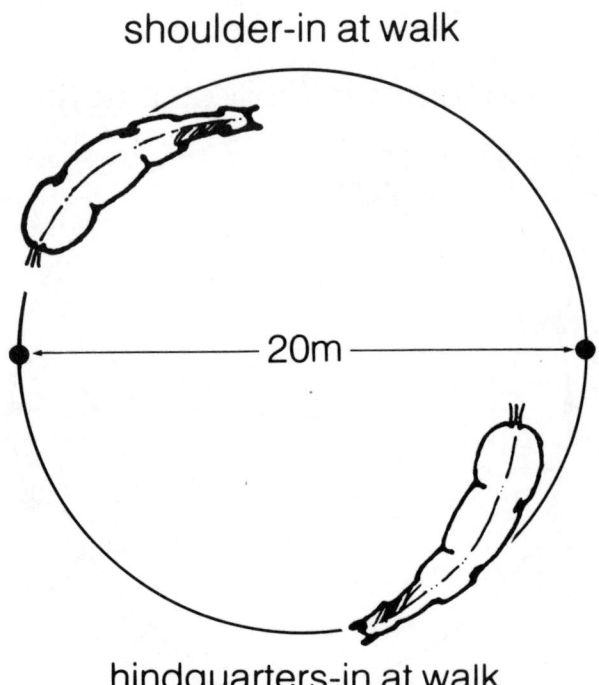

DIAGRAM 24

Hindquarters-in on the long side, and make large circles 10 metres (33 feet) with the hindquarters-in, then continue along the long side.

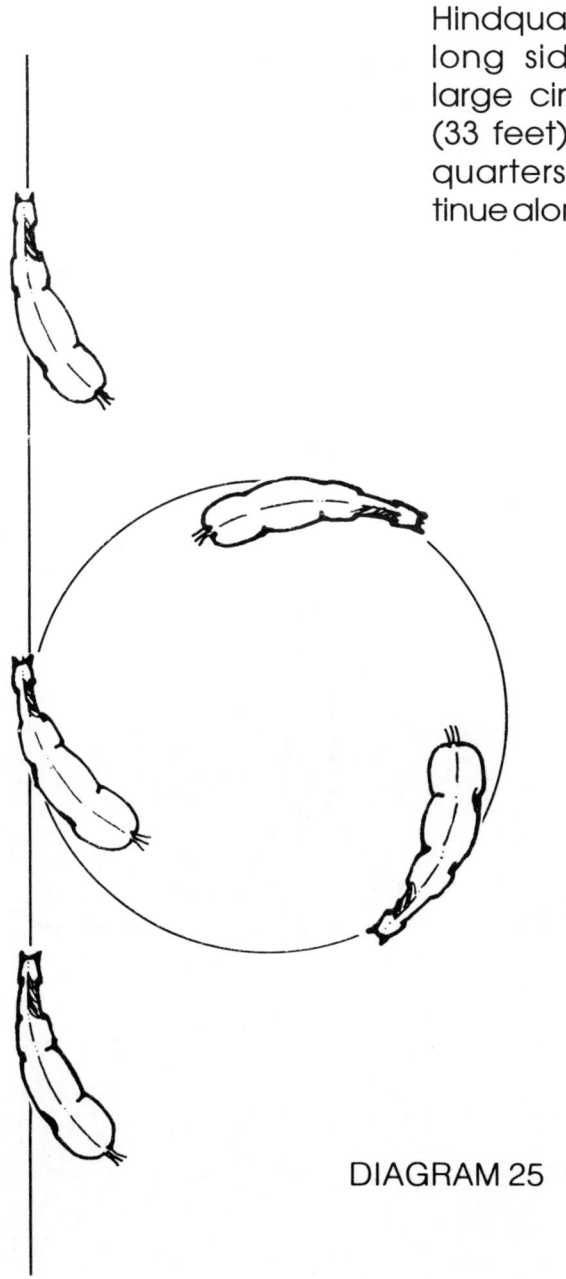

DIAGRAM 25

28

You can do two small circles hindquarters-in, with some steps forward very straight when changing from one circle to the next.

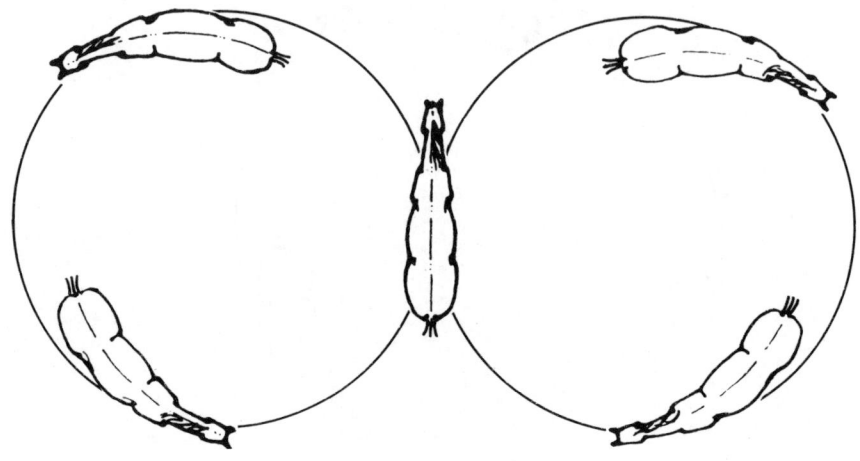

DIAGRAM 26

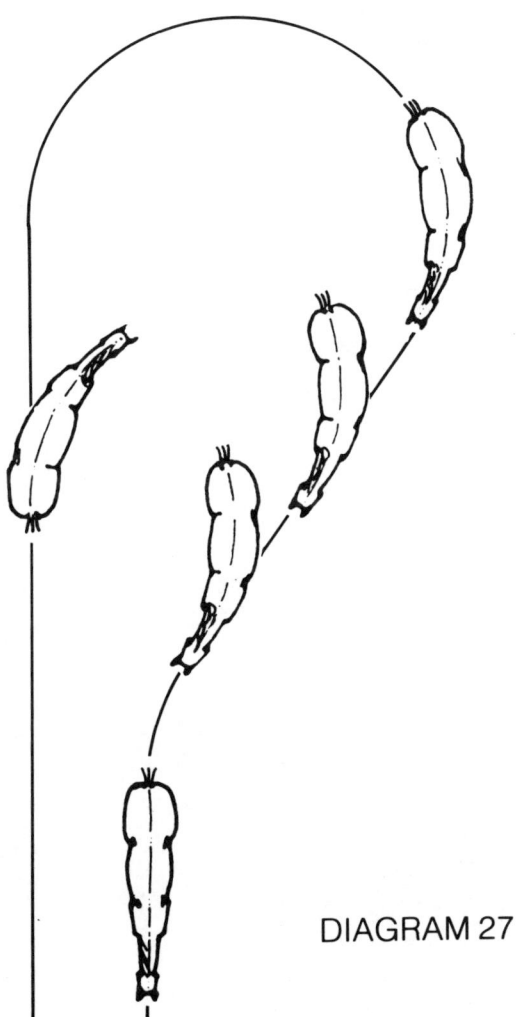

DIAGRAM 27

Start a shoulder-in towards the end of the long side, continue through the corner and along half of the short side, turn down the centre line in the position of shoulder-in, and in this position, and maintaining you're aids for shoulder-in, add hindquarters-in to it, and **wow!** you're doing half-pass!

Relax the aids and walk forward and reward your horse.

Half Pass

When you think about it, the hindquarters-in exercises on the previous pages are really half-pass on the circle with quarters in.

Now, develop your half-pass, in both directions and, when you feel confident on both reins, begin your counter-change of hand.

To avoid the counter-change of hand becoming sloppy and the horse leading with his hindquarters, sometimes include in the zig-zag some steps of shoulder-in.

DIAGRAM 28

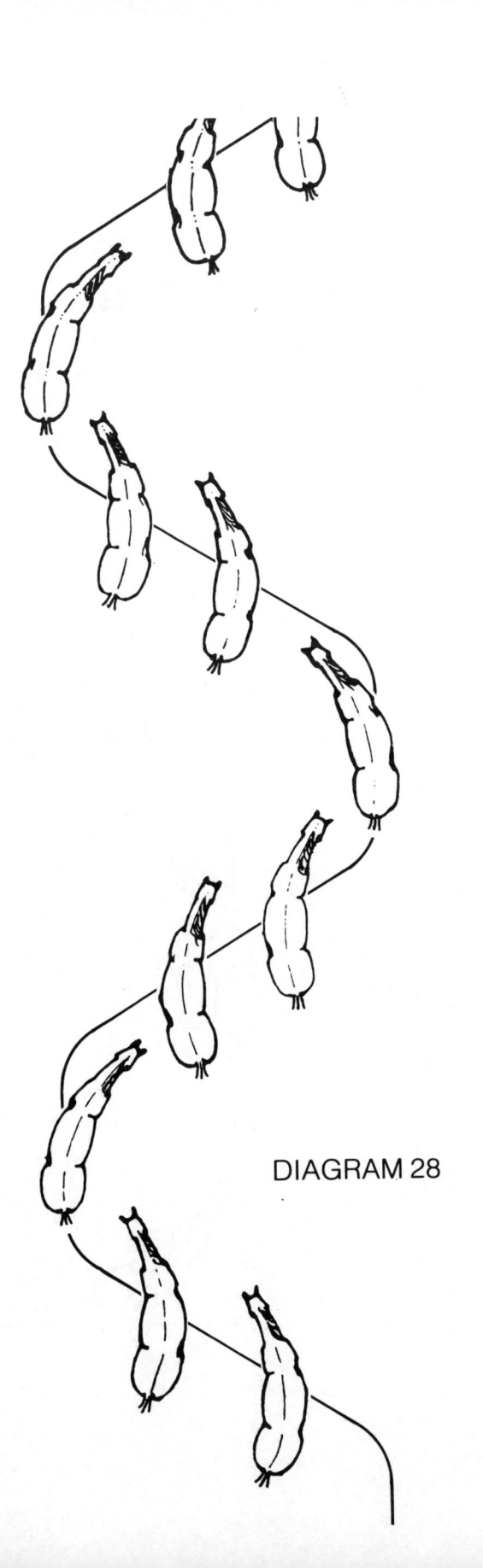

Another Exercise to Help with Half-Pass

At collected trot ride a 10m circle (33 feet) at the short end of the menage as in diagram 29. On returning to the centre line, do one or two steps of shoulder-in and then half-pass towards the long side.

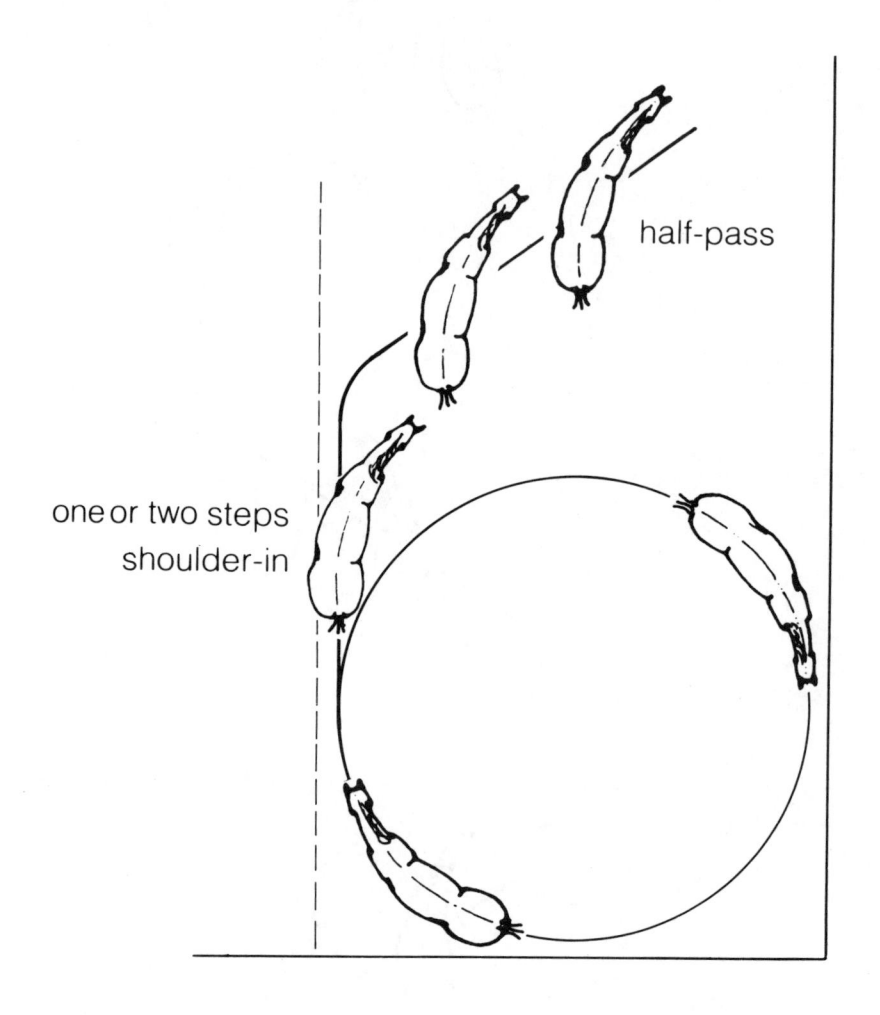

half-pass

one or two steps shoulder-in

DIAGRAM 29

If it is not all happening, go back a step and try the following exercises.

This exercise is good to do down the front drive if you live in the country, otherwise in the menage from the long side to and from the quarter line.

At walk, counter shoulder-in away from the right side of the drive - on arriving at the other side do not change the aids but add the outside leg behind the girth with little taps and push the hindquarters across - and so half-pass back to the right side of the drive and repeat again.

This confirms the aids to both horse and rider, and helps you understand the quotation 'When you understand that the inside leg improves the half-pass, you begin to understand.'

DIAGRAM 30

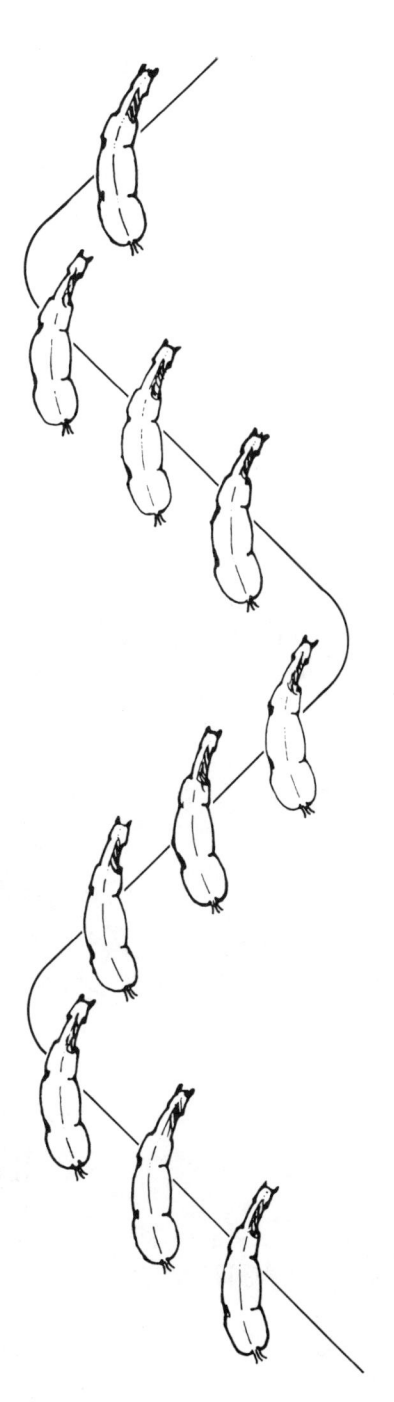

The half-pass ridden with the horse's hindquarters on the track is the Classical exercise called Renvers.

Begin at walk, half-pass towards the long side, and on arriving at the wall slow down the shoulders and make the hindquarters advance the horse still in the position of half-pass.

You can now do an exercise of half-pass around the horse's shoulders at walk.

Gradually, after some time, begin to decrease the diameter of the circle.

When the horse is capable, progress to a light and cadenced collected trot. Always remembering that a little well done is wonderful. So relax your aids and reward your horse.

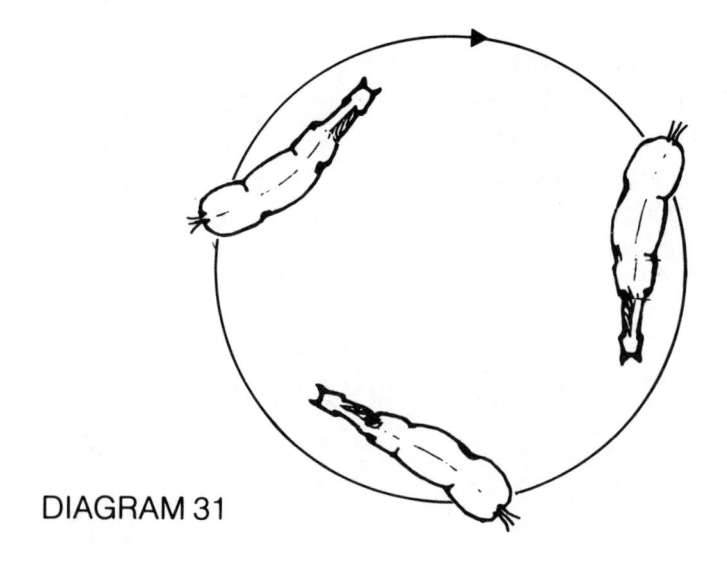

DIAGRAM 31

Notes and Exercises on Developing Collection

Collection should only be obtained from the increased use and power of the hindquarters. This, as any gymnast or body builder will tell you, takes hours of tedious muscle building exercises. It is no different or quicker with the body of a horse.

If collection is obtained from the development of the horse's muscular ability to carry himself he will have that beautiful and elegant collection which is so controlled and light.

"Maximum effort from the horse. Minimum effort from the rider."

So the beginnings of collection can be helped by the following exercises.

At Trot.

Try to lengthen the stride without any increase in the tempo - count 1,2,1,2,1,2,1,2, to yourself like a metronome.

Remember in the downward transitions to use seat and leg first and the hand is minimal, just take and give - do not hang on there!

working trot (sitting)

20m

collected trot (quarter circle)

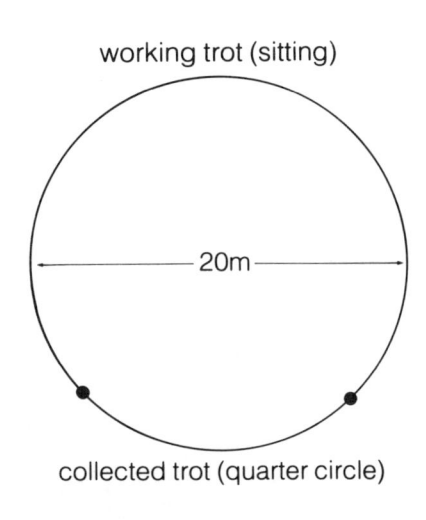

DIAGRAM 32

medium trot

20m

collected trot

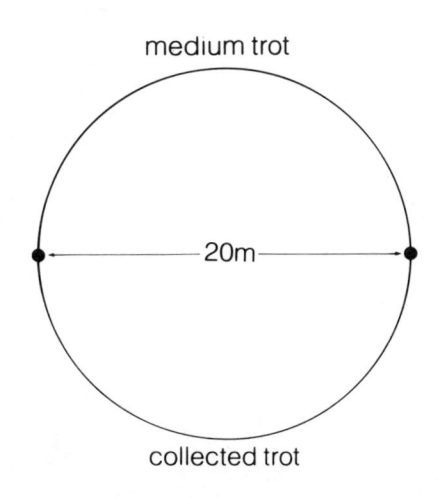

DIAGRAM 33

36

At Canter.

20m

medium canter

collected canter

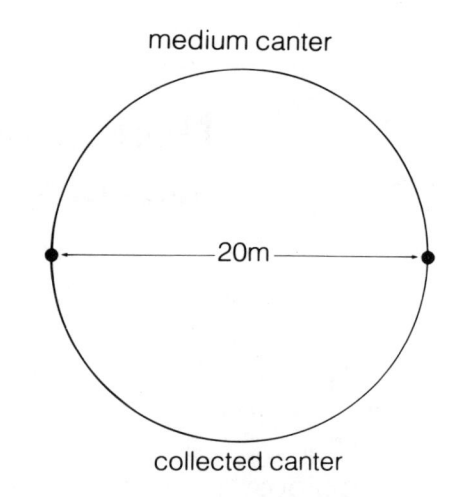

DIAGRAM 34

collected canter

medium canter

20m

medium canter

collected canter

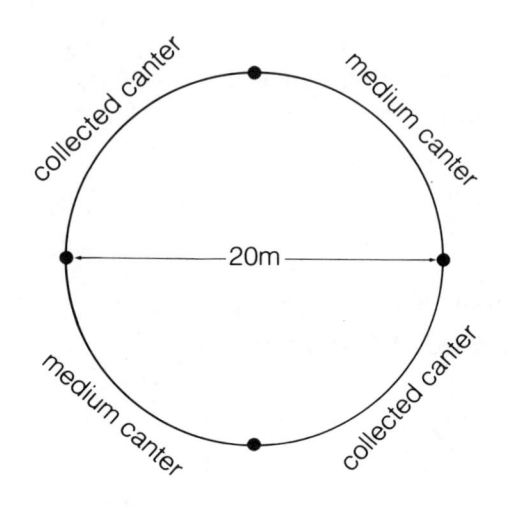

DIAGRAM 35

medium canter

15m

collected canter

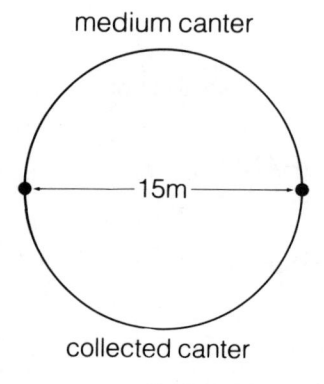

DIAGRAM 36

three to four strides of collected canter

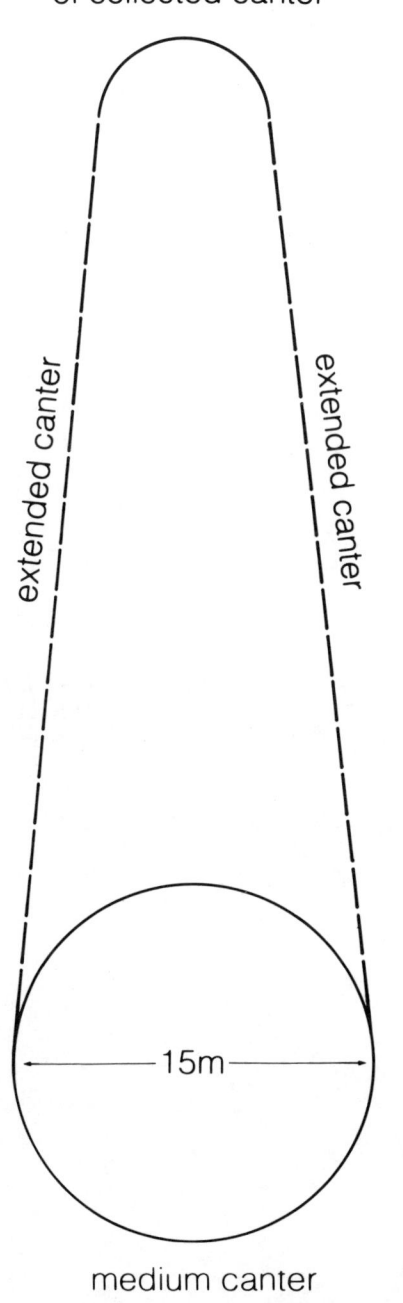

extended canter

extended canter

— 15m —

medium canter

The extended canter must also be the same tempo as the collected canter - so the bounds of the canter become bigger, and you have the feeling the horse is going uphill!

DIAGRAM 37

Counter-Canter

This movement, sometimes known as CONTRA-CANTER, is very easy to do badly - swinging quarters, horse on two tracks, on the forehand.

So do only a little at a time until you are confident.

Start with the curves much bigger than necessary, walk before the horse becomes unbalanced, and then build up the number of steps and reduce the curve until you can do the required serpentine.

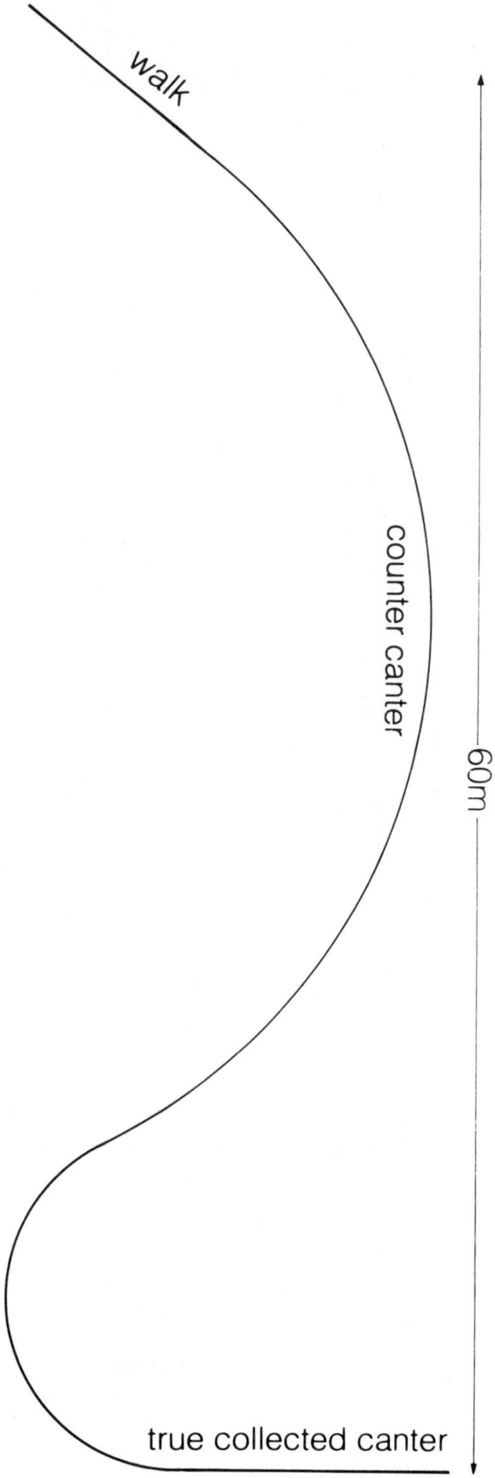

DIAGRAM 38

walk

counter canter

60m

true collected canter

true canter

true canter

counter canter

counter canter

60m

true canter

true canter

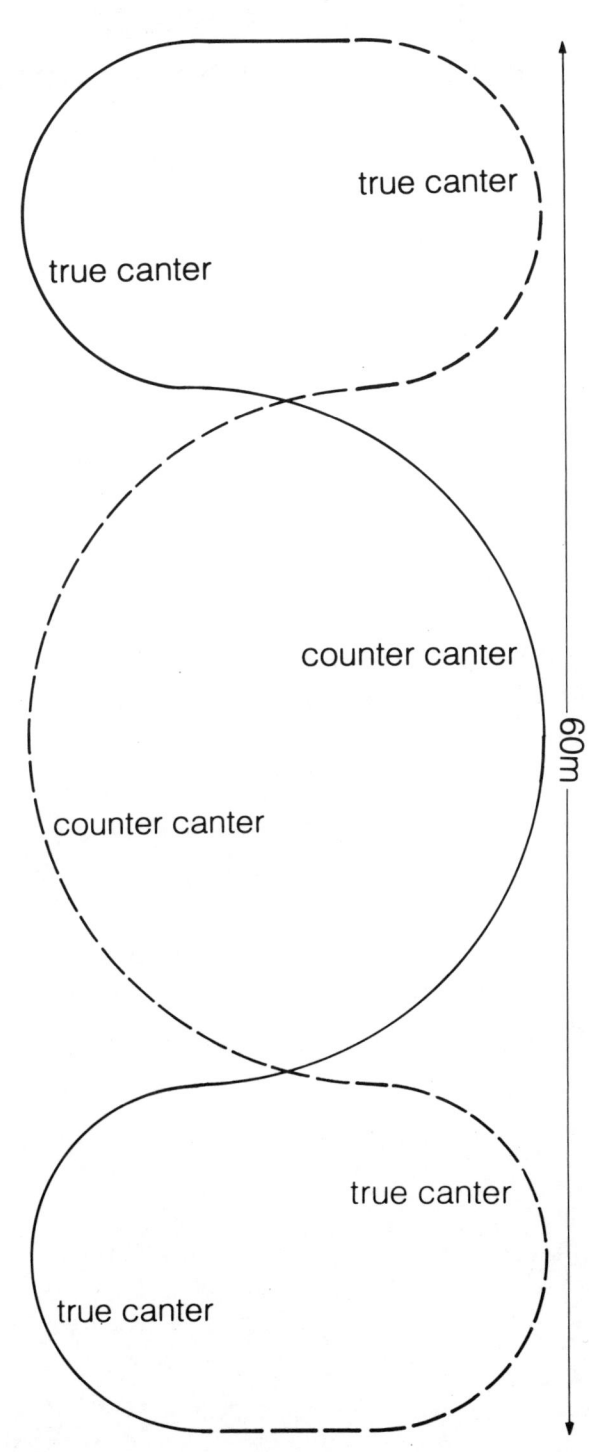

DIAGRAM 39

Exercise to help the Horse Bend His Hindlegs
that is to lower his hindquarters

Begin at walk with large half pirouettes - two to three metres (6 foot 6 inches to 10 foot)- as in diagram 40.

Then at collected trot - down the long side, and a large half pirouette to the right - four to five metres. Return to the long side, trot forward and do a similarly large half pirouette to the left.

This encourages the horse to bend his hind legs and so to 'sit down' a little and begin to carry himself on his hindquarters - that is if he was light in your hands all through the exercise.

This exercise is good for suppling the horse's shoulders, and also makes him straighter.

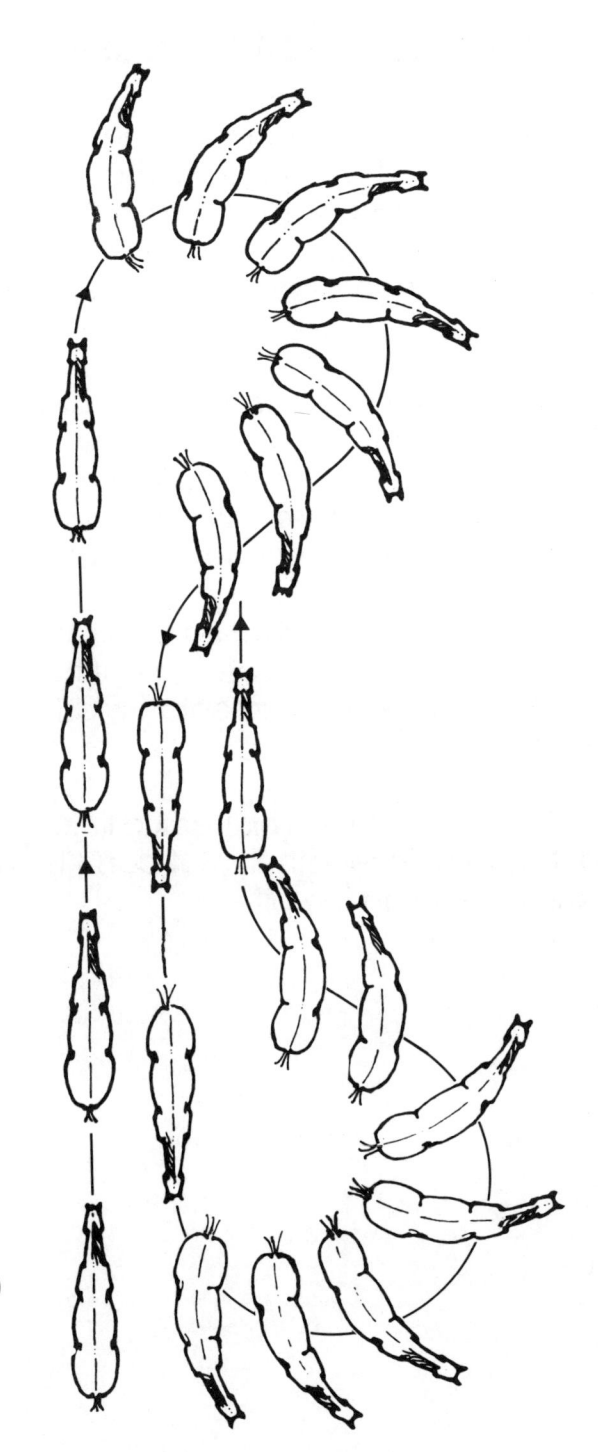

DIAGRAM 40

Extended Trot Exercises

The lengthening and shortening of the horse's stride started a lot earlier in his training. He should be able to do the exercises with medium trot without any change in the tempo. The lengthening must come from the hindlegs coming underneath the horde, not trailing out behind.

So, presuming your medium trot is correct and easily done, the extended trot is just more and more effort asked for until you develop the maximum. Takes Time! But fantastic when your horse carries you on a rounded back with a long elegant and rhythmical stride.

1. Collected trot along the short side, correctly around the corner and the half-pass change of hand twice, finishing before or by B and immediately asking for the extended trot.

Allow the horse to lengthen his neck a little as well as asking for his stride to lengthen. But don't let him 'fall on his face' or lean on the bit.

DIAGRAM 41

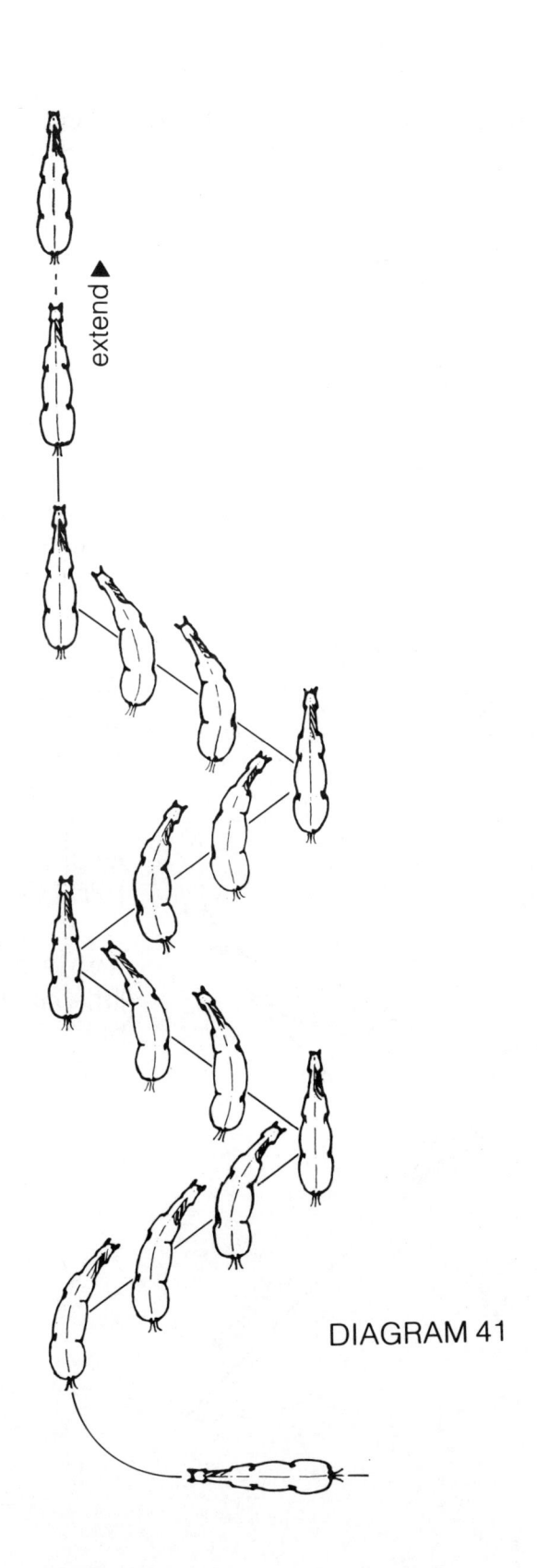

2. Hindquarters-in for three-quarters of a 20 metre circle (66 feet), on arriving at H extend along the diagonal.

Do not ask the horse to extend the length of the diagonal at first. Perhaps just a quarter or half of the diagonal to start with.

Alternatively do the same three-quarters of a circle in shoulder-in and then extend quarter or half the diagonal.

Variation: Also on the diagonals and down the long sides, halt and extend for short distances. Sometimes when halted rein-back and then extend. This rounds the horse's back before asking for the extension. Do not extend forward from the rein-back unless and until the horse is light in hand in the rein-back.

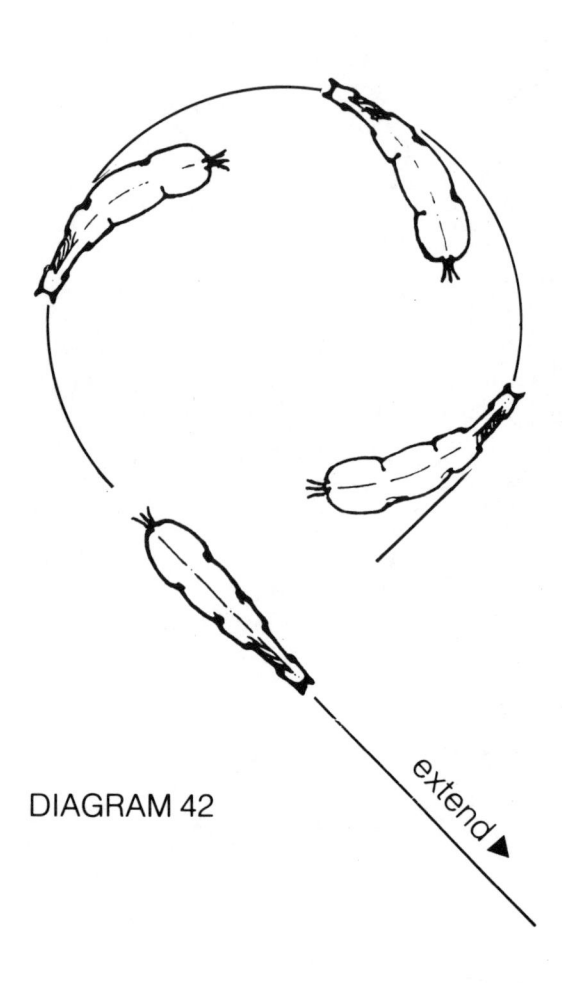

Remember to ask a little and to reward him.

DIAGRAM 42

Preparation for Flying Changes

You must be confident of the strike off to each collected canter, both true canter and counter-canter.

So, do your collected canter strike off around the menage and on circles and the diagonals.

Mix up the canters - true, true, counter, true, counter, counter, true, true, true, counter, true, counter, counter, and so on. Sounds a bit crazy but really makes sure you and your horse are 110% A/OK about strike off.

At this time you can include an exercise doing a definite number of canter strides. That is canter six strides and halt, then, canter four strides, walk, canter six strides, halt, and so on,

When you feel you can - then, combine both the above exercises - making sure the canter retains its bounce, and it is light in hand, in collection, and just does not become slower and heavy in hand, which will become on the forehand and somewhat dead.

An Exercise to Teach Your Horse a Single Flying Change

Prepare your horse - make sure the collected canter is light and cadenced, and do some canter strike off, from walk and back to walk.

At the beginning of a long side (for example H) make a transition from walk to counter-canter and to walk again.

Make several more similar transitions to counter-canter along the long side and at the end of the long side complete a large circle in counter-canter. Walk back to the other end of the menage.

At the beginning of the long side (H) about four to five metres from the corner from the walk, counter-canter four to five steps, then walk. Turn back to the short side in walk and repeat the same transition in the **same** place several times.

If this is all completed in a calm and relaxed manner and the horse's canter remains round, then put the horse in a true canter on a circle near the place where you were doing the last transitions to counter canter.

Canter (true canter) on the circle but go well into the corner (before H) and with the horse very straight, light and round and the rider sitting very straight and still, at the place where you were doing the transitions to counter-canter, do a brief tighten and give of your fingers at the same time a very quick definite tap with your old inside leg (new outside leg).

If your horse has done his first flying change, stop, drop the reins, and reward him.

Now, calmly repeat the canter circle, true canter, and continue down the long side (past H) without any change.

Carefully repeat the exercise at the other end and when you have one flying change in the other direction, get off, make much of your horse, and put him in the stable!!

Another Exercise to Teach a Young Horse His First Flying Change

As in diagram 43, trot across the diagonal, near M, walk two to three steps hindquarters-in, and then trot forward correctly through the corner. Repeat two to three times.

Then collected canter (right) across the diagonal at the same place near M trot two to three steps in hindquarters-in, and then canter (left) through the corner correctly. Repeat two to three times.

When the canter section of diagram 44 has been done calmly and with confidence, then, again, canter across the diagonal, but do not trot on approaching M, instead quickly, firmly, and lightly tap the new outside leg (right) behind the girth and your horse will do his first flying change.

Fantastic!

Stop, drop the reins, and pat him.

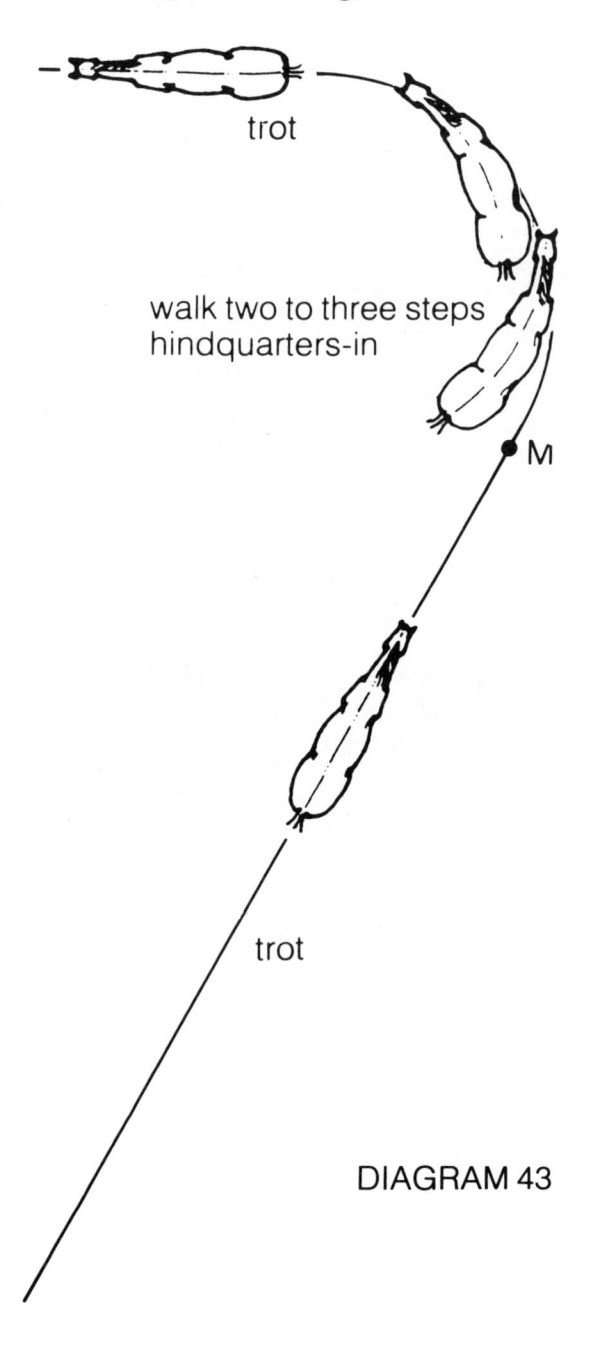

trot

walk two to three steps hindquarters-in

M

trot

DIAGRAM 43

If the change does not happen, do not punish him. If you do, he will always be frightened of flying changes, and do them with tension.

If all is relaxed and calm, and the change achieved, repeat in the other direction, remembering to keep the horse's canter tempo unchanged, the horse straight, and asking for the change from your leg, not from your hand!

When the horse changes, reward him immediately - pat him, give him carrots or sugar, and tell him he is wonderful, and put him back in the stable.

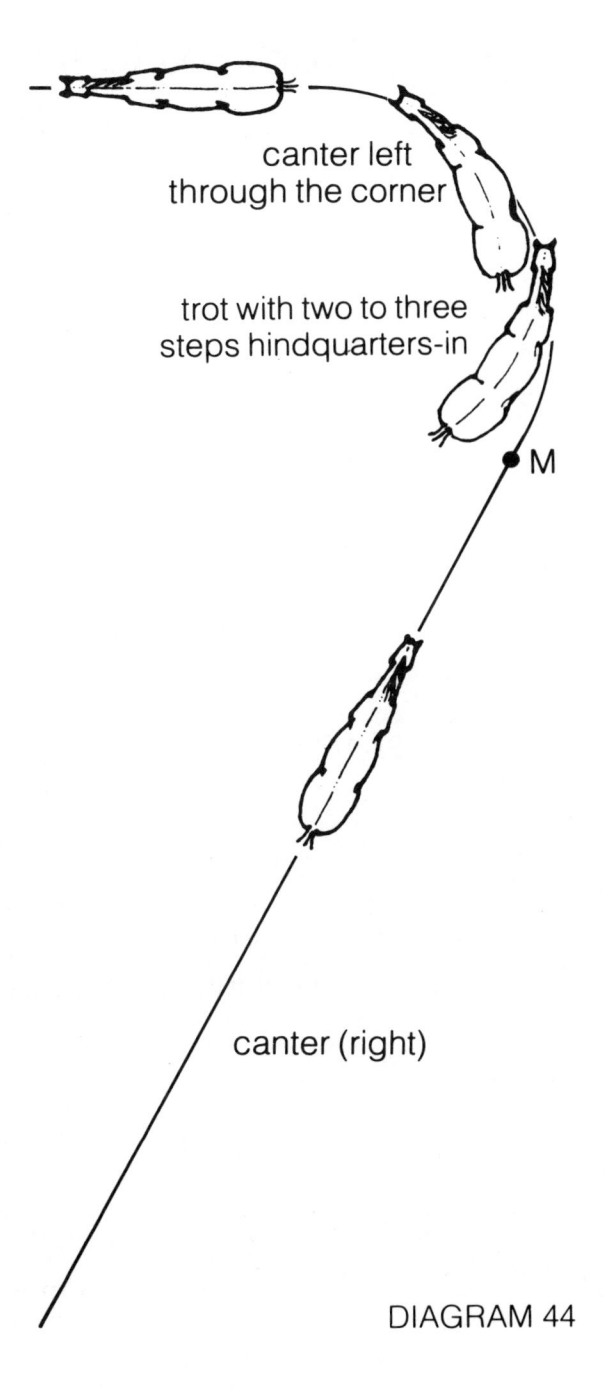

canter left through the corner

trot with two to three steps hindquarters-in

M

canter (right)

DIAGRAM 44

Exercises to Improve Single Flying Changes

When you can do your flying change at the end of the diagonal or along the long side you could try two changes in a circle.

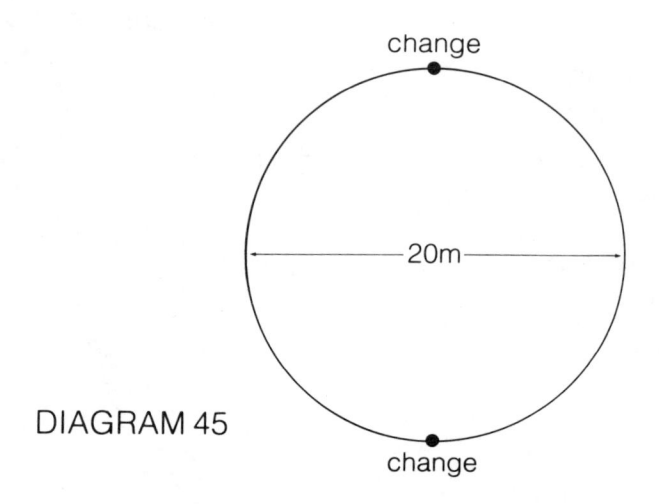

change

20m

DIAGRAM 45

change

To do four changes in a 20 metre circle (66 feet) is much more difficult, but if you keep your horse very straight on the circle, and in a light cadenced canter,

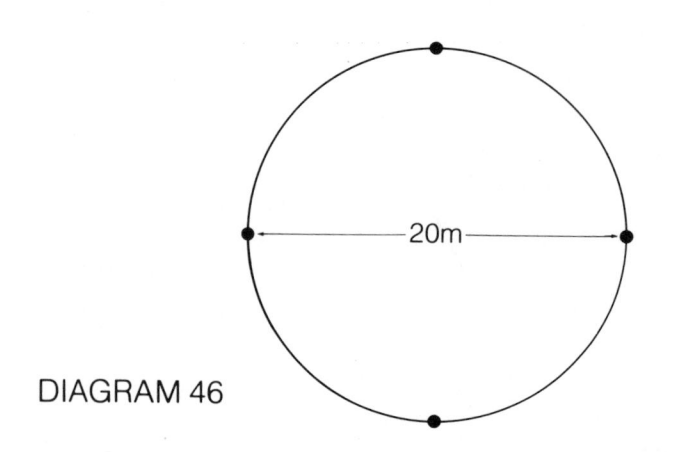

20m

DIAGRAM 46

Another Exercise to Improve the Flying Change

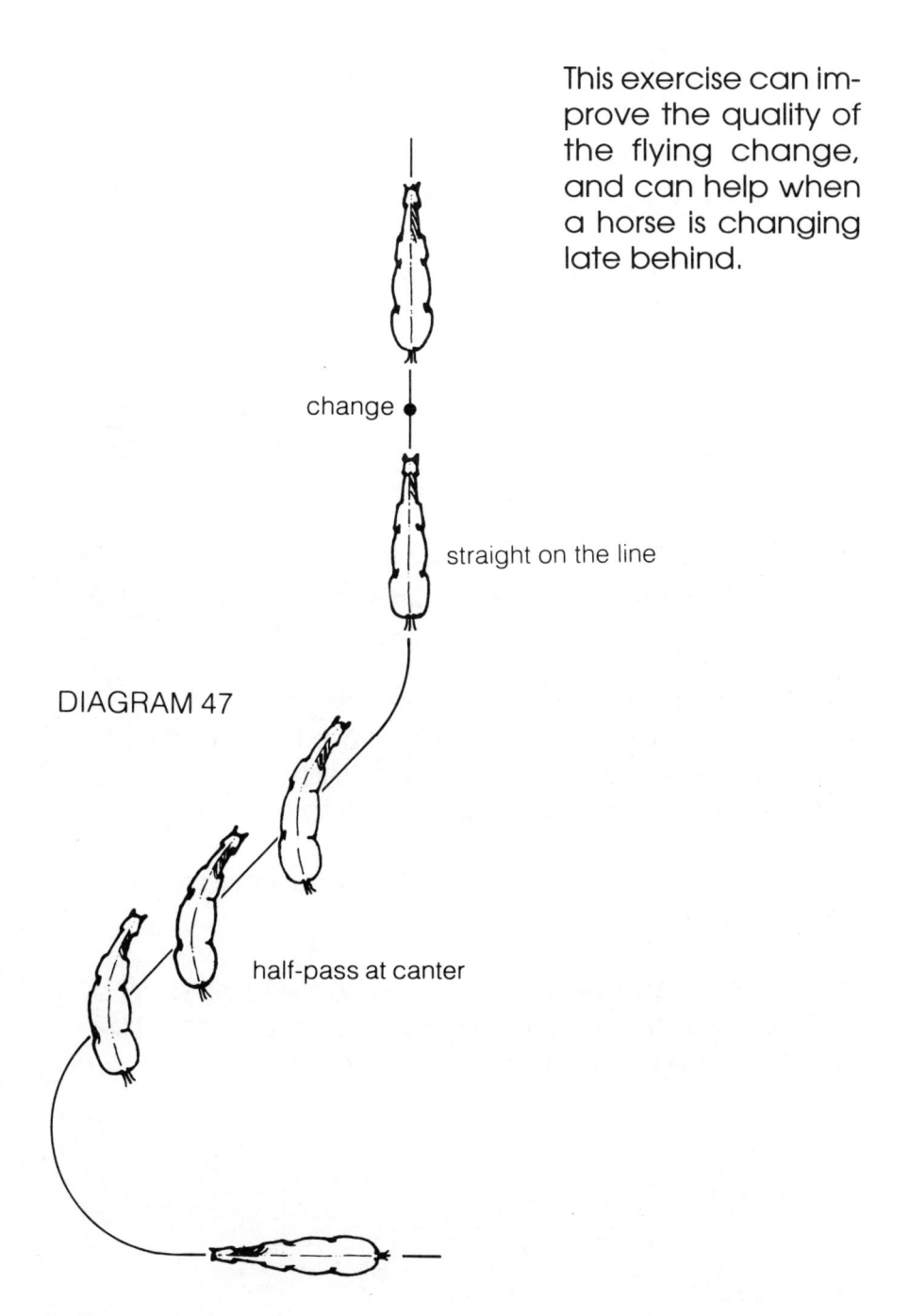

This exercise can improve the quality of the flying change, and can help when a horse is changing late behind.

change

straight on the line

DIAGRAM 47

half-pass at canter

Exercise to Relax and Stretch

When your horse is round and soft and accepting the bit, you can stretch his back and neck muscles by lengthening the reins and encouraging him to stretch forward and down to-wards the ground.

The rhythm must stay the same, and to the rider, the horse will feel very supple, relaxed and rhythmical.

With light contact, almost no weight in the reins, the horse will step rhythmically, with equal steps in a relaxed cadenced trot.

You will feel the horse is really in his own balance, there are no restrictions or force from the rider, and the horse's back will swing.

The lower the head to the ground, the more the horse can stretch all the muscles, especially along the 'topline.'

Try to canter forward without changing the reins or the frame of the horse, and canter some large circles in the same relaxed way. Take care that the trot does not 'speed up' during the transition to canter.

Change directions without speeding up and repeat on the other rein.

This exercise can be very useful when warming up a horse at a competition. It will relax and stretch all his muscles before he has to work in collection.

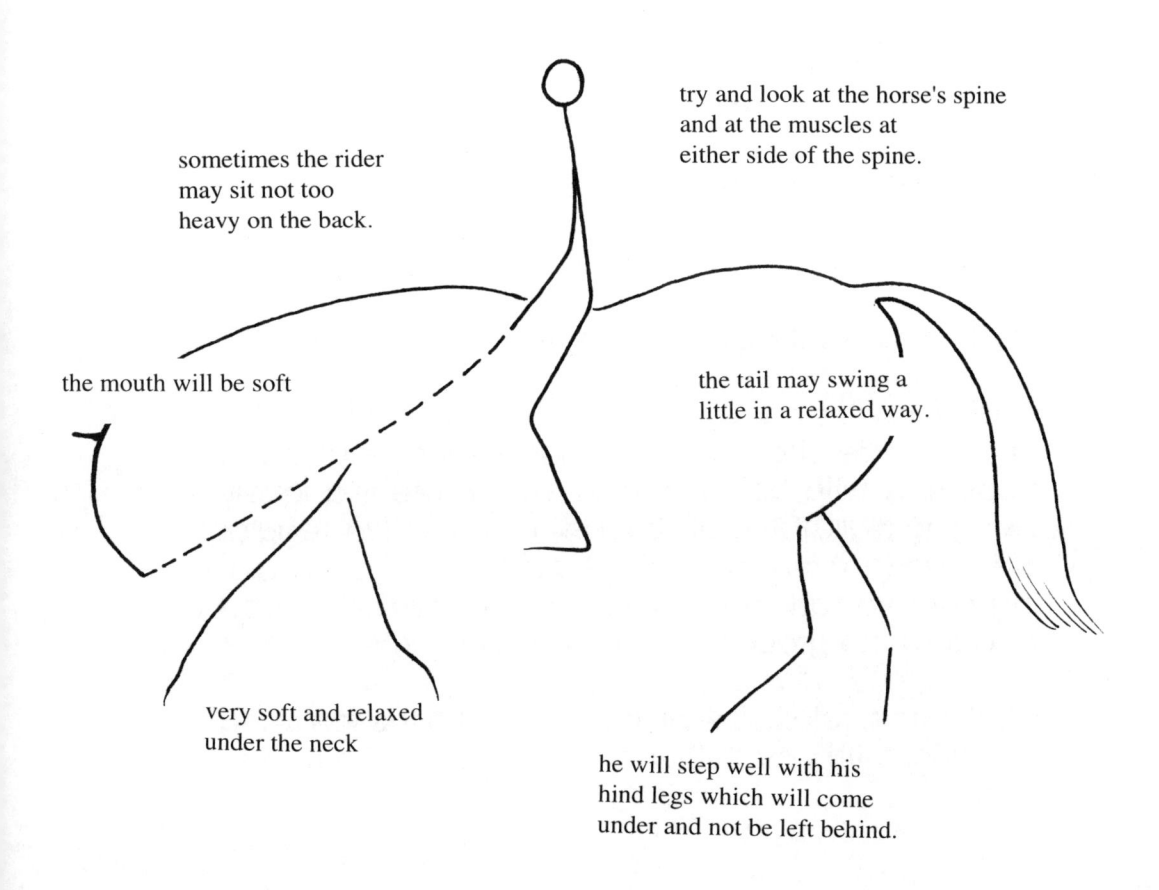

sometimes the rider may sit not too heavy on the back.

try and look at the horse's spine and at the muscles at either side of the spine.

the mouth will be soft

the tail may swing a little in a relaxed way.

very soft and relaxed under the neck

he will step well with his hind legs which will come under and not be left behind.

Active Regular Walk

To finish with an exercise to improve the horse's walk is a good way to finish each day for both horse and rider.

The walk is the horse's gait that is most difficult to improve and the easiest to become lazy. To keep or redevelop his best walk, always walk on a long, or loose, rein with the most active walk you can obtain. This doesn't mean running, or over hurrying, but a clear relaxed active four-time walk.

Count the hoofbeats to yourself.

And when it is a really good walk it will have developed a stride where the horse easily steps over his front hoofprints with his hind foot. You will feel a lovely swinging walk. If you always ask for this active, regular swinging (not running) walk, later in the horse's training when you ask for a collected walk, it will all happen because the ground work is correct.

It is this free, relaxed walk that will make the following exercises with cavalettis not only successful but safer to do.

Exercises With Cavalettis

*Exercises To Help
Dressage Horses
Become More Athletic
And Beginnings For
Showjumpers.*

I thought it would be an idea to add the basic exercises for a young/green showjumper to this notebook.

The following foundation exercises are for teaching a horse to jump to the best of his ability - in a relaxed and confident manner, not from fear.

In this part are exercises which are beneficial for any horse including dressage horses. Dressage riders should accept the independent, balanced seat required for these exercises for the reasons that are given later. Only going back to their deep seat when returning to flat work. By doing this the horse gets the greatest benefit of these suppling exercises.

The Rider's Balance

The best way to get independent balance for rider and horse is to keep your seat a little out of the saddle, but stay in a showjumping position in walk as well as in trot. Your weight is in the stirrups. It is not easy for the rider (it is murder on your legs to begin with!), but very attractive to the horse as he can use any muscle to his fullest extent as his back is free of the rider's weight.

To confirm your independent balance you should be able to walk, trot and canter maintaining your jumping position, (no weight in the saddle) with both hands away from the horse's neck.

That is, you are not assisting your balance by using the reins. Assist yourself with the mane or a neckstrap if necessary

The reason for this "seat just out of the saddle" position is that the horse's back is now free of any weight. This way the horse's back muscles can develop and in turn the hindquarters, and of course, it is the hindquarters that propel the horse over the jump.

Starting of You and Your Horse

Everyday you start jumping exercises you should loosen up your horse with a little ground work.

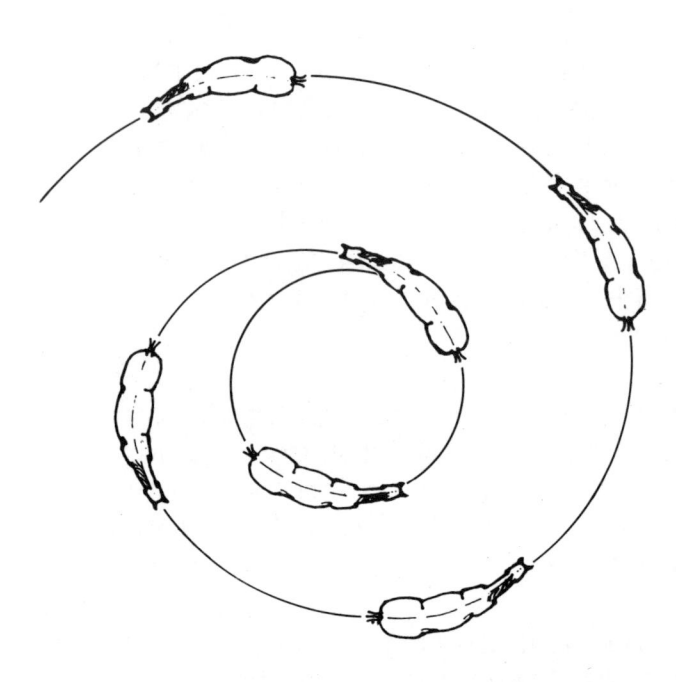

For instance, first, when you get on your horse you loosen him up on a long rein in circles, about 10 metres (33 feet), then go to 6 metres (20 feet), both sides (right and left direction) at walk and then at trot. Also figure of eights, same size 10 metres (33 feet), then 6 metres (20 feet)..

DIAGRAM 48

Secondly, go from small circles in sitting trot to larger circles using your inside leg. Start in sitting trot and enlarge the circle pushing him out and when the circle is larger then do rising trot. Go back to the small circle and repeat in both directions of course. Do the same enlargement of small circles in a canter.

Any time your horse wants to rush make the circle smaller and smaller until he accepts your request (speed/tempo) and becomes light in your hands.

Never forget, that you do not win by forcing or fighting a horse.

The Use of the Cavaletti as a Jumping Foundation

Cavalettis are of various designs and construction but for these exercises should be able to be used at three different heights.

Cavalettis are of most benefit when you have someone on the ground to assist you by doing all the adjustments so as you don't have to keep getting on and off. Doesn't have to be someone with jumping or even horse experience, e.g.. your parents, your aunt, your baby brother, Dame Edna Everidge or your "Perfect Match", just someone who will change the height or the distance when you ask them.

If at any time your horse tries to rush at the cavaletti, just make a little circle left or right as small as possible, five to six metres (16 feet 6 inches to 20 feet), larger when trotting. If he is very restless make two or three circles or a figure of eight, but, don't go over the cavaletti until you feel he is settled. Make sure that you bring your hand out to the direction of the circle that is being made and a little forward (never backwards), because you are going right or left or forward. Do not forget that what you take with one hand you give with the other.

1. Move your hand away from the neck to turn and then back to the neck. Outside rein gives a little but remains steady against the neck to stop the shoulder and consequently the horse falling out on the turn. If you have to use the inside rein firmly, then give a little more with the outside rein.

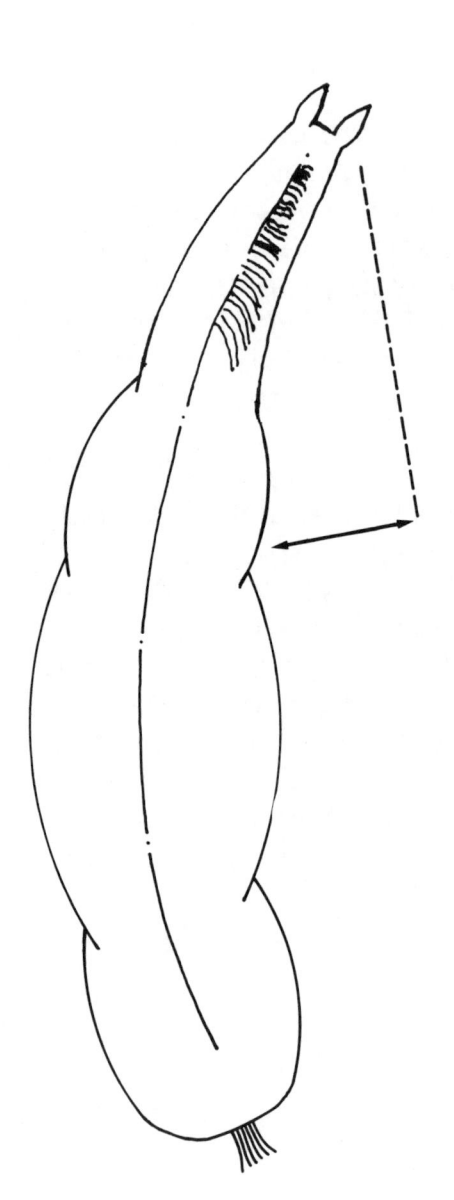

This way of turning keeps the horse's mouth soft because you are not pulling backwards on the inside rein to turn a corner.

Also, you do not lose the forwardness around the turn because you **lead** the horse around the corner.

DIAGRAM 49

2. Begin at a walk with one cavaletti at the lowest height or a pole on the ground. Walk over this a few times maintaining your independent balance - the rider not touching the horse's mouth, except to guide him.

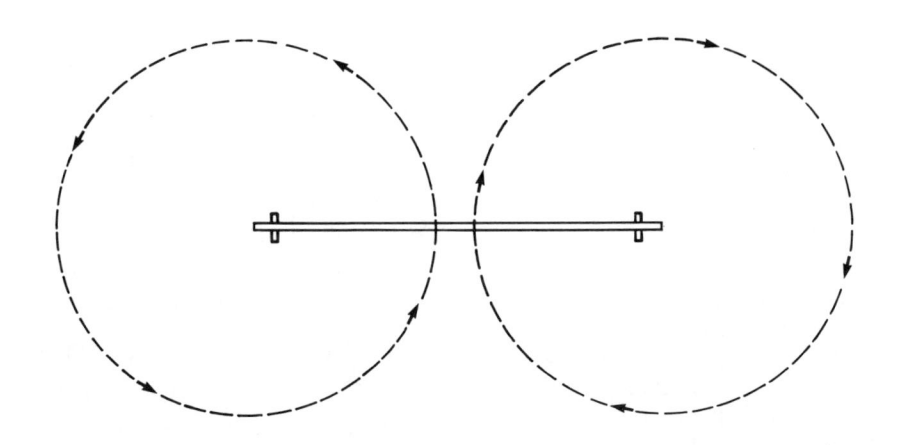

DIAGRAM 50

If the horse is calm and understands, take two cavalettis at the lowest height approximately one metre apart. This distance is of course, slightly different for different striding horses. Perhaps 90-95 cm (2 foot 11 inches to 3 foot 2 inches) for the average and 100 cm (3 foot 3 inches) for a longer stride at the walk.

When your horse is calm and understands the two cavalettis and the riders independent balance is maintained, that is, the rider is not touching the horses mouth - then progressively add the remaining five cavalettis at the lowest height.

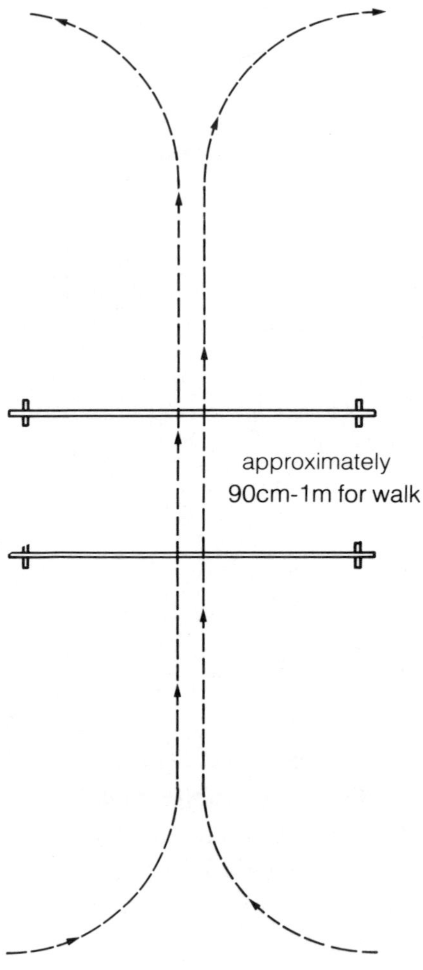

Repeat this exercise at the trot. Starting at the trot with one cavaletti at the lowest height, then two and so on. The space will be 1.50m to 1.83m (5 foot to 6 foot) between each trot cavaletti. Always remembering the main thing is that the rider maintains his balance and does not touch the horse's mouth except to guide the horses direction, whatever unexpected things may happen!

If the horse is not calm or is rushing do not pull against him, just remember to do the small circles taking your inside hand away from the horses neck.

approximately 90cm-1m for walk

DIAGRAM 51

The rider should have a neck strap around the horse's neck to save the horse's mouth if the rider's balance is not good enough should something unexpected happen. Then, if the horse's mouth was not touched, he knows it was his mistake and not caused through the mouth being touched and he will rectify the mistake himself - if not the first time then the second. The bridle should have a very soft bit.

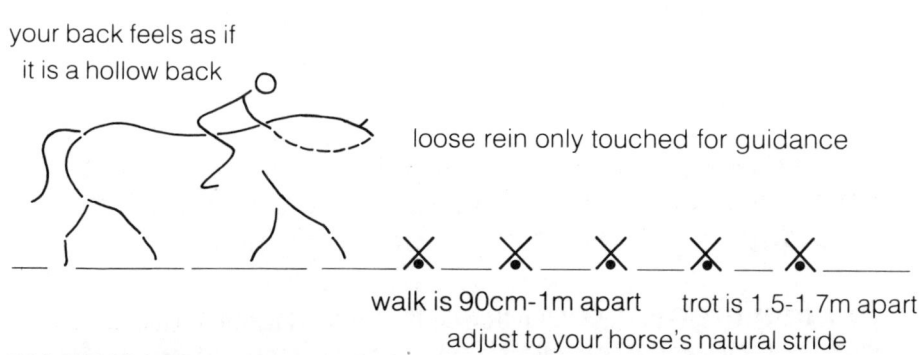

your back feels as if it is a hollow back

loose rein only touched for guidance

walk is 90cm-1m apart   trot is 1.5-1.7m apart
adjust to your horse's natural stride

DIAGRAM 52

Do not touch the mouth for any reason however wrong the horse may approach the poles or whatever may go wrong through the poles. Still not touching the horses mouth, except to guide him, come around and go through again.

Whenever starting to train any horse you must understand that the horses muscles get tired, as do your own when you are doing unaccustomed exercises or a new sport.

Remember this and understand your horse's aches and tired muscles.

So, do your cavalettis. And with a horse that has taken to it easily you may be up to the medium height of the cavaletti by the **second day**.

This has been a strain for your horse, both mental and physical, so you must give your horse a change on the **third day**, go for a ride in the open country.

The **fourth day**, go back to the first height (on the ground) and start again to give the horse a chance to develop his muscles.

The **fifth day**, start at the beginning and if all goes well you may build up to half the cavaletti (four) at maximum height.

The **sixth day**, - spell - Rest day.

The **seventh day**, Start at the beginning again and work up to all the cavalettis at maximum height.

On all the days the horse should first walk and trot through the cavalettis on the ground to loosen his muscles before being asked for more effort.

If fourteen poles are set out on the ground to your horse's natural stride, seven at walking spacing, and seven at trot spacing, this saves a lot of time in adjustments.

So in reality, **each and every day**, you walk through all cavalettis, at all three heights and then trot through at all these heights before asking anything more difficult.

The **eighth day**, loosen your horse on the cavalettis as every other day and start - "In Outs".

"In Outs"

Take the sixth cavaletti and place at its lowest height on top of the seventh. The distance will be right to pop.

Then take the fourth cavaletti and at its lowest height place on the fifth, and then the second on the third, and move the first one in to be 1.5m distance as in the diagram.

This gives you your first "In Out".

Then do it at the medium height and then at the top height.

Do not hurry at raising the heights - be sure the horse is calm and relaxed and the rider's balance is independent.

If at any time a disturbance occurs and the horse takes fright, if for ANY reason through the cavaletti. Stop, and go back to the beginning, to give him his full confidence again. This should be done whenever a rider or horse loses confidence for any reason whatsoever, go back to the beginning.

After about one week of these simple "In Outs", or longer, the horse should have every confidence in the "In Outs". This means he will be doing it all in a relaxed calm and happy way with no interference from the rider.

The rider will be able to maintain an independent balance and the reins will have a small loop, only being used to guide the horse.

If the rider's balance is sufficient and independent, the rider can sing a song or perhaps comb his hair going through the "In Outs".

When the horse gets to this stage, you build a little oxer, two strides behind that "In Out" and then later bring it back to one stride. Build the oxer up to the horses

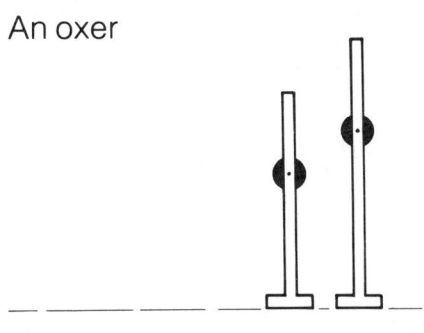

An oxer

Front rail always one hole lower than the back rail

DIAGRAM 53

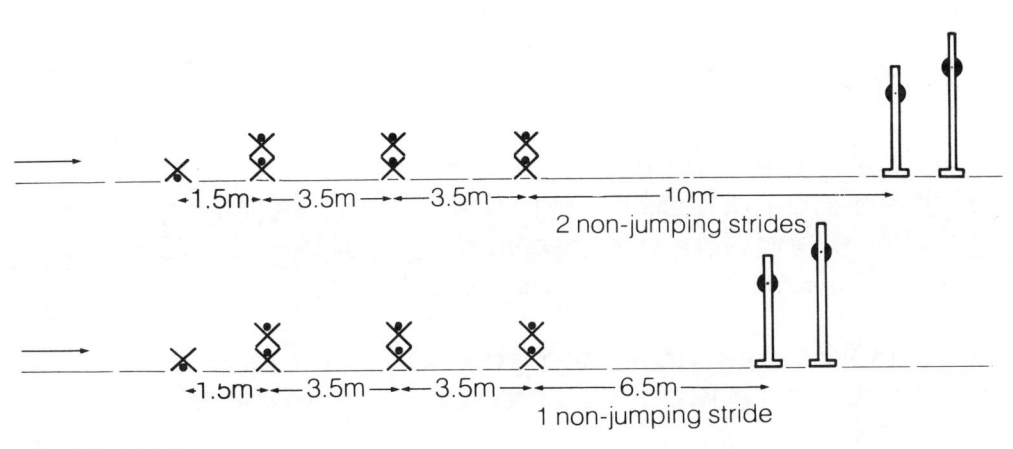

DIAGRAM 54

standard of training and widen it gradually. But not higher than 1.1m (3 foot 7 inches) or wider than 1.2m (3 foot 11 inches) otherwise you are demanding too much of your horse.

All this has been using the horse's natural length of stride at walk and trot. Now we vary the distance to teach the horse to shorten and lengthen his stride which gives you the benefit that he will find his own distance without you pulling against him.

To Lengthen the "In Outs"

When the horse knows well the "In Outs" with the little oxer, the distances can be altered from his natural length of stride.

The time has come that you can have a little bit more in your hands - *a little!*

Start by lengthening the distance between each set of double cavalettis by 30 cms (1 foot), also the distance to the oxer by 30 cms (1 foot).

Go through a few times so your horse understands it is different - longer. If your horse understands and is happy, then lengthen the distance to the oxer another foot.

If you lengthen the three double cavalettis 30 cms (1 foot) each and the distance to the oxer 60 cms (2 feet) you have lengthened the exercise overall by 1.5m (5 feet). Quite a lot for your horse to adjust to.

Do this for a few days then go back to the normal distance for a few days before you begin to shorten the "In Outs".

← ✗ ╳   ╳   ╳   ‖ ‖
   ←1.5m→←3.5m→←3.5m→←——6.5m——→

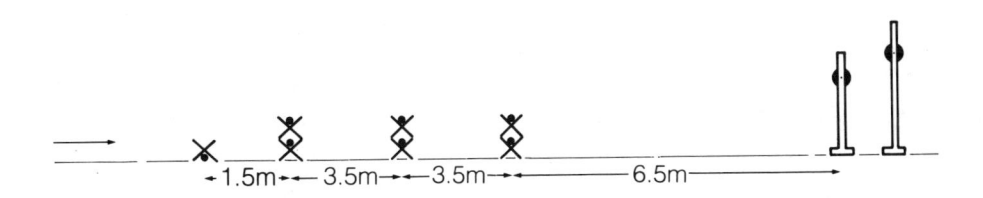

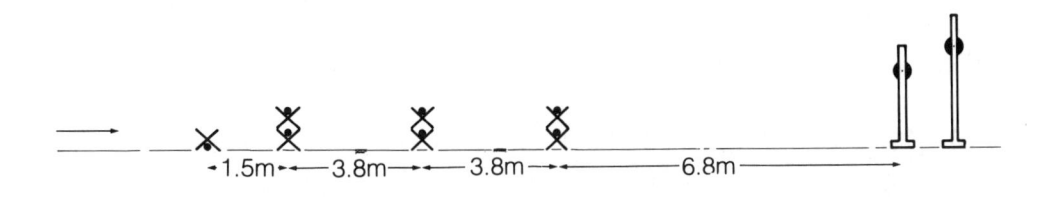

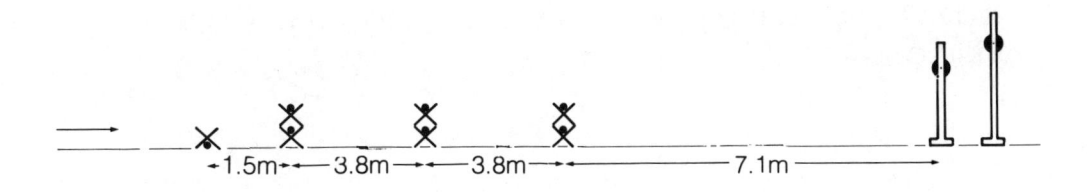

← ✗ ╳   ╳   ╳   ‖ ‖
   ←1.5m→←3.8m→←3.8m→←——6.8m——→

← ✗ ╳   ╳   ╳   ‖ ‖
   ←1.5m→←3.8m→←3.8m→←——7.1m——→

DIAGRAM 55

To Shorten the "In Outs"

Start the same way as for lengthening but do not shorten by as much, 15cm (6 inches) is sufficient between all cavalettis and the distance to the oxer.

Jump through and when your horse is happy you can shorten all the distances by a further 15cms (6 inches). Later bring the oxer another 30cms (1 foot) closer to the cavalettis.

Always remember to approach the first single cavaletti at a trot, **never** a canter.

Remember this is a schooling exercise and always keeping the horse "lightly on the bit" these distances now can be further shortened and expanded.

If by this stage you find that you and your horse have been doing the cavaletti exercises correctly, you have come to the point that you can start jumping a little course.

71

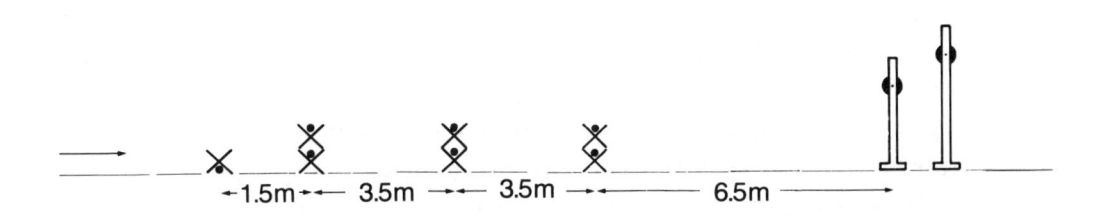

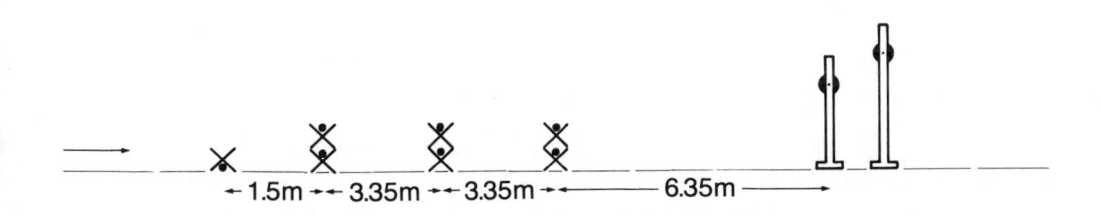

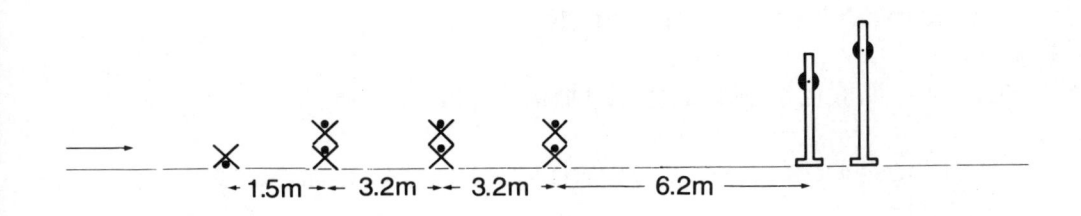

DIAGRAM 56

Trot and Pop

Build some single small, maximum height 60cm jumps (2 feet) to make a course.

These little jumps can be varied from straight to oxer to hogs back, but not ever at this stage, a double bar parallel. There should be approximately 75m (82.5 yards) between each little jump during this course. i.e.. take big loops past the jumps to give you this distance (you do not need an enormous area). This is to give either the horse or rider room to recover between each little jump.

Suggest you still put the neck strap on the horse, particularly if the horse has no mane.

Approach your course of small jumps first at a trot and jump them as single jumps with small and large circles before and after each little jump.

Always trotting with the horse lightly in hand only using the reins to guide the horse, and always the rider maintaining his/her independent balance.

You are, in fact, playing at jumping little jumps.

It is all designed to keep your horse happy, calm and relaxed.

Now do the same at a pleasant canter, not too fast, not too slow, and maintaining the same speed throughout - not always jumping.

So far the only "contact" has been to guide the horse. From now on you start to get your horse a little more in hand. If you have done the right thing up till now your horse has almost unknowingly come lightly on the bit.

CAVALETTI

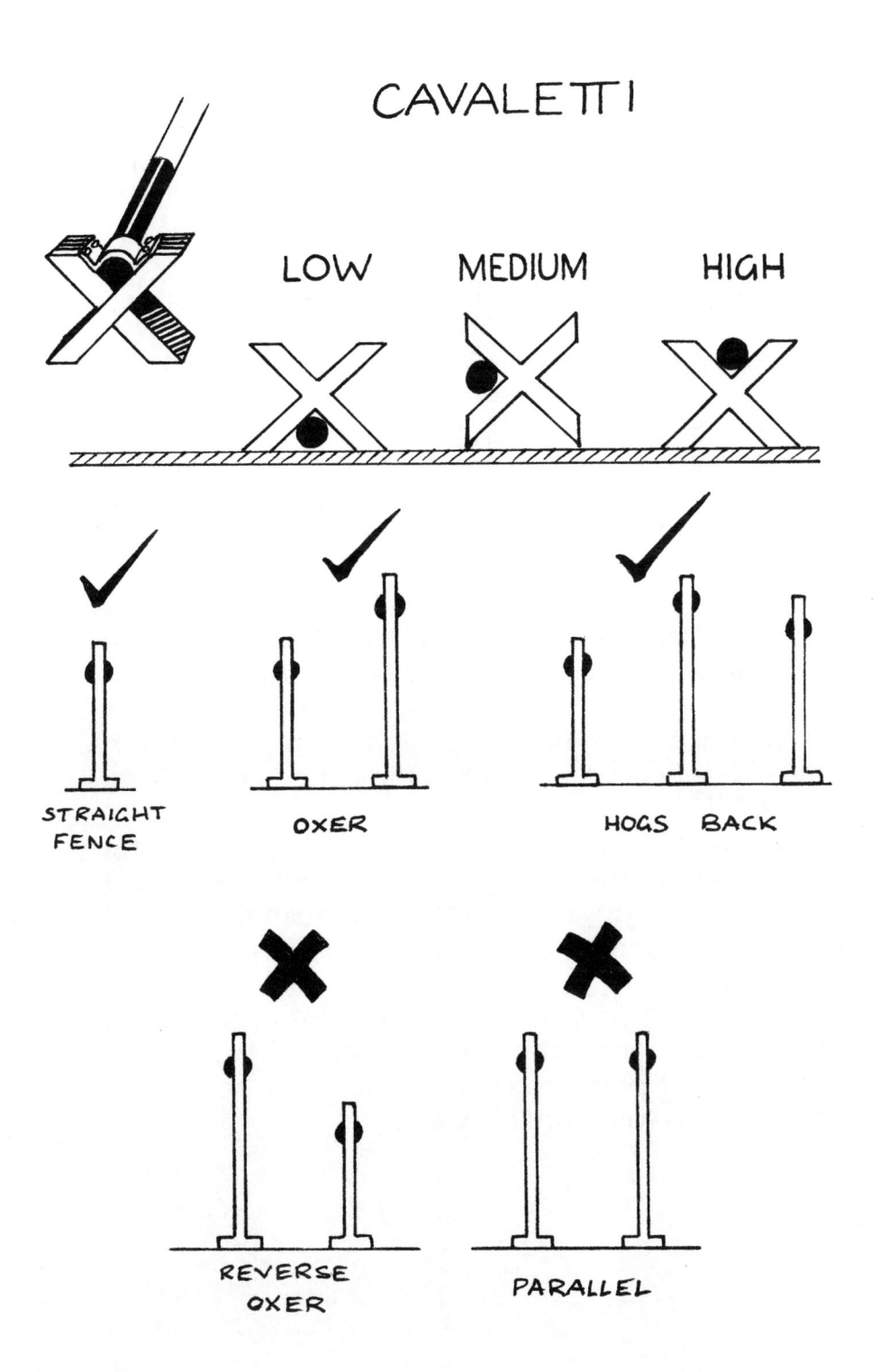

LOW MEDIUM HIGH

STRAIGHT FENCE ✓

OXER ✓

HOGS BACK ✓

REVERSE OXER ✗

PARALLEL ✗

You have come to the stage where you now develop your horses impulsion, collection, lengthening and shortening of stride without losing your "lightly on the bit" contact.

Briefly you can now get your act more together.

We can also now become more technical.

Your horse is approaching a jump at a balanced canter - lightly on the bit - during the last 10 metres (33 feet) before he jumps, his neck should lengthen approximately 1cm per metre (0.5 inches per 39 inches) travelled.

That is, his neck normally should be 10cm (4 inches) longer when he comes to the point of take off.

This will happen if the rider allows the horse to stretch his neck as he engages himself to jump.

The horse must not lose his impulsion, or change his canter tempo, nor does the rider drop the reins and lose contact. If any of these things occur the horse will lose his confidence, and usually stop.

But by having your horse on a loose rein during his ground work and schooling, he has developed his independent balance and will probably cope with any situation with confidence.

Extra Exercises

To help your horse find his distance for take off on any fence.

At canter, start with a 60cm (2 feet) straight fence, then two normal strides (eleven and a half metres or 38 feet 0 to an oxer, 60cm (2 feet) high in the front element and 75cm (2 feet 6 inches) high in the back element with a 90cm (3 feet) spread.

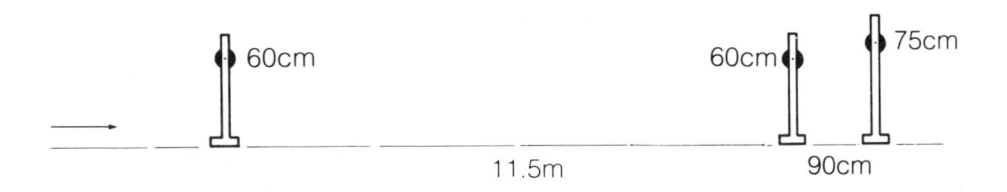

Next step is to leave the straight fence at 60cm (2 feet), build both elements of the oxer up by 15cm (6 inches) - 75cm (2 foot 6 inches) front and 90cm (3 feet) back - but leave the width between the two elements at 90 cm (3 feet). Jump this a couple of times from both left and right.

The third step is to increase the height of the straight fence by 30cms (1 foot) - from 60cms (2 feet) to 90cms (3 feet) - and both elements of the oxer by 15 cms (6 inches) to 90cm (3 feet) front and 1.05 metres (3 feet 5 inches) back. Also increase the width between the two oxer elements by 30 cms (1 foot) to 1.2 metres (3 feet 11 inches).

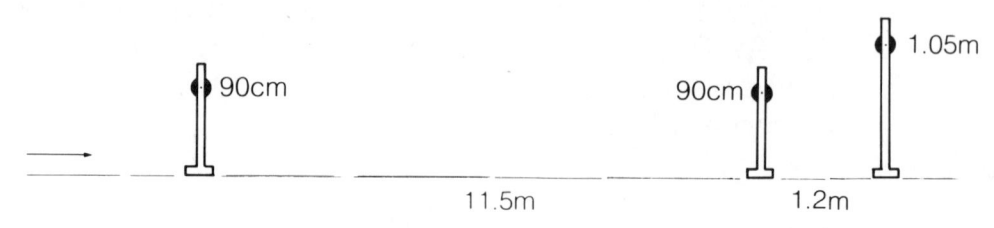

Perhaps raise either or both oxer elements and also widen the oxer elements some more. Widen by leaving the front rail stationary and only moving the back rail away from the front rail.

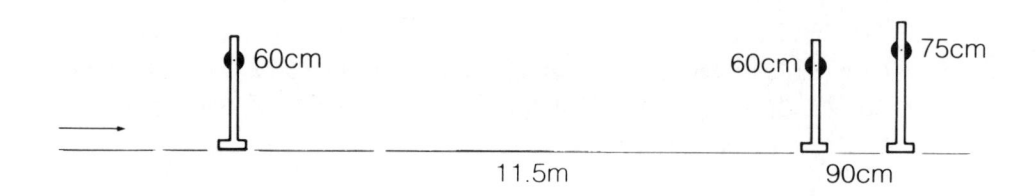

Do this exercise for two to three days, then go for a ride on the fourth day

On the fifth day, lower the straight fence to 60cms (2 feet), and then lower the oxer elements back to 60cm (2 feet) high in front and 75cm (2 feet 6 inches) high at the back with 90cm (3 feet) spread.

```
          60cm                    75cm  ● 90cm
           |                       |     |
    →   ___|_____|_____|___
              11.35m                 1.05m
```

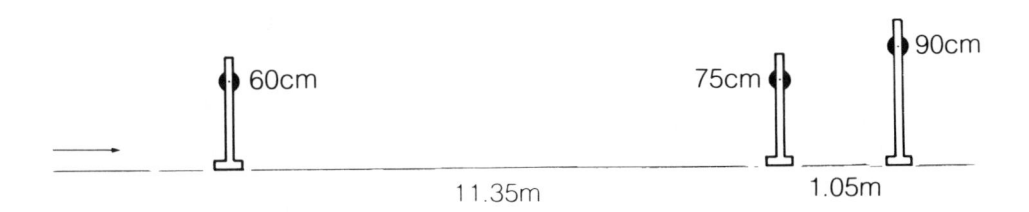

The next exercise involves leaving the straight fence at 60cms (2 feet) and raising both front and the back oxer elements by 15 cm (6 inches) to 75cm (2 feet 6 inches) and 90cm (3 feet) respectively and widening the oxer by placing the front element 15cm (6 inches) closer to the straight fence, reducing the distance between jumps from 11.5 to 11.35 metres (38 feet to 37 feet 6 inches.)

The final exercise involves raising the straight fence to 90cm (3 feet) and both front and back oxer elements by 15cms (6 inches) to 90cm (3 feet) and 1.05 metres (3 feet 5 inches) respectively. At the same time move the front oxer element some 15 cms (6 inches) closer to the straight fence, reducing the distance between the two jumps to 11.2 metres (37 feet).

```
           90cm                    90cm   ● 1.05m
            |                       |      |
    →   ____|_____|_____|___
              11.2m                  1.2m
```

Exercise for an Enthusiastic Horse

1. At canter, if your horse is too enthusiastic, perhaps not quite rushing, you must place another 60cm (2 feet) jump prior to the first one to make an "In Out". Distances should be as in diagram 59.

This exercise is good for all horses, but particularly the horse that is inclined to rush. This teaches the horse to restrain his speed himself, without the rider pulling against him.

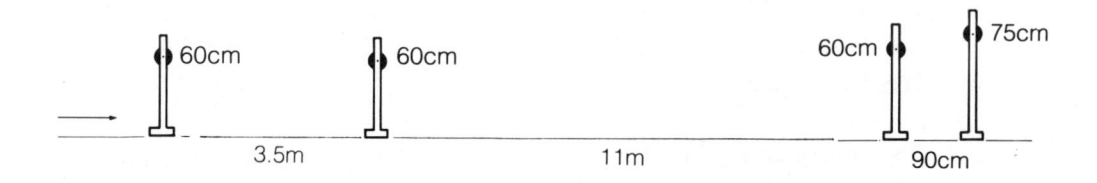

DIAGRAM 59

2. A horse could also be too enthusiastic after landing.

To teach him to maintain his tempo and not rush on landing, place three or four cavalettis approx. 6.2-6.5m (20 foot 4 inches - 21 foot 4 inches) behind the back rail of a 60cm (2 feet) high oxer. The cavalettis are placed 1.5-1.8m (5 feet - 6 feet) apart depending on your horse's natural length of trot stride.

Don't pull against his mouth between the jump and the cavalettis! Allow him to sort it out by himself. As soon as you are through the cavalettis make one or more circles in the same trot to keep him going. If the horse does not stop rushing, keep adding more cavalettis.

Start as in 'A'.

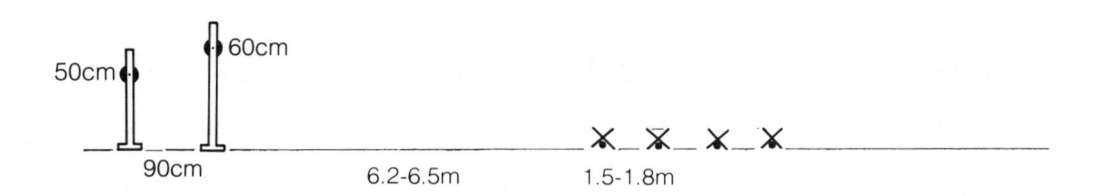

50cm 60cm

90cm   6.2-6.5m   1.5-1.8m

If the horse keeps rushing on landing just keep adding cavalettis 1.5-1.8m (5 - 6 feet) apart as in 'B',

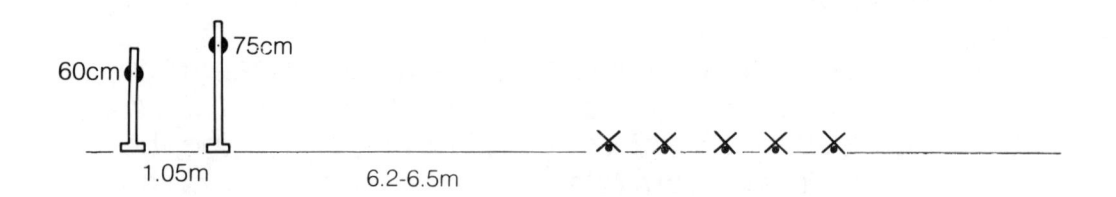

60cm 75cm
1.05m   6.2-6.5m   x x x x x

and later as in 'C'.

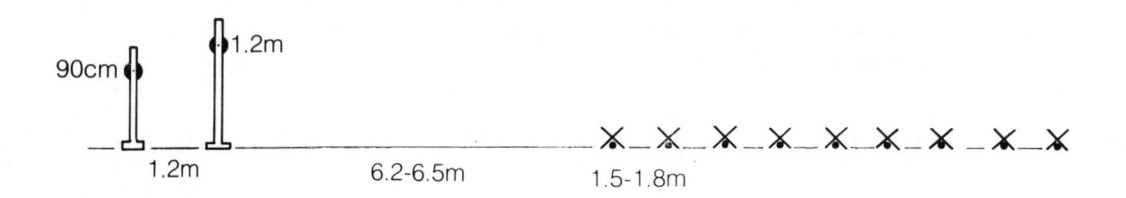

90cm 1.2m
1.2m   6.2-6.5m   1.5-1.8m   x x x x x x x x x

DIAGRAM 60

Remember not to pull against his mouth - just let him sort it out for himself.

Variation on Cavalettis: 1

This is a good exercise for building up the horse's neck muscles.

Cavalettis can also be placed in a half-circle to be lunged over or ridden over.

Start, of course, with one cavaletti at walk and when the horse will walk calmly over all seven cavalettis then start to trot over one cavaletti at the lowest height. And so on, as before, building up to seven cavalettis at the lowest height before raising the height.

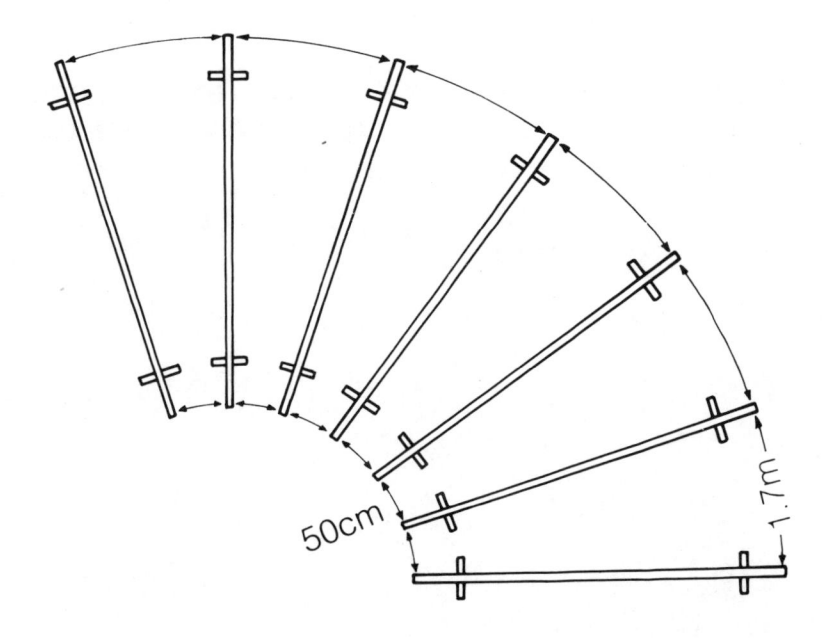

DIAGRAM 61

When lungeing, the horse must be **free** of contraptions (head tied down etc.) so that he is free to put his head and neck down. He will find his own distance and work his muscles correctly but with the added advantage that he is on a circle and bending.

Lunge in both directions.

This exercise gives your horse the most benefit if you wish to lunge over cavaletti.

Do not repeat so often that the horse gets tired or bored, which of course applies in everything!

Take care that the lunge line has an easy contact so that he can find where he wants to trot through.

This lungeing gives only the horse the exercise and the rider misses out, and who usually needs the exercise as much or even more, but the rider?

Variation on Cavalettis: 2

It is the practical and conscientious trainer who knows when to vary an exercise.

Start with one cavaletti at the lowest height at walk and build it up to seven. Still at a walk we raised the fourth cavaletti to the medium height. The horses walked through two to three times, then we raised the second to the medium height and brought the first one fractionally closer (approximately 10cm (4 inches)) but didn't raise it.

The horses walked through two to three times then we raised the sixth to the medium height and brought the seventh approximately 10cm (4 inches) closer.

Again after two to three times walking through, we in turn raised the remaining cavalettis one at a time, that is the fifth, then the third, then the seventh, and then the first.

The effect on all three horses - all with different training experience was startling. The concentration of their faces and the effort required to move all four legs separately was far greater than any trotting cavaletti work.

To the onlooker, it was similar to watching an army trainee crawling through an assault course!

Later with the more experienced horse, we raised the cavaletti one at a time to the maximum height still at a walk. The mental control and concentration showing in horse's face was enormous apart from the variety of muscles exercised.

Variation on Cavalettis: 3

Two way stretch - very good for loosening the shoulders.

When you have loosened up your horse and have seven cavalettis at walk, take four away and place them as in diagram 62.

The horse has to concentrate and think and should turn from one set to the next immediately.

When he is confident of this exercise at a walk, it can be done at a trot.

maximum height   climb through

90-95cm

approximately 4m

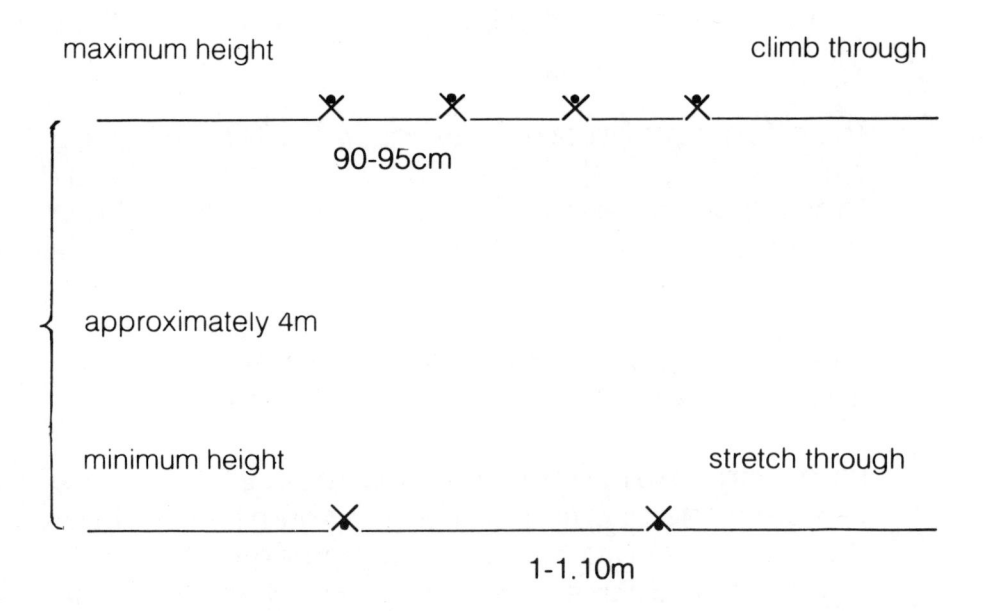

minimum height   stretch through

1-1.10m

DIAGRAM 62

Start from successfully trotting through the seven cavalettis, built up to maximum height.

Take four away and set up as in diagram 63.

The four get gradually raised one at a time to maximum height, perhaps a little closer depends on the horses natural stride.

The three stay at the low height and get stretched. When the horse has to lift and stretch his front legs the cavaletti are far enough apart.

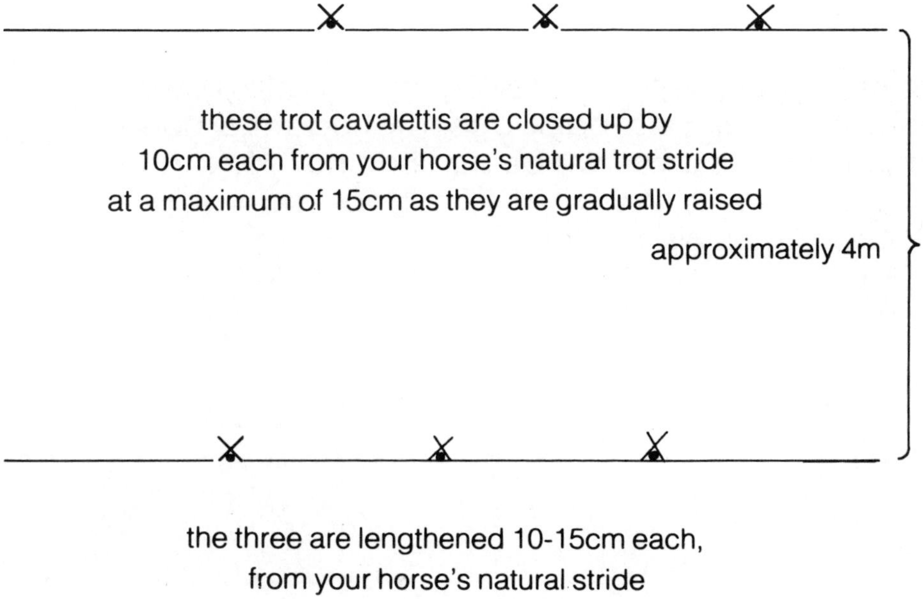

these trot cavalettis are closed up by
10cm each from your horse's natural trot stride
at a maximum of 15cm as they are gradually raised

approximately 4m

the three are lengthened 10-15cm each,
from your horse's natural stride

DIAGRAM 63

Exercise For Turning

Set out the cavalettis as in diagram 63 and beside a small jump that can be jumped from either side, as in diagram 64.

Start by trotting over both lots of cavalettis from either direction then trot over the four, followed by the three, followed by the drums, then turn immediately over the four.

If the horse is cantering let him sort it out and he will remember that he trots through the cavaletti and will check himself. Then the three again and the drums and the four again.

The rider should turn the horse as short and as tight as possible.

Remembering to do it by taking the inside rein away from the neck and back again to lead the horse around the turn. You will be surprised how short and how easily your horse will turn if you do not pull backwards on his mouth!

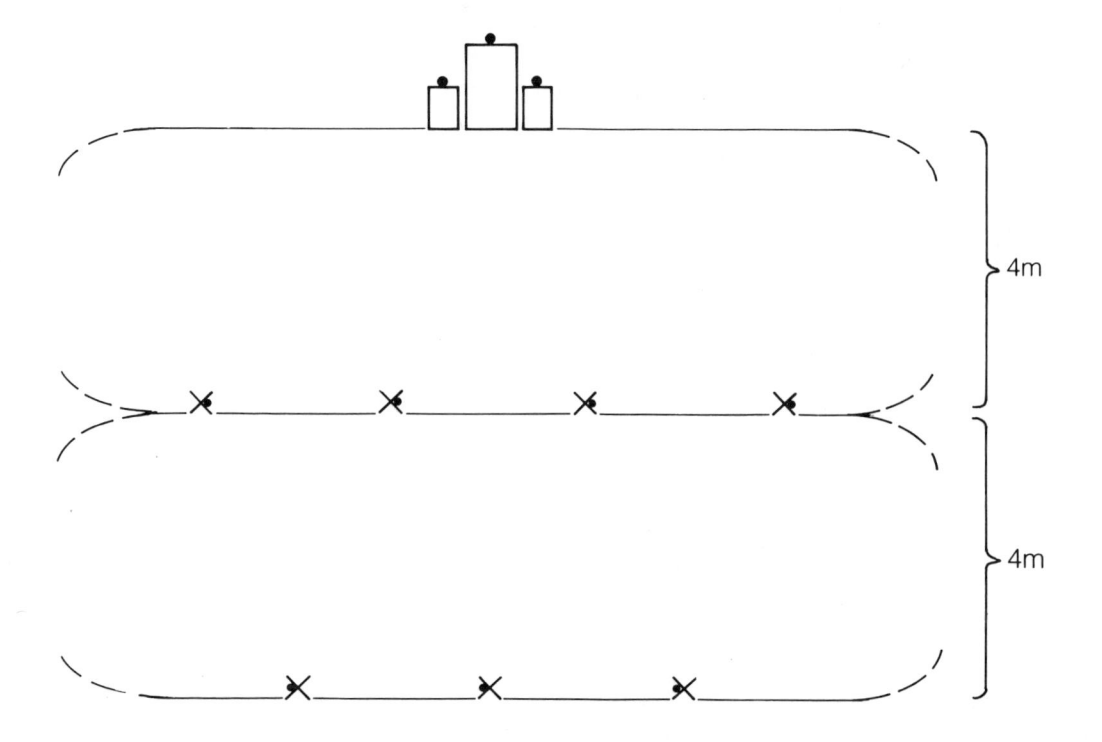

DIAGRAM 64

If all these simple beginning exercises have been done in a careful and thoughtful way and the horse has his independent balance, the rider has his independent balance, then the combination can approach a beginners competition with confidence.

*And most important of all.......
......have fun!!!*

676.99449
M266h

KNAPP BRANCH LIBRARY
13330 CONANT
DETROIT, MICHIGAN 48212
(313) 481-1772

Health Communication and Breast Cancer among Black Women

Health Communication and Breast Cancer among Black Women

Culture, Identity, Spirituality, and Strength

Annette D. Madlock Gatison

LEXINGTON BOOKS
Lanham • Boulder • New York • London

Published by Lexington Books
An imprint of The Rowman & Littlefield Publishing Group, Inc.
4501 Forbes Boulevard, Suite 200, Lanham, Maryland 20706
www.rowman.com

Unit A, Whitacre Mews, 26-34 Stannary Street, London SE11 4AB

Copyright © 2016 by Lexington Books

All rights reserved. No part of this book may be reproduced in any form or by any electronic or mechanical means, including information storage and retrieval systems, without written permission from the publisher, except by a reviewer who may quote passages in a review.

British Library Cataloguing in Publication Information Available

Library of Congress Cataloging-in-Publication Data

Names: Madlock Gatison, Annette, author.
Title: Health communication and breast cancer among black women : culture, identity, spirituality, and strength / Annette D. Madlock Gatison.
Description: Lanham : Lexington Books, [2016] | Includes bibliographical references and index.
Identifiers: LCCN 2016015827 (print) | LCCN 2016016876 (ebook) | ISBN 9780739185155 (cloth : alk. paper) | ISBN 9780739185162 (electronic)
Subjects: LCSH: Breast–Cancer. | African American women–Medical care. | Communication in medicine.
Classification: LCC RC280.B8 H43 2017 (print) | LCC RC280.B8 (ebook) | DDC 616.99/44900896073–dc23
LC record available at https://lccn.loc.gov/2016015827

∞™ The paper used in this publication meets the minimum requirements of American National Standard for Information Sciences Permanence of Paper for Printed Library Materials, ANSI/NISO Z39.48-1992.

Printed in the United States of America

To Annie and Beatrice

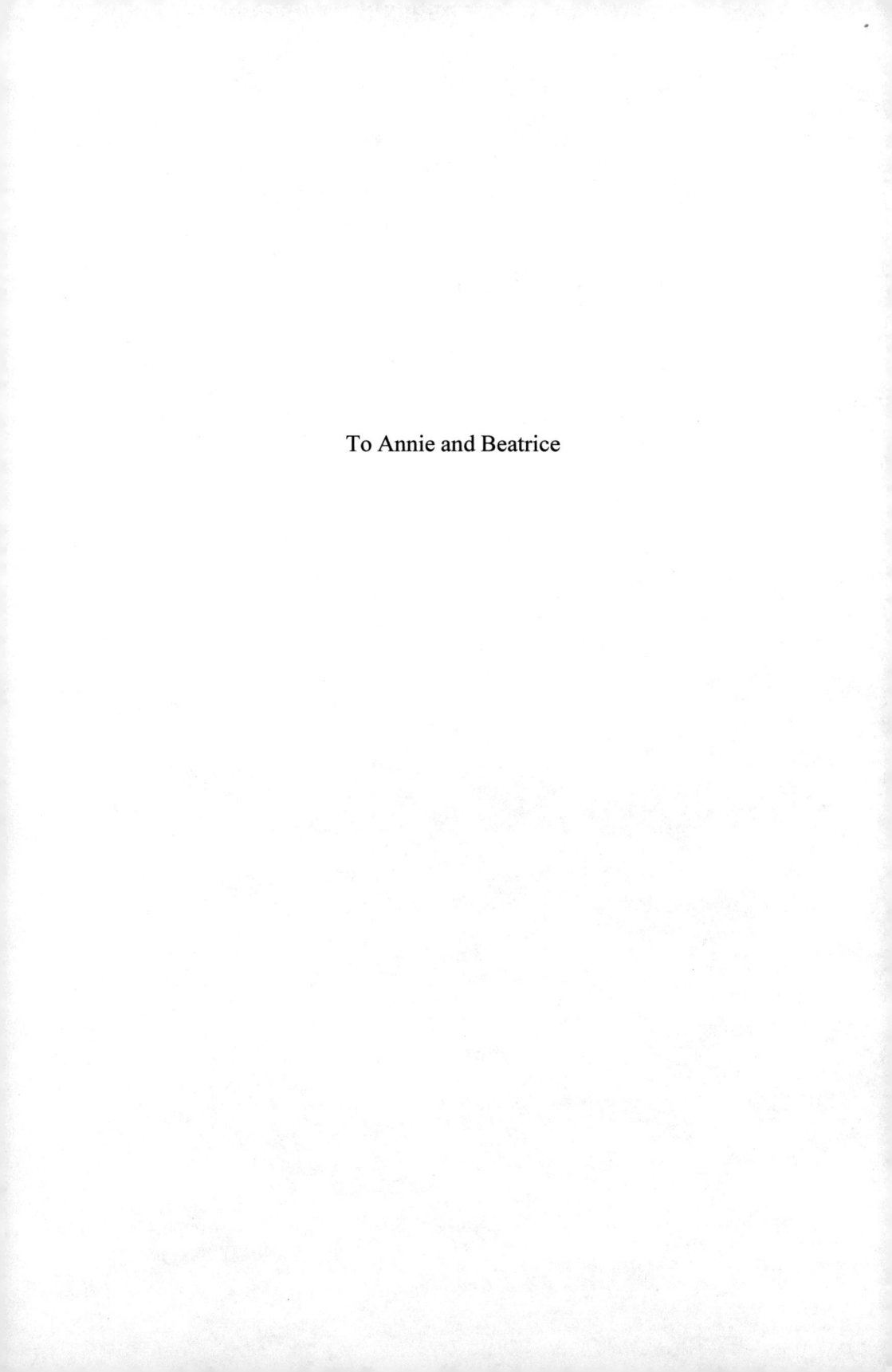

Contents

Acknowledgments		ix
Terminology		xi
Introduction		xiii
1	Background and Theoretical Framing	1
2	Myth of the Strong Black Woman: Asset or Liability	11
3	God's Got It: Faithtalk	21
4	Embracing the Pink Identity: Black Women and Pink Ribbon Culture	37
5	Work and Family	45
Conclusion: Body Politics, Coping, and Reframing the Narrative		59
Appendix: The Pink and The Black Project©: Breast Cancer Culture and Black Women		67
Bibliography		73
Index		83
About the Author		87

Acknowledgments

Bringing this book to completion was extremely difficult and took much longer than I could have ever anticipated. As my body continued to struggle with disease and the aftereffects of treatment, I did not know the emotional toll that my mind and spirit would have to endure as I began the process of analysis and putting words to page. I seriously contemplated not completing this book and just forgetting the whole idea as I had been emotionally immobilized. Immobilized from remembering and reliving my own trauma while sharing in the stories and lived experiences of trauma by other women who are still living and those who have transitioned on since I began The Pink and The Black Project©. However, a community of women inspired me to continue and reminded me that I had to finish in support of those who need to know and understand the trifecta that Black women face when it comes to their health.

Thank you to Dr. Kami Anderson, Ms. Carla Bradford, Ms. Erica Bradley, Dr. Leta Frazier, Reverend Dr. Alika P. Galloway, Elder Deborah Isabelle, Dr. Shirley Jackson, Elder Deborah Bethel Patterson, Ms. Yvette Toko, Ms. Gerri Cotton, and Ms. Dawn White-Bracey. I also have to thank my youngest supporter and biggest inspiration, Mya, who encouraged me on some of my saddest days and said "Auntie Nette, did you write anything today, you can do it." We have to put an end to breast cancer for the sake of our future. Living with a chronic disease like breast cancer cannot be the new normal. That is just not acceptable.

Terminology

African American/Black: African American women are not a monolithic group and acknowledging that African American women differ from other races and ethnicities is only one aspect in the study of Black women's health. To explore both the differences and similarities within the context of health, one must define who is "African American" or "Black" and this can be very complex as the terms are at times used interchangeably and can include many ethnic groups as population shifts and immigration have increased the Black population in the United States. It is important to note that some immigrants from various parts of the Caribbean as an example will at times self-identify as Black or depending on the situation might self-select African-American and forego the hyphen (example: Haitian-American).

The term "Black" itself can mean any person of African descent representing the larger African diaspora throughout the world. However, in the United States the Census Bureau defines "Black or African American" as any person having origins in any of the Black racial groups of Sub-Saharan Africa. The ability for this people group to name themselves is a relatively new phenomenon, as racial identity is a social construct and in previous decades the terms negro and colored were the identity terms used to name the descendants of slaves born in the United States (Madlock Gatison, in press). *Health Communication and Breast Cancer among Black Women: Identity, Spirituality, and Strength* uses African American and Black interchangeably. Capitalization of the word Black in reference to Black women or Black people is not a typographical or spelling error.

Introduction

During an interview in 2010, Jenisha Watts of *Essence* magazine asked noted feminist, scholar, activist, and author bell hooks "What should Black women be paying attention to the most?" hooks' response: "I think the number one thing Black women and Black people should be paying attention to is our health. By that, I mean our physical and mental health."[1] *Health Communication and Breast Cancer among Black Women: Identity, Spirituality, and Strength* was written out of the need to pay particular attention to Black women's health as it relates to breast cancer and the sociocultural norms that influence how Black women communicate about their health. However, I must begin this work with a brief report on the current state of Black women's health, as it deserves attention.

THE STATE OF BLACK WOMEN'S HEALTH

Over the past several decades information about the health of African American women and the factors that influence their health has continued to be collected. Much of this documentation and data have resulted because of Black women's involvement in the women's health movement (Baird, Davis, & Christensen, 2009; Morgen, 2002; Seaman & Eldridge, 2012), which pushed for policies that have required epidemiologic and biomedical researchers to pay specific attention to the health issues of ethnic and racial populations (Fisher Collins, 2006; Madlock Gatison, 2015a; 2015c; 2015e; 2015f). Therefore, I begin *Health Communication and Breast Cancer among Black Women: Identity, Spirituality, and Strength* with a brief status report regarding the overall health of African American women as reported in the scientific data available at the time of this writing.[2] This data is presented because Black women are burdened by a number of chronic illnesses (see table I.1) that impact their quality of life and mortality rates. The following chapters incorporate this statistical data with an emphasis on Black women and breast cancer as seen through a mixed-method research approach that includes autoethnography.

OPTIMAL HEALTH STANDARDS

Whenever one hears about the health of Black women it is often in comparison to white women. This specific binary is the set standard because the indicators for the optimal health of a population are standardized by whomever the research data designates as the healthiest. The standard in the research community is white women as they are more often the healthiest and are normally used as the comparative group for analysis against African American women and other women of color in most studies originating in the United States (Fisher Collins, 2006, p. 1). This fact continues to be the case; therefore this is also the comparative population I use in this work.

Life and Death[3]

Life expectancy describes the likelihood of surviving to a given age at a given time in history based on statistical averages. To determine life expectancy one must consider several variables such as lifestyle, access to health care, diet, socioeconomics, and mortality and morbidity data (Leigh & Li, 2014, p. 65; Mandal, 2014). For African American women life expectancy is not only about how long we are expected to live, but it is also an indicator of how we are meeting the enormous challenges of society, as compared to other women. Socioeconomic status, employment

Table I.1. Health Conditions Common in African American Women

Asthma	Lupus
Breast Cancer	Mental Health Issues & Suicide
Cancer	Obesity & Overweight
Cervical Cancer	Osteoporosis
Diabetes	Pregnancy-Related Death
Glaucoma and Cataracts	Sexually Transmitted Infections
Heart Disease	Sickle Cell Anemia
High Blood Pressure	Smoking
High Cholesterol	Stroke
HIV/AIDS	Tuberculosis
Infant Death	Uterine Fibroids
Kidney Disease	Violence

Health conditions common in African-American women as found on the womenshealth.gov website last updated in March of 2012. U.S. Department of Health and Human Services Office on Women's Health and the National Institutes of Health.

conditions, access to health insurance and health care are macro examples of sociocultural stressors that influence life and death.

Adapted from the Women of Color Health Data Book (Leigh & Li, 2014) and the Center for Disease Control (2010), table I.2 indicates, in rank order, the top five leading causes of death in Black women by age (Clayton, Brooks, & Kornstein, 2014, p. viii;). The statistics also include issues of personal and public safety[4] that are of concern; however, those issues are not addressed in this work.

It is no secret that over the past several decades there have been advances in medicine and improved access to health care for some women of color in the United States. However, the data still provides evidence that Black women are burdened with health challenges more often than other minority groups. According to the U.S. Department of Health and Human Services Office on Women's Health (http://womenshealth.gov/minority-health/african-americans/) of all minority groups, African Americans have the most, and many times the largest, differences in health risks when compared to other minority groups. Overall, African Americans continue to have more disease, disability, and early death. The illnesses and diseases identified in both tables I.1 and I.2 are among the top health concerns facing African American women. For some diseases, genetics play a role in the risk. Many of these health issues are

Table I.2. Leading Causes of Death in African American Women by Age

By Age	Top 5 Major Causes of Death (descending order)				
20–24	Unintentional Injuries/ Accidents	Homicide/ Assault	Heart Disease	Cancer	Suicide
25–34	Unintentional Injuries/ Accidents	Heart Disease	Cancer	Homicide/ Assault	HIV Disease
35–44	Cancer	Heart Disease	Unintentional Injuries/ Accidents	HIV Disease	Stroke
45–54	Cancer	Heart Disease	Stroke	Unintentional Injuries/ Accidents	Diabetes
55–64	Cancer	Heart Disease	Diabetes	Stroke	Kidney Disease
65+	Heart Disease	Cancer	Stroke	Diabetes	Alzheimer's Disease

Leading causes of death for African American women as found in the Women of Color Health Data Book, 2014, and the 2010 report of the CDC at http://www.cdc.gov/women/lcod/2010/womenBlack_2010.pdf.

chronic, which means they last a long time and even worse, sometimes forever. They are also simultaneous, meaning that Black women suffer from multiple chronic conditions at the same time.

As noted earlier, various societal stressors influence the lack of access to health care or adequate quality health care, both of which play a large part in some of the health conditions listed in both tables I.1 and I.2. While African American women are less likely to receive health care, when they do get care, they are more likely to get it late. This means, for instance, a problem like breast cancer is not found early, when it is most treatable. Or, the chance to prevent or delay diabetes is lost. Societal stressors also include generations of racism and poverty, which influence attitudes about seeking and receiving health care. The lack of trust in the medical system, cultural differences (Hooks-Anderson & Anderson, 2015), problems accessing care, and a lack of knowledge about the importance of tests to screen for major health problems are of major concern.

There are many reasons for this gap in mortality rates, overall health, wellness, and quality of life for Black women. *Health Communication and Breast Cancer among Black Women: Identity, Spirituality, and Strength* takes a purposeful look at three overlapping sociocultural influences, which are only a fragment of the burden but carry significant power in and on the lives of some Black women.

VISIBILITY OF BLACK WOMEN'S HEALTH

Poet and activist Audre Lorde (1988) stated that "Caring for myself is not self-indulgence, it is self-preservation and that is an act of political warfare." As Black women have started to care for themselves and become concerned with their health both medically and politically it has brought increased visibility. As one, medicine, does not work without the other, politics.

The increased visibility of Black women's health has not gone unnoticed by the public or by scholars across disciplines. As it pertains to Black women much has been written about access to health care, affordability of health care, quality of health care, sociocultural influences such as family, religion (Campesino, Saenz, Choi, & Krouse, 2012; Gregg, 2011), economics, and media. Vivian W. Pinn in her forward to *African American Women's Health and Social Issues* (Fisher Collins, 2006) has written extensively on the health and social status of African American women and, like me, acknowledges two important aspects. First, research has been done on how social issues like racism, poor education, poverty, diet, and the environment affect health status and not much has been done to change these issues. Second, individuals other than Black women have done the majority of the published research and writing on Black women's health. In this work I provide a needed voice in the research community as it pertains to Black women and their perceptions of their health and sociocultural affects.

There are four cancer-related identities that influence the well-being of Black women living with a breast cancer diagnosis, that of survivor, patient, victim, and person with cancer (Park, Zlateva, & Blank, 2009). *Health Communication and Breast Cancer among Black Women: Identity, Spirituality, and Strength* focuses on the survivor identity found in breast cancer and pink ribbon narratives. This work is unique in that it looks at the ways the discourse of strength constructs the identity of Black women even during times of chronic illness. *Health Communication and Breast Cancer among Black Women: Identity, Spirituality, and Strength* calls attention to the burden of breast cancer on Black women's health and quality of life. *Health Communication and Breast Cancer among Black Women: Identity, Spirituality, and Strength* not only calls attention to the physical health challenges it also calls attention to the mental and spiritual challenges Black female breast cancer survivors face with a disease that is now normalized in our society. The expectation is that one selflessly lives and works through breast cancer without showing fear or any sign of weakness. The expectation is set for breast cancer survivors to be tenacious and victorious.

CANCER JOURNALS OF INSPIRATION AND COURAGE

The Cancer Journals by Audre Lorde appeared in my life at the right time and was and continues to be my inspiration. Lorde's work provides a different type of motivation for victory and tenacity. *The Cancer Journals* caught my attention as I was browsing a used bookstore in Wisconsin during a period of remission in 2008. I was reflecting on my life and my journey with breast cancer at that time, something that I continue to do regularly as I am a Black woman who has been diagnosed with breast cancer twice, in 2003 and 2009. Both times I had been treated using the standard protocols of lumpectomy, chemotherapy, and radiation. This was followed by a bilateral mastectomy with reconstruction in 2012. Verbally sharing my thoughts and concerns with others about breast cancer was not a part of my process for living and coping with this disease. I read whatever I could get my hands on and wrote in a journal given to me by a friend.

I do not recall hearing about *The Cancer Journals* prior to 2008 although I was somewhat familiar with Lorde's work as an advocate for women and social justice, but somehow I missed her breast cancer story. This particular book, out of the many books I have read since my first diagnosis, is the one that has made the greatest impression on me to do more than donate to the cause of breast cancer, purchase pink products, or march for a cure.[5] While all have value I needed to do more. The first thing I needed to do was find *my* voice. It was Lorde's introduction to *The Cancer Journals* that garnered my attention as it spoke of women living in a self-imposed silence. This resonated with me as I worked and lived in silence about breast cancer not really wanting to talk about "it" unless it was absolutely necessary.

The necessity of speaking about my own experience presented itself in two main ways, first out of sheer necessity in discussion with health care providers or employers, and at the request of a family member or friend. It is necessary to discuss prognosis and treatment plans with one's health care team. In the case of an employer it is necessary to discuss the particulars so one can negotiate time off from work to receive said treatments. With family members or friends it is necessary to talk about breast cancer for two reasons: (1) friends and family want to know how you are doing, and (2) you become the go-to person if friends or family know of someone else who has been newly diagnosed with breast cancer. Both of these experiences force a breast cancer survivor to speak about, revisit, and begin to rationalize all of the feelings that subsumed and pushed one into silence. In my case, friends or family would want me to talk to the recently diagnosed individual about my experience. I am not sure if anyone ever considered that it could be too painful for me to talk about. With some reluctance I would share. Yet, I truly did not want to keep reliving a negative experience and it was agonizing. However, I also knew the anguish and fear of being told that I had cancer. As a result, I would gracefully and respectfully share my experience. Reliving the story is part of the life of a breast cancer survivor. The anguish and fear is always there in the background at varying intensities even when you have achieved remission. By speaking about it, the crack in the silence begins.

For some, the diagnosis of cancer can infiltrate and take over one's life. Some women try to live as if nothing ever happened, remaining in silence and pretending that "it" will go away if you do not think about "it." For me, I have been overtaken by breast cancer and what it does to the mind, body, and spirit of the lives it touches. What it does to the lives of breast cancer survivors, their family members, or those who have transitioned to the next life is unimaginable. Every waking moment is filled with what if scenarios: What if I die? What if I live? What if I get cancer again? What will my life be like? What about the kids? What about my job? What about the bills? What if the cancer metastasizes? What if I have to have my breasts removed? (I do not have to ask myself that question anymore.) Nevertheless, the question of "what if?" remains. During those and other moments one might try to draw strength and fortitude from faith traditions, possibly praying or meditating one's way through the agonizing thoughts that appear and reappear. An individual tries these particular self-help strategies, as a means to cope. Yes, there are other coping strategies, but the focus here is on faith and internal strength. Being stoic and never complaining means simply being that infamous strong Black woman who lives through some of the "what if" scenarios that come to pass and just deals with them. By falling in line with the march of the pink ribbon as a (s)hero, a warrior, a breast cancer survivor, and a strong Black woman of faith, one is in a way, being forced into a type of silence. As I worked to break my silence and find my voice, I found that I was expected to talk about breast cancer survivorship in a certain way; one that reinforced the imagery and metaphors of strength, resiliency, and survival.

This book developed from the positioning of my voice as well as the intersections and commonalities my voice shared with other breast cancer survivors of color. As I began to assert my own voice, I realized how many other Black female breast cancer survivors were also struggling with silence and voice. Through this work I acknowledged this struggle and the nature of silence within the Black community. Using health communication as well as standpoint and womanist theology theories, this book will conceptualize the true nature of being African American, living with or surviving breast cancer with the lens of the "pink culture" as a tool that both includes and excludes Black women.

To navigate what some call the new normal of living as a breast cancer survivor, there are words that can truly have an impact on ones psyche. Particularly when said by someone who has experienced the trauma of breast cancer and mastectomy. That is why Audre Lorde's *The Cancer Journals* made such an impression on me. She gave voice and named the self-imposed silence that I was experiencing and witnessing in the other breast cancer survivors I was in contact with. It was the first time I had read anything by a Black woman that got down to the truth of how I was feeling, that did not make me feel ashamed, feel like a failure, or feel like I was being punished by God for some "sin" for which a diagnosis of cancer was an extreme price to pay. I had read a lot of information about breast cancer, other types of cancer, and a host of other works about health issues that burden Black communities here in the United States and abroad. But, if one believes in divine providence, maybe it was just that when my eyes fell upon the words from the introduction of *The Cancer Journals* that follow:

> Each woman responds to the crisis that breast cancer brings to her life out of a whole pattern, which is the design of who she is and how her life has been lived. The weave of her every day existence is the training ground for how she handles crisis. Some women obscure their painful feelings surrounding mastectomy with a blanket of business-as-usual, thus keeping those feelings forever under cover, but expressed elsewhere. For some women, in a valiant effort not to be seen as merely victims, this means an insistence that no such feelings exist and that nothing much has occurred. For some women it means the warrior's painstaking examination of yet another weapon, unwanted but useful.

> I am a post-mastectomy woman who believes our feelings need voice in order to be recognized, respected, and of use.
>
> I do not wish my anger and pain and fear about cancer to fossilize into yet another silence, nor to rob me of whatever strength can lie at the core of this experience, openly acknowledged and examined. For other women of all ages, colors, and sexual identities who recognize that imposed silence about any area of our lives is a tool for separation and powerlessness, and for myself, I have tried to voice some of my feelings and thoughts about the travesty of prosthesis, the pain of amputation, the function of cancer in a profit economy, my confrontation with mortality, the strength of women loving, and the power and rewards of self-conscious living.
>
> Breast cancer and mastectomy are not unique experiences, but one shared by thousands of American women. Each of these women has a particular voice to be raised in what must become a female outcry against all preventable cancers as well as against the secret fears that allow those cancers to flourish. May these words serve as encouragement for other women to speak and to act out of our experiences with cancer and with other threats of death, for silence has never brought us anything of worth. Most of all, may these words underline the possibilities of self-healing and the richness of living for all women.
>
> There is a commonality of isolation and painful reassessment, which is shared by all women with breast cancer, whether this commonality is recognized or not. It is not my intention to judge the woman who has chosen the path of prosthesis, of silence and invisibility, the woman who wishes to be "the same as before." She has survived on another kind of courage, and she is not alone. Each of us struggles daily with the pressures of conformity and the loneliness of difference from which those choices seem to offer escape. I only know that those choices do not work for me, nor for other women who, not without fear, have survived cancer by scrutinizing its meaning within our lives, and by attempting to integrate this crisis into useful strengths for change. (*The Cancer Journals*, 1980, p. 1)

Audre Lorde's words inspired and encouraged me. It was as if she reached across time and space and said to me: "It is your turn. It is your turn to rest when you need it, but be free to rest. Not only talk the truth, but to do so without impunity." We need to understand how our lives, our bodies are not our own when our health is legislated and commodified. As such we have the right to speak up and take a stand. We have the right and we must act upon this right.

To understand how women's experiences with breast cancer influence their self-perceptions, the views others have of them, and their ability to express their needs and concerns, I developed The Pink and The Black Project©. As the project progressed, I learned how breast cancer survivorship and the lingering effects of treatment affected the balance of work, family, and overall quality of life. The notion of being a Strong Black Woman intersected with women's belief about the role of faith on health and illness, and the common survivorship rhetoric in pink ribbon culture. My research from The Pink and the Black Project© forms the analysis of this book.

In this work, I explore how breast cancer culture, faithtalk, and the myth of the strong Black woman influence the quality of Black women's lives when facing breast cancer diagnosis and treatment. It describes how Black women use faithtalk to negotiate their identity as breast cancer survivors while balancing life and work, exposes the expectations of the survivor whose *words* should be full of hope, and explains the implications of talking too openly about the physical and emotional toll of breast cancer and treatment. In reviewing the history of the pink ribbon and breast cancer culture, I show how warrior metaphors and triumphant survivorship can be detrimental to Black women who must negotiate three societally scripted identities, that of the pink ribbon warrior, the mighty woman of faith, and the myth of the strong Black woman—the combination of which creates a *trifecta of strength* and a new cultural ideal in the *Pink and Black Superwoman*. This controlling image creates unrealistic expectations that cast illness as a sign of weakness or lack of faith and silences those whose breast cancer experience does not fit within this rhetoric.

Autobiographical reflection was used to inform the data analysis from my perspective as a breast cancer survivor. From the time those words were first uttered, "you have breast cancer," there were things I needed to know that went beyond disease-specific medical facts and statistics. Those closest to me thought I was managing quite well as I did not "look sick" and they perceived me as a "strong Black woman" with "strong faith." I thought this problematic but kept those feelings to myself. If anyone were to ask how I was feeling I found it stressful to provide an answer that went beyond, "I am doing okay." At that time I did not really think I was doing well at handling the magnitude of the physical, mental, and spiritual changes brought about by those four words uttered by my doctor. But I found it hard to talk about my illness because I did not want to be perceived as complaining or weak.

As I traversed my way through healing circles and breast cancer survivor support groups I began to see patterns in the conversations of women who were long-term (longer than five years from first diagnosis) breast cancer survivors. They oriented around strong Black womanhood, faith talk, and pink warrior metaphors. I wondered how these conversational devices either helped them to cope or keep them silent. Maybe they were like me, keeping quiet in order to "look strong." My personal experience in, and with, breast cancer culture led me to think about the kinds of conversations survivors engage in when they are asked about their health. Conversations that change of course depending on the audience (family members, friends, other survivors, health care providers, employers, and others). But they also change in relation to core beliefs that tend to revolve around two key issues. For Black women facing breast cancer, where they land on the spectrum of pink ribbon culture (i.e., embracing to rejecting) is important as are their beliefs about Christian faithtalk, spiritual healing, and disease.

My personal experience with breast cancer provides a lens through which to understand the disease and the culture that surrounds it, particularly as a Black woman. This insider status as an African American female breast cancer survivor also provided an opportunity for me to connect more fully with the women that participated in The Pink and The Black Project©. As African American female breast cancer survivors we share some similarities in our disease experience and cultural heritage attributes that I found crucial for navigating the cultural terrain of Black women and breast cancer survivorship.

Catherine Fisher Collins in her introduction to the second edition of *African American Women's Health and Social Issues* (2006) addresses many of the influences on Black women's health that include biological, familial, cultural, economical, emotional, psychological, behavioral elements, and her sociopolitical environment (Fisher Collins, 2006, p. vii). Some of these are areas consistent with the data collected during The Pink and The Black Project©. "We know that some illnesses are fueled by social problems such as racism, poverty, low levels of education, and poor lifestyle choices such as smoking, drug use, unprotected sex, lack of physical activity, and inadequate dietary choices" (Fisher Collins, 2006, p. 1). All of these have some influence on the life expectancy of African American women breast cancer survivors.

Meaning of Survivorship

We should ask ourselves what does it mean to be a survivor. We see and hear the word *survivor* all the time as it relates to breast cancer. According to Sulik (2010), what started out as a way to "refer to anyone who has been diagnosed with and treated for cancer" or as a place for "diagnosed women to validate their experiences" and "advocate for their own bodies" has become a double-edged sword. It is now a term to silence women about the true nature of breast cancer and its impact on the body and encourages women to put on a brave face. "In pink ribbon culture, the survivor has become an obligatory status that prioritizes the trauma of suffering, gives the impression that diagnosed women are not dying, and diverts attention from issues related to quality of life while focusing almost exclusively on years survived" (Sulik, 2010, p. 318). In my own feeble attempt to resist this counting years of survivorship I keep track of each occurrence of breast cancer individually. In essence I reset the clock. I find it somewhat humorous that when I do this I am corrected. I am told I am "not counting right." Do the number of years survived really matter when your quality of life is questionable due to the disease and disharmony a woman is experiencing? As the count starts from the time you were diagnosed, not the time you finished treatments or no longer suffered from any side effects of the treatment.

This counting of survivorship years with no recognition of what happens during those years gives a false perception of longevity, which leads to a false perception of the quality of life for a survivor. This is an additional layer of strength that complicates the lived experience of Black women breast cancer survivors. Five women interviewed for The Pink and The Black Project© are in their third, fourth, and fifth occurrence with breast cancer. There is one other who indicated that she is facing metastatic[6] disease. I find it remarkable that these women are still here fighting for their lives every day while working outside their home and managing family and community responsibilities[7] and were willing to share their experiences. Without them and others like them this work would not have been possible.

NOTES

Publisher's Note: The interviews used as supplemental research in this text were all conducted with the participants' knowledge and agreement that these interviews would be used in a later publication.

1. bell hooks. Interviewed by Jenisha Watts for *Essence* magazine (2010). Retrieved from http://www.essence.com/2010/03/03/bell-hooks-self-esteem.

2. National Institutes of Health Office of Research on Women's Health, Women of Color Health Data Book, October 2014.

3. See also K. D. Kochanek, E. Arias, R. N. Anderson. How did cause of death contribute to racial differences in life expectancy in the United States in 2010? NCHS data brief, no 125. Hyattsville, MD: National Center for Health Statistics. 2013. Please note that all material appearing in National Center for Health Statistics data brief, no 125 report, July 2013, is in the public domain and may be reproduced or copied without permission.

4. Issues of domestic violence are of concern as it relates to homicide.

5. The Susan G. Komen Race for the Cure® Series is marketed as the world's largest and most successful education and fund-raising event for breast cancer ever created. The series of 5K runs and fitness walks, started in 1983, raises significant funds and awareness for the breast cancer movement, celebrates breast cancer survivorship, and honors those who have lost their battle with the disease. It is significant to note that in April 2010 Sisters Network Inc. made history by hosting the 1st National Black Breast Cancer 5K Walk/Run in Houston, Texas. The Stop the Silence® 5K Walk/Run attracted over 4,000 participants from cities across the United States. Funds raised from Stop the Silence® will benefit Sisters Network® Inc. Breast Cancer Assistance Program (BCAP), which provides assistance to women facing financial challenges after breast cancer diagnosis. This program offers financial assistance for mammograms, medical-related lodging, co-pay, office visits, prescriptions, and transportation.

6. Metastatic cancer happens when cancerous cells travel from the breast to vital organs and other parts of the body: bones, liver, brain.

7. While preparing this manuscript four of the women that participated in the individual interviews or focus groups transitioned to the next life/passed away.

ONE
Background and Theoretical Framing

The advances in cancer treatment that have been made in the more than three decades since Audre Lorde's *The Cancer Journals* (1980) was first published have not really changed the cancer burden faced by Black women or women in general. Breast cancer continues to be one of the most common cancers among Black women. It is also the second leading cause of cancer death among Black women (Blackwomenshealth.org), surpassed only by lung cancer. The rate at which Black women die from breast cancer is higher than other racial groups. They are 40 percent more likely to die of breast cancer than are white women (American Cancer Society, 2016; BreastCancer.Org, 2009; 2016; McCarthy, Jianing, & Armstrong, 2015). The reasons for this involve many factors, including the likelihood of Black women having more aggressive forms of cancer, such as "triple negative" breast cancer (Stead et al., 2009), and to have fewer social and economic resources (Centers for Disease Control, 2012). Much of the research into health disparities and the higher mortality rates among Black women focuses on access to affordable health care, quality of care, breast cancer screening rates, and attitudes toward mammography (American Cancer Society, 2016; BreastCancer.Org, 2016).

One significant change in breast cancer research is that the five-year survival rates for breast cancer survivorship are no longer considered the gold standard. Some types of breast cancer have become like other kinds of chronic illnesses with some women moving in and out of remission with repeated relapses of breast cancer, occurrences of new cancers, or the development of metastatic cancer. Survivor success should be measured in terms of quality of life, not only mortality. This is especially true when one considers the rate of breast cancer among Black women. Yet these are not the only issues Black women face. There are various environmental and social stressors that contribute to breast cancer that have gained the attention of researchers from various disciplines.

In an exploratory study of middle income Black women, Claudia Coggin and Mary Shaw-Perry (2006) found that this particular group of women identified a variety of needs to help them deal with breast cancer, such as medical and support services that are affordable, accessible, acceptable, and appropriate; a caring and loving family; more than a generic list of contacts for information about breast cancer symptoms or related health problems; an intimate relationship with God; and adequate resources for self and family care, such as financial assistance with living expenses and help with housework and children. This study highlights the fact that socioeconomic status is not always a barrier to the needs of Black women who survive breast cancer, meaning that some Black women are aware of breast cancer and have access to mammography, other medical care, and insurance. Therefore, some research studies are missing a crucial part of the breast cancer story as it relates to Black women. It must be taken into account that other social and cultural factors also shape and contribute to how Black women's experience of the disease is different than that of white women. There are mitigating factors that must be considered when one wants to understand why breast cancer can develop in Black women not only at a younger age but also much more aggressively than in white women. By focusing only on access and resources, the voices of Black women are missing not only from the larger cancer survivorship narratives but play a role in their marginalization.

Lorde's sharing of her experience has inspired me to speak beyond the prescribed narratives and metaphors of strength and survival. I carried *The Cancer Journals* with me everywhere and provided copies to family members and friends hoping they would read and understand the sense of urgency that had overtaken me. Lorde's work helped me to break my silence and not to be afraid to express my fears and limitations, while at the same time understanding that being a strong Black woman is about knowing when to say you have had enough and want to find a way to do something different. That is why I began The Pink and The Black Project© which resulted in *Health Communication and Breast Cancer among Black Women: Identity, Spirituality, and Strength*.

There is a notable deficiency of research on how Black women manage their breast cancer or its impact on their lives following diagnosis particularly for long-term survivors. During the literature review for *Health Communication and Breast Cancer among Black Women: Identity, Spirituality, and Strength* I found that much of the research continued to focus on issues of access to health care, quality of care, obesity rates, and comorbidities (American Cancer Society, 2016, pp. 7–8, 10; Campo & Mastin, 2007; Mastin, Campo, & Askelon, 2012) as they relate to Black women's health. It is only in recent years that research has taken a different approach by examining the sociocultural affects of stress on the mental and physical health of Black women. *Health Communication and Breast Cancer among Black Women: Identity, Spirituality, and Strength* is unique in that it looks at a trifecta of strength narratives that Black women must face as they manage their illness—that of the strong warrior fighting breast cancer, the strong woman of faith, and the strong Black woman. Previous research does not explore these three strength narratives collectively, rather they are explored separately as strong Black women, religion/faith and spirituality (Conway-Philips & Janusek, 2014; Lynn, Yoo, & Levine, 2014), and breast cancer culture.

Health Communication and Breast Cancer among Black Women: Identity, Spirituality, and Strength has three objectives. First this book seeks to add to the research and literature by providing a space for women to share their experiences as Black female long-term breast cancer survivors on how they negotiate their identity around the trifecta of strength narratives. Second, it seeks to challenge the existing notions of what it means to be a Black woman surviving and living with breast cancer in the 21st century. Thirdly, it hopes to provide strategies for coping with long-term illness that promote long-term wellness. Finally, important information for those seeking to change the standard assumptions and hypotheses concerning strategies for health promotion, chronic disease management, and prevention (United States Department of Health & Human Services, National Institutes of Health, 2005) has been made available.

I delve into the survivors social support network of family and friends, as they are the ones who initially provide empathy and understanding of the trauma associated with the onset of cancer diagnosis and resulting treatments. The question of long-term survivorship becomes twofold as one wonders about the impact of a diminishing support network that understands the psychological and physical problems of the illness and the role of breast cancer culture, faithtalk, and the myth of the strong Black woman. In doing so, I discuss how breast cancer culture, faithtalk, and the myth of the strong Black woman influence the expectations placed on Black female long-term breast cancer survivors in a professional or work setting.

This work also critiques the role breast cancer culture, faithtalk, and the myth of the strong Black woman has on the expectations Black women place on themselves to live up to the she-ro ideology, the pink and Black superwoman identity, even at the detriment to their health. Yes, sometimes we have to wear the cape. Furthermore, it is the role that cultural images play in the shaping of health behaviors of Black women and perceptions of Black women in the illness/work-life balance narratives that must be a part of the historical record with a call toward change. This call for change is one that promotes the notion that Black women are worthy of a true time of rest for healing and wellness. It is my hope that this book will lead this call.

Chapter 1
THEORETICAL FRAMEWORK

As a communication scholar there are many theoretical models that could be used to explore the trifecta of strength that runs through the narratives of breast cancer culture, faith and spirituality, and the strong Black woman ideal. This work calls for a theoretical framework that speaks directly to the standpoint of the participants of The Pink and The Black Project© study as well as the author. There are two theoretical perspectives that both include and embrace Black women and the breast cancer survivorship experience. This section outlines the Black Feminist Thought and Womanist Theology frameworks that can be applied to better understand Black women's survivorship experience with breast cancer. Hoffman (2006) argues "feminism's primary focus on gender issues has frequently been interpreted as a lack of concern with ethnicity and race" (p. 359). Black Feminist Thought centers on understanding Black women's everyday lived experience with racism, sexism, and classism (Hill-Collins, 2000; hooks, 2000; Sumi, Crenshaw, & McCall, 2013). This perspective is crucial to this discussion as issues of race, social class, and sexism influence access to health care, treatment by health care providers, employers, and family members. Additionally, Black female breast cancer survivors with insurance face challenges to receiving adequate and appropriate health care as do their counterparts without medical insurance. By adopting this lens, Black Feminist Theory allows the opportunity to highlight those issues and concerns that are unique to Black women and breast cancer. It provides the centric thinking necessary to bring Black women to the center of discussion around survivorship and breast cancer. It provides the space to focus on the unique characteristics that accompany Black women and breast cancer in a way that historically has not been done.

I begin by using Alice Walker's definition of womanist as it first appeared in *In Search of Our Mothers' Gardens: Womanist Prose* (1983). The term refers to outrageous, audacious, courageous, or willful behavior, as well as strength and commitment to the health and wholeness of all people, men and women. Womanist Theology goes further and looks at the intersection of race, class, and gender juxtaposed to the church and the role of faith and religion in the lives of Black women in the United States (Cannon, 1995; Grant, 1989). In the context of The Pink and the Black Project© the women who participated have a strong sense of faith and a connection to their family and larger community which influences their overall well-being and how they negotiate their identity as Black women living with breast cancer. The contribution of this project is that it brings to the fore negotiations of faith and survivorship. Furthermore, it strives to identify intercultural implications in health communication as it pertains to Black breast cancer survivors and family members.

Both Black Feminist Thought and Womanist Theology empower the voices of Black women. This is particularly salient as Black women breast cancer survivors face obstacles to their survival when seeking treatment for breast cancer, the prevention of future cancers, and the management of their spiritual and mental health needs. All of their self-care occurs while they are engaged in providing care and concern for others.

Communication

It is widely understood that basic communication theory explores "who says what, in which channels, to whom, and with what effects." Communication theory investigates how messages are created, transmitted, received, and assimilated. The information presented in this work applies the agency-identity model as a metatheory that looks at three aspects of identity, intrapersonal, interpersonal, and sociocultural. Villagran, Fox, & O'Hair discuss the three aspects of agentic identity in the *Handbook of Communication and Cancer Care* (2007). They go on to explain that intrapersonal aspects of identity are created over time and a cancer diagnosis can create a sense of disconnect from a person's previous concept of self. Villagran et al. state that the interpersonal aspects of identity are developed through relationships with family, intimate friendships, and coworkers while the sociocultural aspects of identity are rooted in a specific cultural belief system and ideology (pp. 134–139). Table 1.1 below provides a summary of some of the concepts within these three aspects of identity.

Identity is an important concept of both Black Feminist Thought and Womanist Theology. *Health Communication and Breast Cancer among Black Women* will assist those concerned with Black women's health understand the role that the trifecta of strength narratives play in their identity, coping strategies, and decision making. This work provides important information for the development of future research designs and health communication message construction. When applied to public health problems, such as breast cancer in Black women, the central question theories of communication might seek to answer is, "How does communication affect behavior change (i.e, health care decisions, self-care, interaction with medical professionals, family, employers, etc.)?"

METHODOLOGY

The Pink and The Black Project© sought to investigate the silence that comes with the intersection of breast cancer culture and pink ribbons, faithtalk, and the expectations of being a strong Black woman. A combination of qualitative research methods were used to collect information about the lived experiences that shape the lives of breast cancer survivors

Table 1.1. Summary of Concepts Within Three Aspects of Identity

Aspects of Communication Agency-Identity	Self Concepts
Intrapersonal Identity	Information Processing
	Decision Making
	Personality Traits
	Emotional Needs
	Behavioral Responses
	Self-Concept
Interpersonal Identity	Family Relationships
	Intimate Relationships
	Friendships
	Co-Worker Relationships
	Computer-Mediated Support Groups
	Impression Management
Sociocultural Identity	Gender
	Ethnicity
	Age
	Sexuality
	Ability
	Social Status
	Group Affiliation

Villagran, Fox, & O'Hair, 2007, p. 131.

as related to breast cancer culture, faithtalk, and strong Black woman ideology. Those methods include: autoethnography, ethnography, participant observation, focus groups, individual interviews, and content analysis of survivor narratives. Qualitative research was considered the most appropriate methodology for The Pink and The Black Project© as it allowed for richness in data analysis that quantitative methods or numbers alone are unable to provide (Davis, Gallardo, & Lachlan, 2010). It is from this earlier work that *Health Communication and Breast Cancer among Black Women: Identity, Spirituality, and Strength* emerged. The combination of qualitative research methods provides rich data that requires an intimate, detailed discussion with participants.

Ethnography and participant observation were used to examine social situations from an insider's perspective. I participated in the social environment that I observed as a researcher and survivor, systematically recording and classifying my observations (Rubin, Rubin, & Piele, 1996, p. 224.) with known breast cancer survivors while at events and activities, some specifically targeted at breast cancer survivors and others that took place at general community events and activities. I not only relied on my own observations, but also on information supplied by members of the various organizations sponsoring or hosting the events and activities where breast cancer survivors would gather. The data I collected from The Pink and The Black Project© challenged me to provide a space that speaks directly to the womanist theological perspectives as they pertain to Black breast cancer survivors. I do not portend to dispel all myths, but it is my hope that providing this space for discussion will allow for a more centric approach to understanding breast cancer communication as it relates to African Americans women.

Content Analysis

Content analysis was employed in this study as it allows an exploration characteristics of communication messages found in specific artifacts and creates yet another avenue to learn about both the content of messages and those who produced them (p. 220). As part of The Pink and The Black Project© I performed content analysis on calendars from the years 2000–2013. Each calendar features a different survivor and her survival narrative for a specific month. A total of 168 (12 narratives x 14 years worth of calendars = 168) narratives were reviewed, categorized, and coded for references to strength, faith, family, friends, and breast cancer warrior metaphors.

The results from the analysis of the survivorship calendars confirmed two of my hypotheses, the first being that over time the narratives survivors created began to include greater levels of self-disclosure and more discussion about interaction with medical professionals and the afteraffects of medical treatment. Second, the analysis also confirmed that the stories survivors told for public consumption discussed being strong Black women, were consistently hopeful, included faithtalk, and referenced the warrior metaphors of breast cancer culture. A detailed discussion of the breast cancer survivor calendar narratives is not the focus of *Health Communication and Breast Cancer among Black Women* but further suggests that survivors create personal narratives for varying audiences. It would have been ideal to include all 168 women featured in the survivorship calendars in interviews or focus groups, however that was not feasible for many reasons and fell outside the scope of the original project plan.

Focus Groups

The preliminary investigation took place in a prominent Northeastern city with additional participants from cities in the Midwest and West Coast. The investigation included women over the age of 18 who self-identified as Black or African American breast cancer survivors. Through a snowball approach, women were initially recruited through written and verbal announcements at a breast cancer survivor's group meeting. Subsequent contacts were made with survivors through word of mouth by those who participated or shared the information with potential participants. Flyers, both business card size and postcard size, were distributed at survivors meetings and various community organizations that catered to Black women. An informational website was also developed to provide additional information about the research project to encourage participation and share consent information for those interested in participating. The website was taken down at the conclusion of the study. Please see the appendix for more information regarding participant recruitment.

A total of 27 women from the aforementioned regions participated in the study. Five of these women were also featured in the survivorship calendars that I noted earlier. The focus groups were divided into two groups and the participants for each group were selected randomly. Six women participated in focus group A, ten women participated in focus group B, and eleven women participated in in-depth individual interviews. The participants ranged in age from 25 to 70. Years of breast cancer survivorship ranged from one to twenty-two years. The participants believed it necessary to share their experiences so others would not be alone in trying to figure out how to find balance in their lives while creating "a new normal" after their breast cancer diagnosis and treatment. The study included additional one-on-one interviews of eight individuals who themselves were not cancer survivors but had a relative or family friend who had been diagnosed with breast cancer. These individuals had heard about the study and wanted to provide their insights. These are briefly discussed in chapter five.

Autoethnography

Autoethnography: combining ethnography, biography, and self-analysis, a qualitative research method that utilizes data about self and context to gain an understanding of the connectivity between self and others within the same context. Some scholars see personal experience as "evidence" in academic research to be problematic. Buzard (2003), for example, argues the trouble with this methodology is that researchers spend too much time observing just a few individuals. Additionally, the use of personal experience is perceived as intentionally using biased data. Leon Anderson (2006) "proposes the term analytic autoethnography to refer to research in which the researcher is (1) a full member in the research group or setting, (2) visible as such a member in published texts, and (3) committed to developing theoretical understandings of broader social phenomena." I consider this work part of the genre that Anderson purposes.

Research is an extension of researchers' lives. This research is an extension of my life. As a social scientist in the communication discipline I have been trained to guard against subjectivity—self-driven perspectives—and to separate self from research activities. This is an impossible and difficult task as scholarship is inextricably connected to self, personal interest, experience, and familiarity. Moreover, being trained as a scholar activist connecting life and research affords credibility when working with groups and individuals that share a common life experience or history. This is particularly evident as a researcher who is investigating the effects of breast cancer culture, spirituality, and the grand narrative of strong Black womanhood on the work/life balance of Black women breast cancer survivors. As a researcher, survivor-advocate, my life story creates a pathway of trust for others to openly dialog about the intimate details and challenges of living with breast cancer.

There is a deep mistrust of those who want to gaze upon, and work within, the Black community that goes beyond the now infamous Tuskegee Syphilis Experiments that studied the progression of untreated syphilis in Black men who thought they were receiving free health care from the U.S. government (Tuskegee.edu, 2015) or the theft of genetic material belonging to Henrietta Lacks, a Black woman whose cultured tumor cells were used to create the first human "immortal cell line" for use in medical research (Mukherjee, 2010; Skloot, 2010). Harriet Washington, in her book *Medical Apartheid: The Dark History of Medical Experimentation on Black Americans from Colonial Times to the Present* (2006), provides a comprehensive historical account of the mistreatment of African Americans and other socially and economically disadvantaged groups who were unwitting participants in medical research. With a history of unethical treatment in the name of research, individuals are wise to be suspect of outsiders who come to "do research" or "ask questions," particularly when the results of the research do not directly benefit their community. There are now improved ethical practices, Institutional Review Boards to protect human subjects, and researchers who abide by ethical standards, but mistrust lingers.

Connecting personal experience to research imparts credibility when establishing trust and working with those who share a common life experience or social history. This was particularly true for me as one with insider status. Black women were willing to tell me about their lives and experiences with breast cancer because they saw me as one of them. I cannot stress enough that to create the conditions for open dialog, trust is important. As a researcher survivor-advocate my life story created a pathway for others to talk about the intimate details and challenges of living with breast cancer and its aftermath, one that has physical and psychological repercussions around body image. The shared experience of wondering if breast cancer will return or metastasize to other parts of the body, the immediate and residual effects of treatments, such as chemo brain, nerve neuropathy, lymphedema, loss of hair, or even the loss of teeth were of utmost concern and provided common ground in which to share. I conducted my focus groups and interviews in familiar settings to create a comfortable environment for women to discuss these often private and emotional details.

In the next chapter I discuss the uneasy mythology of the strong Black woman. Each participant was asked questions regarding the ideology and rhetoric of the strong Black woman and if this particular message of strength had any influence on her ability as a breast cancer survivor to discuss what is happening to her mentally, physically, and spiritually. Does this expectation of strength hamper her ability to discuss with her friends, family, coworkers/employer, and health care team any issues related to her needs and concerns? Insight into this question is critical for those constructing health communication messages targeting African American women.

TWO
Myth of the Strong Black Woman
Asset or Liability

"Sometimes, sometimes, I just don't want to be strong, I'm just tired, too tired, too tired to be strong all the time." —Survivor

"We work hard at everything so people don't think we are lazy." — Survivor

"A child of God, definitely; a phenomenal woman, maybe; a strong Black woman, some would say; a superwoman, I don't think so; I am not every woman—at least in private." —*Writings of an Insomniac*, 2011[1]

Walking in the valley of the shadow of death, Black women breast cancer survivors carry the mantle of the strong Black woman trope as they navigate their diagnosis, treatment, and survival. Stereotypical images of Black women are at the foundation for Black women's stressors related to self-image, wellness, and healing. As Black women, we must challenge the myths and stereotypes that are detrimental to our mental and physical health. Black women are fighting ever-present stereotypes that they must look and behave like a strong Black woman in America regardless of how unwell they may be. I contend this is detrimental to Black women's breast cancer recovery and long-term survivorship. In addition it also impacts the prevention of breast cancer and other diseases in Black women because they are perceived as being able to handle anything that comes their way, even when their lives are in jeopardy.

Even in illness Black women must fight against the "isms" of racism, sexism, and classism that create an environment of persistent stress that feed the multitude of health and other types of disparities faced in Black communities. Many scientific studies reiterate the fact that while Black women are least likely to get breast cancer when compared to other racial and ethnic groups, they are more likely to die from it because of systemic societal challenges. Poverty impacts access to health care beyond just screening, diagnosis, and treatment and the lack of aggressive treatments to fight equally aggressive forms of breast cancer. When quality health care is available, survival rates are low as cultural and societal narratives call for them to be strong, fight the good fight of faith, and kick cancer's butt while continuing to maintain home, family, employment, and other responsibilities, and in essence be model strong Black women and the model breast cancer survivor. They are forced to proudly wear the mantle of strength, even if it is detrimental to their health.

Although the "relationship between stress and health in African American women is not fully understood because of limited information about African American women's experiences of stress and their stress-related coping strategies" (Woods-Giscombé, 2010), focus group participants and individual interviewees clearly identified stressful life events before, during, and after diagnosis and treatment. They recounted stressful life events that they were expected to cope with and survive as strong Black women.

HISTORICAL CONTEXT

Where did the idea that "I must live the role of the strong Black woman" come from? Where did my sister survivors get the idea that they must be strong Black women in spite of their illness? What does that mean for Black women who defy the statistics and survive? And what does it mean for those who do not?

The origins of the idea and concept for the strong Black woman have been well documented by many Black feminist scholars (Beauboeuf-Lafontant, 2009; Gillespie, 1984; Harris-Lacewell, 2001; Hill-Collins, 2000; hooks, 1993; Wallace, 1990). Historically, the root source of the strong Black women ideology originated as a rationalization or justification for slavery, because Black women were touted as physically stronger and more resilient (Harris-Lacewell, 2001). Black women were perceived to be able to bounce back from adversity unscathed. They were able to raise their own children and those of the master. They birthed babies and immediately went back to work in the fields. The outsider interpreted these feats of forced labor as Black women being unbreakable and "strong" but do not acknowledge the punishments they faced if they failed to do so.

This mythical image was appropriated and recreated within Black communities in response to other derogatory images of Black womanhood. The strong Black woman image presents a picture to the world that Black women are inherently strong and resilient, self-reliant, able to confront myriad challenges, and provide encouragement to self and others during times of adversity. These images foster the belief that Black women are courageous warriors. Any sign of vulnerability or weakness is tantamount to failing oneself, family, and community. The strong Black woman ideology does not allow space for Black women to express their feelings related to traumatic experiences (much like the ways in which Black women swallowed sexual violence on their bodies during slavery and today as victims of intimate partner violence). The strong Black woman trope has become a barometer of how Black women's behavior should be evaluated in adverse situations (Harrington, Crowther, & Shipherd, 2010).

The mule or workhorse is another stereotypic image that presents the picture of Black women being inherently strong. The following quote from Zora Neale Hurston's *Their Eyes Were Watching God* (1969) describes this image:

> "Honey, de white man is de ruler of everything as fur as Ah been able tuh find out. Maybe it's some place way off in de ocean where de Black man is in power, but we don't know nothin' but what we see. So de white man throw down de load and tell de nigger man tuh pick it up. He pick it up because he have to, but he don't tote it. He hand it to his women folks. De nigger woman is de mule uh de world so fur as Ah can see."

Gail Wyatt (1997) writes about the workhorse stereotype and describing the characteristics of the workhorse as a Black woman who was thought to be so strong that she could tolerate all types of physical abuse. Through hard, backbreaking work, she develops useful skills and excels in her work while contradicting the stereotype that she is lazy. The contemporary version of the workhorse is that of the educated, career-driven, professional Black woman. It is assumed that nothing bothers this type of woman because she has pressed on and defied the odds. Wyatt goes on to say that the workhorse is akin to how Zora Neale Hurston (1969) describes Black women as "the mules of the world."

When I read this description of the workhorse, it brought me to my early journal entries where I had written down the entire quote from Hurston. This is where I discussed my feelings and concerns about the physical and cognitive limitations I experienced while undergoing chemotherapy and radiation treatments. This was the safe space in which I could disclose how these limitations were manifesting themselves while I continued to work full-time and maintain a household, concerns that I did not feel I could share with anyone. As a result, I put on a brave face and did what was expected of a strong Black woman. I kept everything inside. I did not act like someone who happened to be fighting her way through breast cancer.

Patricia Hill-Collins (2000) writes about the four main stereotypes or controlling images for Black women. These stereotypes are the Mammy, the Matriarch, the Welfare Mother, and finally the Jezebel or the whore. According to Hill-Collins, these are images that were used to oppress Black women. Traditionally, the Mammy was "the Black mother figure in white homes." The faithful, obedient domestic servant who knows her place, she has accepted her subordinate role. Mammy represents the normative yardstick used to evaluate all Black women's behavior. By loving, nurturing, and caring for her white children and "family" better than her own, the Mammy symbolizes the dominant group's perceptions of the ideal Black female relationship to the patriarchal power structure of the white elite. She understands that you take care of others before yourself and your own. This message of selfless care and placing others first holds true for some survivors as the needs of others supersede the need for self-care. It is assumed that the survivor will ignore personal pain, both physical and emotional, in order to make sure the needs of her family are prioritized.

The Matriarch represents "the Black mother figure in Black homes." A less often discussed aspect to the Black Matriarch dimension is that she serves as the foundation for family cohesiveness. The most often discussed Matriarch image is that of the "bad" Black mother, the overly aggressive, unfeminine, emasculating woman who fails at her traditional "womanly" duties. The Matriarch spends too much time away from home working and cannot properly supervise her children or hold on to her man. This is a double-edged sword as Black women are working outside of the home to provide financially for our families often as the major or sole breadwinner. Many Black women survivors are the primary wage earners or a part of a co-dependent financial relationship that does not allow room for time away from work as it will impact the survival and well-being of the entire family. In essence, when it comes to Black women breast cancer survivors the Mammy and Matriarch serve as the primary silencers to letting others know how they really feel.

The Welfare Mother, commonly referred to as the welfare queen, comes from the racial stereotype that African Americans overall are lazy, do not want to work, and are immoral beings who simply have as many children out of wedlock as they can in order to stay home and collect government welfare. As the women in the focus groups discussed these stereotypes of Black women, the welfare queen stereotype was singled out for their wrath, as it was not viewed in its singularity but as an overlap with the Mammy and Matriarch stereotypes that were in no way true for most mothers receiving government assistance.

The women interviewed for The Pink and The Black Project© are at various middle-income levels and the idea that Blacks are lazy had the women seething as they recounted the work ethic shown to them by their parents, grandparents, aunts and uncles, or the fact that they pulled themselves up by their own sheer will and determination. These women also talked about the effort and time they put into caring for their families, elderly parents, sick relatives, and their jobs, some survivors worked multiple jobs at times to make ends meet in the care of their immediate or extended family. Most of the women I spoke with did not take any significant time off during their health crisis. The visceral reaction of the Welfare Mother stereotype seemed to be the unconscious driving force for embracing the Mammy and Matriarch tropes as necessary for the public face. The very real fear of confirming negative stereotypes can keep us from all-important and necessary self-care.

Finally, the last of the four stereotypes is the Jezebel, the sexually aggressive whore. Initially based on Jezebel first described in 1 Kings and 2 Kings in the Old Testament this image of the sexually aggressive woman was used to justify rape and dominate the bodies of Black women. Black women are seen as hypersexual and out of control. The oppression and commodification of Black female bodies is perpetuated by the notion that if she is raped or assaulted she was asking for it. In a conversation with a survivor in her late twenties she revealed that "Being considered the object of any man's fetish or fantasy is no longer an option. Not that I am talking about being whorish, but your body is not the same. . . . Who is going to want you with broke down titties, or missing titties? Sorry for phrasing it like that." As we discussed the meaning of the Jezebel stereotype some of the women felt it was just an appropriate place to bring up the topic of sex. I mention this only to indicate that body image, sex and sexuality are on the minds of the Black women breast cancer survivors I spoke with who ranged in age from 25–70. However, the primary focus here is on the overall implications of the strong Black woman stereotype.

Society's expectations can be powerful, controlling forces, particularly if we come to accept them. As Black women and breast cancer survivors we tend to accept them whether we want to or not. Some of us accept these images kicking and screaming all the way—either out loud or under our breath in our quiet places. The Strong Black Woman in this survivor circle is a mythic amalgamation of the Mammy and Matriarch stereotypes (Hill-Collins, 2000) and the workhorse (Wyatt, 1997). In a conversation with a survivor she told me that she asked someone close to her "What is it about me that makes you feel like I should not be taken care of?" His response to her was, "You can take care of yourself. You do not need anyone. You're a strong Black woman." Her response to his answer to her question was physical—"I thought I would be sick, my stomach turned." She explained that she never found an opportunity to tell him that she was diagnosed with breast cancer immediately. It was not until after her hair fell out and she could no longer hide the physical effects anymore that she told him. At that stage the stress experienced by loved ones offers two options: stay and support her at all costs or leave her to suffer alone. He chose the second option.

THE COST OF STRENGTH

Black women breast cancer survivors are women living through the throes of their illness and are rarely seen as vulnerable, but are defined by strength. This is expected, not only through the social construction of what it means to be a Black woman but also through the pink lens of breast cancer culture. The rose-colored glasses of the pink ribbon reinforces the expected virtues of bravery and courageousness that complicate the road to recovery and wellness for Black women. Emily Abel and Saskia Subramanian (2008) also note the role of the ideology of the strong Black woman in the narratives told to them by survivors experiencing some of the long-term side effects of chemotherapy, radiation, and other adjuvant treatments for breast cancer. Black and Woods-Gliscombe (2012) concur, noting, "strength is identified as a culturally prescribed coping style that conditions resilience, self-reliance and psychological hardiness as a survival response to race-related and gender-related stressors"; the very same coping style expected of and performed by Black female breast cancer survivors.

Tamara Beauboeuf-Lafontant (2009) in her book *Behind the Mask of the Strong Black Woman: Voice and the Embodiment of a Costly Performance* argues that the "performance" of strength is costing Black women their health in the form of eating disorders, particularly obesity and depression. This same "performance" of strength is one of the causes for the higher incidence of mortality in Black women diagnosed with breast cancer. Furthermore, studies indicate that Black women may be at an increased risk of breast cancer in their lifetime due to higher obesity rates (American Cancer Society, 2016; United States Department of Health and Human Services, 2011). Prevailing research pays particular attention to socioeconomic status, access, or lack of access, to health care. It has only been in recent years that some attention has been paid to other environmental and psychosocial stress factors that affect Black women's health. Black women have always known these stress factors exist and now we know that they are impacting our health.

Taylor and colleagues' (2007) study on the influence of racial discrimination as a specific stressor and the incidence of breast cancer in Black women concluded that there is an association between stress and breast cancer. Using data from the Black Women's Health Study from 1997–2003, they reviewed two decades of research that examined the extent to which psychological stress influenced breast cancer and other diseases. The results from the review were mixed; some studies show no association of risk while others indicate an increased risk of breast cancer among women with high stress levels. When it comes to stress, all things are not equal. More research needs to be done in this area as it pertains to the environmental and psychological stress experienced by Black women.

The internalization and embodiment of the Strong Black Woman is deeply embedded in the psyche of the survivors I spoke with in focus groups and privately. It permeated entire conversations around the idea of faith, faithtalk, and the pink ribbon warrior metaphors. Terri Williams (2008) in her book *Black Pain: It Only Looks Like We're Not Hurting* discusses being overworked, undervalued, and under pressure. She states, "I have come to believe that as Black women our threshold for pain is too high. We have embraced very destructive beliefs about our ability to 'handle it all,' our power to overcome in the face of trauma, our ability to put ourselves aside as we tend to the needs of our employers, partners, children, family—everyone but ourselves!" It is evident that the survivors in this work have a high tolerance for pain. When the conversation moved to the expectations, we broadly discussed two questions: (1) Does the mythology of the strong Black Women influence self-expectations? and (2) Does the mythology of the strong Black women influence the expectations others have of breast cancer survivors? There was no hesitation in how the women responded as every woman was well aware of what was expected of her. She was expected to maintain and continue with minimal interruptions. She not only expected this of herself, but others expected the same:

- "I think I am holding myself to impossible standards and others have come to expect the same."
- "You keep pushing yourself and thinking if I don't do it who will?"
- "I don't have anyone to fall back on."
- "I was never taught that someone, anyone, would take care of me, I was taught to take care of myself."
- "Relax! What does that mean?"
- "We have to rely on ourselves."
- "Strong Black woman. Hmmmph! I think that's just code for we don't have to do it she'll take care of it."

Cheryl Woods-Giscombé (2010) developed a conceptual framework called the Superwoman Schema (see figure 2.1), which specifically explores the idea of strength in Black women and how it impacts mental health, physical well-being, and health decisions. The four areas of the Superwoman Schema include: characteristics of the Superwoman role/Strong Black Woman, contributing contextual factors of the Superwoman role/Strong Black Woman, perceived benefits of the Superwoman role/Strong Black Woman, and perceived liabilities of the Superwoman role/Strong Black Woman. Each area of the schema was substantiated during The Pink and The Black Project© focus group discussions and individual interviews. The Strong Black Woman narrative in the lives of breast cancer survivors is significant and is used as coping strategy even with known negative outcomes.

Shardé Davis (2015) developed a theoretical framework called the Strong Black Woman Collective (SBWC). She contends "the idea that Black women construct strength through communal communication practices by imbuing their assembled voices for might and fortitude." She goes on to suggest "Black women regulate strength in themselves and one another," and that this "re-appropriation of the strength image enables refuge from and collective resistance against larger oppressive forces, as well as validation and celebration of a distinctive Black woman identity." Regardless of how much the participants of The Pink and The Black Project© embrace the idea of the Strong Black Woman as a place of strength and a way to cope with health and other adversities, they also recognize the harm in the strength narrative and unknowingly created space for other breast cancer survivors to express their emotions, vulnerabilities, and areas of stress associated with survivorship. It was important for them to allow other women to express how they were really feeling. As one survivor stated, "We have to create our own safe spaces to share thoughts and feelings."

Making room for others to openly communicate their weaknesses is part of the audience analysis and conversation monitoring that breast cancer survivors perform. This is a performance skill that participants indicated they learned over time, knowing when it is okay to discuss and share their vulnerabilities. This openness to discuss weakness and vulnerability with in-group members is in contrast to what Davis (2015) describes as the SBWC reinforcement of the strength ideal, which can stifle expression of emotion, acknowledgment of vulnerability, healing, and sharing of weaknesses.

Villagren et al. (2007) believe that "Communication becomes more salient as cognitive, affective, and behavioral responses to a cancer diagnosis become additional barriers for the patient to overcome and that an agentic identity provides cancer patients the opportunity and responsibility to analyze the context and available options for care." Villagren et al. (p. 129) also surmise that personal agency is a way for cancer patients to advocate for themselves and make better health care decisions. I contend that the agentic identity model does not account for the social construction of an identity that embodies strength. Specifically the sense of perceived strength that the strong Black woman ideal provides as this ideal provides a false sense of agency for Black women that results in silence about what their health care needs truly are. This is a liability.

The weight of strength is heavy on Black female breast cancer survivors and at times some have an image of themselves that differs from the one imposed on them by others. However, they often find it necessary to enact the script provided. Layered beneath the mantle of the Strong Black Woman is the shroud of faith, the foundation for which the women in my conversations gain additional strength and courage to continue in the role of the Strong Black Woman. Being a Strong Black Women of Faith is

Myth of the Strong Black Woman 19

a sociocultural narrative of strength identified in this research and has been given the label of "Faithtalk" which is the focus of the next chapter.

Superwoman Schema Conceptual Framework

The Superwoman Role

What are the Characteristics?
- Obligation to manifest strength
- Obligation to suppress emotions
- Resistance to being vulnerable or dependent
- Determination to succeed despite limited resources
- Obligation to help others

What are the Contributing Contextual Factors?
- Historical legacy of racial or gender stereotyping/oppression
- Lessons from foremothers
- Past history of disappointment, mistreatment, or abuse
- Spiritual values

What are the Perceived Benefits?
- Preservation of self/survival
- Preservation of African American community
- Preservation of African American family

What are the Perceived Liabilities?
- Strain in interpersonal relationships (e.g., romantic, familial)
- Stress related health behaviors (e.g., postponement of self-care, emotional eating, poor sleep)
- Embodiment of stress (e.g., anxiety, depressive symptoms, adverse maternal health, overall poor health)

Figure 2.1. Superwoman Schema Conceptual Framework. *Superwoman Schema Conceptual Framework adapted and used with the permission of C. L. Woods-Giscombé.*

NOTE

1. *Writings of An Insomniac* is the title of the section of notes from the author's personal journal written during countless sleepless nights while undergoing treatment in both 2003–2004 and 2009–2012.

THREE

God's Got It

Faithtalk

"If someone quotes another scripture to me I am going to punch them!" —Survivor

"I will not put any of the diseases you are afraid of on you, but I will take all sickness away from you." (Deuteronomy 7:15)

In previous decades conventional medical practice often overlooked or denied the significance of religiosity and spirituality in the lives of patients. However, there is a growing body of literature with scientific evidence that connects the importance of spirituality and religious practice to improved overall health and quality of life for breast cancer survivors and their families (Schneider, 2007; Sterba et al., 2014). Some have even gone as far as to say that the lack of a personal faith belief or prayer life should be considered a risk factor to an individual's health (Kutz, 2004; White, Peters, & Myers-Schim, 2011). It should be noted that while there are studies that have positive implications and outcomes for breast cancer survivorship through the use of religious and or spiritual practices, there are also those that are concerned with the negative implications. For example a study completed by McLaughlin et al. (2013) sought to understand how religion, specifically "deferring control to God" or "putting it into Gods hands" affected psychosocial health outcomes. The researchers determined that women who deferred control to God employed a passive coping style as they felt that they were in less control of their fate or illness. As a result, the authors concluded that these women may be hesitant to take actions that involve caring for themselves. McLaughlin and colleagues suggest that a positive outcome of this passive coping strategy was a reduction in stress and anxiety about breast cancer. Yet, there was a greater potential for increased mortality rates.

In addition to the interest in the affects of religion and spirituality on health outcomes and quality of life, there is also a growing acceptance of holistic treatments. These are found in some of the leading cancer treatment centers and hospitals. For example, Yale New Haven Hospital's Smilow Cancer Center has an outdoor meditation garden on an upper-floor patio and a radiation waiting room with a large tropical fish tank to assist with visual relaxation, as well as offering consultations with nutritionists, reiki, a Japanese technique for stress reduction and relaxation (thereikicenter.net),[1] and hot stone massages to its patients. All of the breast cancer survivors who participated in The Pink and The Black Project© indicated that they have participated in some type of holistic treatment in addition to prayer or meditation, and church attendance. Participants indicated that these practices added value to their journey as breast cancer survivors. In doing so they found strength and hope (Lynn, Yoo, & Levine, 2014).

BLACK FAITH TRADITION

It is well documented that spirituality and religion serve as the foundation of the Black community's faith experience. The historical roots of Black religious practices and faith traditions are varied and complex. Enslaved Africans, from whom the majority of African Americans descend, brought with them their cultural religious practices and linguistic patterns. This became supplanted by Eurocentric Protestant and Catholic religious traditions resulting in the loss of purely African traditions where both practices and meanings were lost (Cone, 1969; 1970; 1975).[2] Nonetheless, the importance of spirituality and connecting to God remained constant. Religion and spirituality include traditions and values that may affect an individual's understanding of the causes of illness, their acceptance or compliance with regard to treatment and medical recommendations, and even feelings of optimism or fatalism about disease outcomes (Harris & Gibson, 2011; Gullate et al., 2010; Phillips, Cohen, & Moses, 1999).

When considering the influence of religion and spirituality on the ideas about health and illness, it is important to distinguish between the two since they refer to different levels of involvement in organized religious practices. Scholars do not always agree on the meaning of the terms but Gibson and Hendricks make clear the distinctions. *Religion* is usually defined as a series of spiritual practices and behaviors within an organized structure (e.g., African Methodist Episcopal, Baptist, Catholic, Seventh Day Adventist), which in some cases may also recommend, require, or inspire specific health behaviors (e.g., vegetarianism). *Spiritual-*

ity is a larger concept that includes an individual's values, questions about the meaning of life, and potentially, some level of involvement in organized religious activities (Gibson & Hendricks, 2006). Both religion and spirituality can play a key role in the way breast cancer is perceived and addressed in the Black community and this perception is part of the contributing contextual factors and perceived benefits presented in the Superwoman Schema in figure 2.1 found in the previous chapter.

POWER OF THE SPOKEN WORD

Nommo

When initially starting my research on how health, religion, and spirituality intersected in the lives of Black women breast cancer survivors I began with the origins of faithtalk and the simple premise of *nommo*. *Nommo* is an Afrocentric term used by Dr. Molefi Kete Asante[3] that refers to the power of the word to generate and create reality. I also recalled the words of Dr. Melbourne S. Cummings,[4] who discusses the work of Asante and the concept of *nommo* as a way to create harmony out of disharmony. This struck a chord with me as I equated this with the Judeo-Christian creation story found in the book of Genesis, which describes how God spoke the world and humanity into existence. The concept of *nommo* did not create any dissonance with my religious education or spiritual grounding, as I believed in the power of positive speaking and positive thinking. However, it is ideology that kept me silent in the early days regarding my own challenge with breast cancer. Breast cancer is a disharmony withinin the body. I questioned if talking about the disease would bring about harmony and healing or continued disharmony and disease? Why? Because the bible says in Mark 11:23:

> For verily I say unto you, that whosoever shall say unto this mountain, be thou removed and be thou cast into the sea, and shall not doubt in his heart, but shall believe that those things which he saith shall come to pass, he shall have whatsoever he saith.

Out of fear I did not want to say anything that would prolong the disharmony in my body. The fear of speaking about breast cancer seemed to cause a kind of mental anguish or disharmony. I wondered if it were possible to talk about breast cancer while at the same time creating harmony. In 2 Timothy 1:7 it says: "For God hath not given us the spirit of fear; but of power, and of love, and of a sound mind." My mind was conflicted and I was not sure what to do. So, I remained silent.

Depending on the audience, faithtalk can hinder open discussion regarding health concerns. Some see talking about your illness and the resulting side effects from the treatment as a faithless act—speaking about the negative brings about the negative. In this situation, words must be carefully framed around the acknowledgment that God is in control and that His will be done. One participant asked, "Who wants to be seen as complaining all the time?" Another respondent replied, "We are not complaining just stating facts about what our bodies are doing and how we are feeling. No disrespect to God's will by any means."

Name It and Claim It

Digging deeper into the Judeo-Christian aspect of the power of the spoken word led me to research the Faith movement[5] and prosperity gospel teaching which comes from the New Thought movement of the late 1800s (Anderson & Whitehouse, 2003).[6] This type of gospel teaching has two well-known edicts. First, God grants all his faithful followers abundant life through physical health and financial wealth. Second, God's followers or believers claim their divine born-again right to wealth and health through positive confession or positive declarations (which I refer to as *faithtalk*), financial offerings/tithing, and continued faith that God must fulfill His promises as it states in His Word, the Holy Scriptures/Bible. Based on my own observations and notes from various evangelical and nondenominational preachers this type of gospel teaching is known by various names—Name it and Claim it, Blab it and Grab it, Seed-Faith, Word of Faith, Gospel of Wealth and Health, Prosperity Theology, or Abundant Life. This particular type of teaching and thinking has been popularized by televangelists and preachers such as: Kenneth and Gloria Copeland, Creflo Dollar, Kenneth E. Hagin,[7] Benny Hinn, T. D. Jakes, Eddie Long, Joyce Meyer, Joel Olsteen, Fredrick K. C. Price, and Paula White. These individuals have gained prominence through global television ministries such as the Trinity Broadcasting Network (TBN), Daystar Television Network, The Word Network, and other cable network. The media reach of these ministries allows for the intersection and crossing of mainline or traditional denominations as many Christians who are members of either mainstream denominations or traditional Black churches consume the writings, attend the conferences, and watch the broadcasts of these and other televangelists.

I must confess that my indoctrination into the Faith movement was heightened during my first occurrence of breast cancer in 2003–2004. Friends, family, and coworkers provided numerous amounts of faith-based listening and reading material, I mention here four of the many gifts I received because I still find them useful. First, an audio CD entitled *Healing Scriptures* by Kenneth E. Hagin[8] in which he reads various passages from the King James Version of the Bible related to healing and faith is of significance because Romans 10:17 states: "So then faith cometh by hearing, and hearing by the word of God," this again is a significant concept for Christian believers. Kenneth Hagin opens the audio readings with passages from Proverbs 4:20–22[9] which reads:

> My son, attend to my words; incline thine ear unto my sayings. . . . Let them not depart from thine eyes; keep them in the midst of thine heart. . . . For they are life unto those that find them, and health to all their flesh.

Hagin discloses that in the margins of his Bible he has written that the Word of God is medicine for His people. The second item of significance was the book *Through the Fire and Through the Water: My Triumph Over Cancer* which tells the story of Betty R. Price, wife of Faith movement preacher Fred K. C. Price. The third item was a healing devotional written by Mark Brazee that contains scripture references, short narratives of encouragement, and recitation prayers for the reader. The final item was a journal that inspired me to not only write but to keep writing. I have since written volumes! This allowed me to keep track of my lived experience over the years and provided the reflective notes that I share here.

Support Groups

The introduction to faithtalk did not stop with gifts as it also included an invitation to attend *"Healing School."* This was my first encounter with a faith-based support group in Minnesota sponsored by a prominent nondenominational mega-church that is part of the Faith movement. I entered a large room filled with mostly white men and women with various diseases and physical impairments who were talking about their faith and hoping for a miracle. While I never witnessed any miracles (as no one stood up from their wheelchair and started walking) there were plenty of stories about vision returning and mysterious anomalies disappearing from x-rays and CT scans. I have no doubt that something did happen to the individuals who reported these healings. However, there were many others who did not have any tangible manifestation of healing. As a result it became rather depressing to continue attending this healing school since there seemed to be so little of it. This added to my feelings of disharmony and dissonance discussed earlier, and my departure was also seen by some as a lack of faith and patience.

As a breast cancer survivor with a support network from a variety of strong Judeo-Christian, faith-based communities, I was surrounded by individuals near and far insistent on quoting biblical passages as a means of support and encouragement. As this continued I became weary of these verbal affirmations. I also felt bad about the way I was feeling while at the same time having great appreciation for the verbal support and encouragement I received. The socially accepted response to the question "How you are doing?" is to respond with the customary "I am fine" or "I am doing okay." These responses are often given for fear that if one were to be honest about how they are feeling, the interaction can become awkward if the responder goes off script.

As human beings, logic and practicality drive our senses. However, at times we desire and crave something much more tangible, particularly during times of crisis. We are aware that something is out of sync, even if we do not know exactly what it is. Thus, when someone asks how we are feeling, we may want to tell them so that hopefully we can feel better. Hebrews 11:1 states that "Faith is the substance of things hoped for and the evidence of things not seen" thus, the fear of talking and thinking about the trauma associated with breast cancer was disheartening as was sharing it with others. During these times, I questioned my faith as did other survivors I have met.

To question one's faith is a normal process, but to have others misunderstand and assume you lack faith or trust in God is different. It is particularly hurtful when one begins to talk about breast cancer, the disease, and the disharmony it brings as a form of healing and coping. In other words, they want you to "get it all out" if you will. My faith is strong and I wholeheartedly believe in spiritual self-care such as prayer, meditation, or any other spiritually-based practices that promote continued personal development and well-being in times of health and illness (White, Peters, & Meyers-Schim, 2011). I consider myself to be in a constant state of prayer for my health and well-being. This is something that will not change and is consistent with a womanist[10] viewpoint that includes the betterment of the community, not just self. This shift in how I interpreted scripture emerged after spending time reading the works of womanist theologians Katie Cannon (1988, 1995), Jacquelyn Grant (1989), and Delores Williams (1993).[11] I was introduced to their work by womanist theologian Rev. Dr. Alika Galloway during my time of recovery and as I renegotiated faithtalk. Rethinking scripture through a womanist lens of liberation allowed me to speak openly and freely about breast cancer to heal myself and to help other women in the community by telling my story.

Most breast cancer survivors have those "Why me?" moments. However, as I started to discuss openly about how I was feeling about the trauma I was experiencing and concerns for my family, it quickly became apparent to me that I could not share with just *anyone*. This realization was confirmed while at a faith-based cancer support group for women at a traditionally Black church. To my surprise and that of some of the other women in the room I was verbally attacked and chastised for speaking so negatively "out loud" about having breast cancer, I was warned "You need to keep that sort of thing to yourself" and criticized, "What makes you so special that you should not get it?" It was even suggested that illness is a form of punishment and that I must have done something wrong or else I would have been spared from the disease. I was shocked and could not respond to the tirade against me because I did not want to appear to be disrespectful to my elders. I realized that I had made a huge mistake straying away from an unspoken group norm where you were not supposed to say how you really felt. I had forgotten one of the first things I was taught as a communication scholar—audience analysis. I had been lulled into a false sense of security by a church group of older women. I learned a hard lesson as a novice support group seeker—not all support groups are supportive. This experience heightened my awareness and the realization that breast cancer survivors needed to adjust their conversations and level of disclosure for different spaces and places; that even among other survivors one may not be able to truly express one's feelings. As noted in chapter 2, the tropes associated with Black womanhood force Black women to deny vulnerability for strength and resilience. Despite the physical and emotional toils of treatments as the result of expectations of family, society, and even the breast cancer culture, they must be courageous and strong.

FAITHTALK AND BREAST CANCER

The entire chapter 11 of Hebrews is a list or historical account of the acts of faith performed by God's people. Hebrews 11:1 for instance reads, "Faith is the substance of things hoped for and the evidence of things not seen." Metaphorically, by speaking, Black women breast cancer survivors can create their own performative faith list that parallels the aforementioned passage. This specific scripture reference to the word "hope" is often depicted with the pink ribbon symbol to encourage awareness of breast cancer and often representing the strength and courageousness associated with breast cancer survivorship and of course, hope for a cure.

In an attempt to understand the influence of faithtalk on Black women breast cancer survivors I sought answers to the following questions:

1. What role does faithtalk have on your ability to openly discuss health concerns?
2. What role does faithtalk have on self-expectations?
3. Does faithtalk influence the expectations others have of breast cancer survivors?

When I began this work, answering the questions was an informal process done by keeping track of observations and conversations in journals. It was The Pink and The Black Project© that provided the impetus to formally ask these questions of other Black women breast cancer survivors.

The concept of faithtalk was described to focus group participants as any type of verbal confession or declaration of faith made in conversations with others outside of prayer or meditation and any reference to the belief in a higher power for healing and strength in the Christian tradition or belief of having faith in God or Jesus as a healing power based on biblical passages. Many of these passages were referenced and include:

- "While the sun was setting, all those who had any who were sick with various diseases brought them to Him; and laying His hands on each one of them, He was healing them." Luke 4:40
- "And He was not able to do even one work of power there, except that He laid His hands on a few sickly people [and] cured them." Mark 6:5
- "Let us all come forward and draw near with true (honest and sincere) hearts in unqualified assurance and absolute conviction engendered by faith by that leaning of the entire human personality on God in absolute trust and confidence in His power, wisdom, and goodness, having our hearts sprinkled and purified from a guilty (evil) conscience and our bodies cleansed with pure water." Hebrews 10:22

In addition, Christian slogans such as: "Too blessed to be stressed," "God will never give you more than you can bear," "God will never lead you where His Grace cannot keep you," "God's got this," "God is good all the time and all the time God is good," "By His stripes I am healed," and other sayings or slogans are included as examples of faithtalk.

As the survivors began to discuss the questions and provide answers the following general responses were provided to confirm their stance on faith:

- "I think I can speak for everyone here, we all know that God is a healer that is our belief, with the different trials and tribulations of our life he has carried us through."
- "If there is no test, there is no testimony."
- "If you just turn it over to God, you have nothing to worry about."
- "I know he has healed me and carried me through a lot of things."
- "I cannot imagine not having it (faith)."
- "That is what has carried me."
- "I can't imagine anyone that doesn't have something or somebody to believe in besides the doctor."

All of the general responses talk about faith as part of the healing and coping process which are corroborated by other studies that look at religion and spirituality (Gibson & Hendricks, 2006; Gregg, 2011; Lynn et al., 2014; McLaughlin et al., 2013). Additionally, some of the responses were specific slogans or faithtalk that one might hear in other conversations or contexts, (e.g., "If there is no test there is no testimony" and "If you just turn it over to God, you have nothing to worry about").

When the women were asked, *"What role does faithtalk have on your ability to openly discuss health concerns?"* it prompted two conversations. Most women indicated that they do not discuss their health concerns in detail while other survivors indicated that they were willing to discuss certain aspects with family, friends, employers, or even strangers on an as needed basis. Specific responses were:

- "Hmmm, I never really thought about it that way. . . . I guess I don't talk about it much."
- "I try not to be too negative or talk about the 'bad stuff.' It makes people uncomfortable, even family."
- "I can talk to my family about anything."
- "I do not have a problem, my family is strong."
- " I can talk to my doctors but it is harder with family and friends, I don't want them to think I'm always complaining."
- "Sometimes it sounds like complaining when you're not."
- "I have a hard time with that name it and claim it . . . it's like, if you talk about it you're giving power to the enemy."
- "You do have to be careful who you talk to. Not everyone is understanding . . . they will pretend like they care and are interested."
- "It's hard to know who to trust with your feelings."

When asked about faithtalk, self-expectations, and expectations others have of them, this group of survivors was in agreement that it was their faith, the mental and verbal affirmations, that kept them going. However, this idea of expectations opened up into a discussion on being strong Black women, as one survivor explained "When you are at your lowest point, when you feel like just giving up, we are strong black women. We have to be strong. Our faith helps us be strong." Another concurred, noting "People expect us to be strong. We were born strong."

The group also delved into media representations of survivors, explaining that, "not many are Black women," and "in the early days, you never saw any of us. That is changing now though." It was acknowledged that the Cancer Treatment Centers ad featuring "Dawn," a survivor who is depicted in the advertisement going to her treatment appointments and meeting with members of her care team, was getting close to a real representation, but one of the focus group members also noted that "Dawn" is always alone, "No one from her family is ever with her, just doctors and nurses."

The group concluded that *faithtalk* has its challenges depending on the audience. Furthermore their use of *faithtalk* is part of their coping mechanism for living with breast cancer's aftermath. Faithtalk keeps the survivor encouraged. When we are alone, we have no one to motivate us but ourselves. This is the place where we can speak freely about what is going on with our mind, body, and spirit. The voices of the women are instructive as they noted the importance of sharing ("We know that God hears us and He knows we are not complaining"). Faithtalk influences a survivor's expectations of self. ("We must not only encourage ourselves in private, we must also encourage ourselves in public. We have to live up to that Proverbs 31 woman. She did everything. Never once did she discuss her ailments, having a bad day, or anything like that.") Living up to the expectations that others have of us keeps some of us trying to maintain that level of work and support we provide to others. As one survivor put it: "We are naming and acknowledging the disease that we have, but we are not claiming it, we are not claiming death. We are claiming survival!" To close this chapter I include the story of Elder Vernell Smith, who chose to tell her story using her real name. Using her words "to be a living testimony of God's healing power."

As women claim their strength through faith, they also claim their strength through breast cancer culture by embracing the pink ribbon, warrior metaphors, and other symbolisms found in this particular narrative (Johansen et al. 2013; Sulik & Deane, 2008). Chapter four provides a brief historical background of the pink ribbon and breast cancer culture while providing insight into how some Black women breast cancer survivors accept or reject the associated symbolisms and metaphors.

INTERLUDE
Survivor's Story in Her Own Words: My Story
Vernell Smith

My hope is built on nothing less than Jesus blood and righteousness. I dare not trust the sweetest frame but Holy lean on Jesus name. On Christ the solid rock I stand all other ground is sinking sand. In 2005, as I sat at work at Prayer Tabernacle Church of Love in early summer at my desk, I started feeling pain in my left breast. I attributed the pain to hitting my breast on the desk when I would answer the telephone, saying to myself it would go away and that what I don't know won't hurt me. Boy was I wrong.

To comfort myself, I would hold my breast with my hand or take 2 Tylenol, there were times that I had to do both and the pain would subside. One afternoon while having lunch with my sister and friend Lottie Brown, she noticed me holding my breast and asked what was wrong. I told her about the pain. She said I'm going to pray for you and that I should get checked out. I, of course said okay and that I would see the doctor.

In mid-October, 2005 I had a doctor's appointment for my yearly physical and a follow up visit for a TIA I had the prior year in November, 2004. To make long story short, I was examined by a female doctor and was told, "that everything looks okay" and to get dressed. She came back in and as I was fully dressed she asked me how I was feeling overall and I remembered the pain in my left breast. She had me undress and did a clinical exam of both breasts and said to come back the next day for an ultra-sound. Well, I wonder about two things, first why the clinical breast exam was not done as a part of my physical and second why she did not inquire about my "overall feelings" at the beginning. I also have to ask myself, why I did not speak up about the pain in my breast when I walked into that appointment. Mind you I had a mammogram in April of 2005 and was told that all was well. In retrospect it is possible that I was holding on to that report.

The next day, I believe on a Thursday I got a call before I was to leave for work, which stated the ultra-sound showed live cancer cells. It was then that I was informed that I had breast cancer. My reaction was okay and I came downstairs and told my mother and she said very confidently and assuredly you will be all right we serve a God that heals all forms of sickness and diseases.

I left for work and went in to talk to the man of Faith, the late Bishop Kenneth H. Moales, Sr., who also spoke faith and healing to me. And thus my journey begins.

I went in for a biopsy and it confirmed what the doctors had said. We began to seek other options as to what path to follow. Some said treatment first in the form of radiation, others said cut it away to never return. We prayed and the decision was made to cut it away. We were referred to one of the best surgeons at Bridgeport Hospital and the Norma Phrein Breast Cancer Center but that particular surgeon was booked solid.

I was taught that God will give you favor which in most cases in better than money. My mother worked for Dr. Vincent Sica in earlier years and even though he is deceased his son became my mother's doctor. My mother made a call to the young Dr. Sica and he made a call and I had an appointment in December 2005 to meet with Dr. Mary Pronovost. She said we would proceed with surgery in January 6, 2006 and she wanted me to have another mammogram, which I did and the cancer did not show. I was told that because of the density of our (African Americans) breast skin and tissue that we should request an ultrasound.

I continued to work until January 5, 2006. I had mastectomy on January 6, 2006. Was told by Dr. Pronovost that she would try to save the breast if possible. My Mother, Bertha Patterson; my daughter, Ashley Smith; my pastor and spiritual father Bishop Moales; my sisters: Judy Fletcher, Martha Melvin and Deb Pullen; and my spiritual brother Sigmund Morriar to name a few of my concerned friends and family were with me at the hospital. All who loved me and could not be there in person were with me in prayer. My family far and near were bombarding heaven with prayers on my behalf.

After surgery my mother and sister Judy were the first ones I remember speaking to and they assured me that all went well. I remember asking Judy did Dr. P save my breast and she laughed and said no but that I could have one of hers and we smiled at each other.

I was in the hospital for one week and every morning my sister, Wilhelmina Jackson, who is a midwife and doctor at Bridgeport Hospital would come to my room and say "Nell I'm just glad you are still here." While I was also glad I did not really understand the urgency of her statement. But, I would soon find out.

The pathology reports came back and I was assigned to an oncologist and a radiologist. Who both explained their findings and what was ahead for me. There is this old saying that you hear what you want to hear. Well, that is what happened to me. I suggest and say to everyone, never go to the doctors by yourself, someone has to hear and listen for you. My Mother, Bertha Patterson, and my sister, Judy Fletcher, went with me. My sister Judy always took notes and would ask questions if we had any during and between visits to the doctors in preparation for my treatment and during treatment.

I was told that my treatment plan would include extensive chemotherapy and radiation treatments. This was due to the grade and stage of the cancer in my breast. I was stage 3 getting ready to be stage 4. Stage 3, which means the tumor is no larger than 5 centimeters (2 inches or the size of a lime) and has spread to the underarm lymph nodes or nearby tissue. The tumor can be any size and the breast cancer has spread to the chest wall or the skin of the breast, which would cause the breast to become swollen or appear lumpy. At stage 4 the tumor can be any size and the breast cancer has spread to other parts of the body, such as lungs, liver, bones or brain. Stage 4 is also called advanced or metastatic breast cancer. Stages are used to help choose and or determine the breast cancer treatment options that are right for you.

I went through chemo, which was a very tough time in my life. At one point it had to be stopped after the first two doses. The initial chemo medicines I was prescribed were the drugs Cytoxan and Arimidex which both of with are extremely toxic to the body and were administered intravenously. After two doses of this toxic mix of drugs my chemotherapy treatments had to be stopped because I almost died. Yes, I lost my hair, lost weight and became deathly ill. My blood levels were all out of control, I was unable to keep food in my body; lived off Coke Cola and ginger ale. BUT GOD...

After that week was over I was admonished by then Bishop Kenneth Moales, Sr to come to church because the people needed to see me and know that God is and can do anything but fail. His visit to the hospital was with my brother Pastor Thomas Grant who came from Jacksonville, FL to see about me. I went to church that Sunday in April, 2006 where Pastor Grant and Bishop Moales prayed and ministered to me. Bishop Moales said that death came for me BUT GOD said not yet. Jeremiah 29:11 says: "I know what I'm doing. I have it all planned out—plans to take care of you, not abandon you, plans to give you the future you hope for (the Message Bible)."

I had to resume chemo for two more doses of Cytoxan and Arimidex. They were so strong they were administered once every two weeks. I finished that drug treatment only to continue with 13 additional weeks of Tamoxifen pills and Herceptin shots this was no walk in the park. The side effects from the tamoxifen caused me to lose the feelings in my fingertips and toes. I also lost the ability to taste food, everything began to taste the same. At the end of chemo I told Bishop that I would not wish chemo on my worst enemy.

It was after the chemotherapy treatments that my radiation journey began and again this was not a walk in the park. This was also a 13-week journey that I endured for 5 days a week, every week, for 13 weeks. The damage to my skin was horrific. My skin was burned to the point where the white meat was showing. This also had to be stopped to allow my skin to heal some only to be burned some more.

I remember days that I did not want to go to the hospital for treatment, and I had questions. Not of the health care professionals but of God. Why me? Was my question. I did not want to question God as to why me, and I was really afraid to question God. Until one day I was talking to that sister/friend Lottie and told her I would not dare question God and she said to me why not. Why not question Him?

So I did, as I did not understand why me out of all the people in the world. So I asked: Lord, why me? In my conversation with the God I explained to Him how I saw it: Lord, my God, I have served and lived for you since I was in high school and now this! Why me? So one day while I had my face to my wall and was asking God why. God sent my daughter Ashley in to my room to minister to me. She said "Ma, you know why God let you have breast cancer?" I said "no, why" and she said "because He knew you were a strong tower and that you could bear it." Well needless to say I got myself up and got ready and went for treatment.

Yes, I still have scars to show and I believe they are reminders of the wonderful works of God.

God remained Faithful to me. I had to preach one Sunday morning and God gave me the word UNSTOPPABLE. In 2007, I had another scare with the right breast but I did not lose this one. I once again had to have radiation treatment 5 days a week for 13 weeks. So glad I made it, I made it through.

Psalm 37:25 states: "I once was young, now I'm old"—not once have I seen an abandoned believer, or her kids out roaming the streets.

As a breast cancer survivor you always live with the fact that the cancer could come back. I believe that if I did not have a strong faith in God and a support system second to none that I would not be here today to share my journey. I believe if I had given into the hopelessness and fear that can come with a cancer diagnosis and the belief that I have cancer and I'm going to die that I would not be here today. I thank God daily for my hope and trust in him. I was told by that great man of Faith that we would not visit this again. I believe God.

Right now in 2015 I am nine years cancer free. God did it and I am grateful. So what I didn't know did hurt me but I am here to tell you that God can and will deliver and keep you

NOTES

1. From thereikicenter.net—Reiki "is administered by 'laying on hands' and is based on the idea that an unseen 'life force energy' flows through us and is what causes us to be alive. If one's 'life force energy' is low, then we are more likely to get sick or feel stress, and if it is high, we are more capable of being happy and healthy."

2. The writings of James H. Cone on Black Liberation Theology and Black Power provided the historical information.

3. Dr. Molefi Kete Asante is a Professor of Black Studies at Temple University and author of over 74 books and 400 articles on politics, African and Black thought, global culture, and communication. See Afrocentricity (rev. 2003) and Afrocentric Manifesto (2008). http://www.asante.net/books/.

4. Class notes on Nommo. Dr. Melbourne S. Cummings, noted communication scholar, and retired Professor of Communication from Howard University.

5. Cathrine Bowler at Duke University has written on the history of the Faith Movement, http://thefaithmovement.com/history.html.

6. New Thought was a movement dominated by women during the Victorian era that focused on mental and bodily healing.

7. Kenneth Hagin is recognized by scholars as the father of the contemporary Faith movement.

8. All of the passages read aloud on the CD can now be found online at http://hopefaithprayer.com/scriptures/healing-scriptures-kenneth-hagin/.

9. Many of the gifts I received referenced Romans 10:17, Proverbs 4:20–22, or Mark 11:23 in the card from the giver.

10. The term Womanist was developed by author Alice Walker in her first collection of non-fiction, *In Search of Our Mothers' Gardens: Womanist Prose* (1983), and referred primarily to African American women, but also to women in general. In her own words: "A Womanist is to feminist as purple is to lavender."

11. Womanist theology is a religious conceptual framework, which reconsiders and revises the traditions, practices, scriptures, and biblical interpretation with a special lens to empower and liberate Black women in America.

FOUR
Embracing the Pink Identity

Black Women and Pink Ribbon Culture

> "I never really liked the color pink. But I guess I will wear it anyway. I mean that pink ribbon." —Makeda

Black women have a standpoint which shapes the way we think about breast cancer and pink ribbons. As such, I consider breast cancer and any other chronic illness or disease a form of oppression for Black women evidenced by their higher mortality rates. Patricia Hill-Collins (1995) discusses two interlocking components that characterize Black women's standpoint in terms of how we view our own oppression:

> First, Black women's political and economic status provides them with a distinct set of experiences that offers a different view of material reality than that available to other groups. The unpaid and paid work that Black women perform, the types of communities in which they live, and the kinds of relationships they have with others suggests that Black women as a group, experience a different world than those who are not Black and female. Second, these experiences stimulate a distinctive Black feminist consciousness concerning that material reality. (p. 339)

When we think about these components in terms of breast cancer and Black women's health they are different from the experiences of white and other women of color. These differences can be seen in the early media images that shape breast cancer culture and pink ribbon rhetoric that call for white women to be strong and hopeful *during a particular moment in time*. Which differs for Black women as the idea of strong Black womanhood and faith describe how we are to act *during all times*. Thus, the expectation is that this is no different from how we should act during other periods in our lives. We continue to fight against the controlling image that stereotypes us as strong Black women even among a sea of pink ribbons.

If you ask most people what they think of when they see a pink ribbon they are likely to say breast cancer, survivors, women, hope, mammograms, money, marches, Susan G. Komen walks or runs to help find a cure. For some African Americans the response to this question also included "white women." When a Black breast cancer survivor sees a pink ribbon, she might think about giving a response that includes the rhetorical messages as mentioned above. But if she is able to be honest she might include statements such as "fear," "death," "dying," "can't stand the sight of it," or "too commercial." The first set of responses are those one might expect to hear from a breast cancer survivor. The second are not popular (and as my own experience showed, even among those one might think would be supportive) and must be uttered cautiously in a safe space if one is going to speak in such a negative way about the lovely pink ribbon.

Gayle Sulik (2010) in her book *Pink Ribbon Blues* remarks that "Pink ribbon culture in the United States has become more than a cultural trend or a successful industry: it has become a distinct cultural system that is integrated into the fabric of American Life. Grounded in advocacy, deeply held beliefs about gender and femininity, mass mediated consumption, and the cancer industry, pink ribbon culture has transformed breast cancer from an important social problem that requires complicated social and medical solutions to a popular item for public consumption." She goes on to discuss the negative aspects of pink ribbon culture and the detrimental impact it has on women's health overall.

Rhetoric or dialogue about breast cancer and breast cancer survivorship in the media often include these broad categories: (1) mammography—who should get one and at what age; (2) fund-raising such as Susan G. Koman or AVON runs and or walks for a cure; (3) popular pink ribbon warrior metaphors; and (4) purchasing pink products from a variety of manufacturers as a show of support. These are the major themes identified through my personal observations and confirmed in conversations with other survivors when discussing what we remembered from breast cancer advertisements in print or on television.

Noelle-Neumann's (1984) *Spiral of Silence* posits that media representations of social issues are often indicative of public opinion. People live in perpetual fear of isolating themselves and carefully monitor public opinion to see which views are acceptable. When their opinions appear out of favor, they keep silent. Television's constant repetition of a single point of view biases perception of public opinion and accelerates the spiral of silence. Most published accounts of breast cancer are told from one perspective: that of white middle- to upper-middle-class women of a privileged position who according to some research have the inclination, literacy, and leisure to write their stories, and the contacts to get them published (Couser, 1997). I take issue with the idea that Black women lack inclination and literacy to tell their stories. Black women are inclined to write and share their stories, however in addition to the cultural silencing there is also the issue of "leisure." Leisure time is unavailable for most Black women. As a Black female academic who is in the profession where writing is required, it has taken much longer for me to complete this book than I would have liked. In addition to health challenges along the way, I am still expected to perform at a level that goes beyond teaching classes, grading papers, and committee work (Madlock Gatison, 2011a). When it comes to work and home, leisure is not an option. Like other scholar activists, "work" fills the "leisure" time that is missing in Black women's narrative of breast cancer. Thus they must create spaces where women can tell their stories and share their experiences (Carter, 2003; Grimes & Hou, 2013; Herndl, 2006). Black women with breast cancer are living within a cultural norm that favors silence about illness.

In the Black community it is not uncommon to be uninformed regarding any family history of chronic physical or mental illness. Family medical history is not discussed unless deemed absolutely necessary. For example, it was not until I was well into the recovery stage of my second occurrence of breast cancer that I was told about my paternal grandmother being diagnosed with breast cancer. She had succumbed to it. During focus group discussions every participant told story after story about not getting family health information about earlier generations. Each participant also indicated that they have since changed this family information sharing dynamic and freely share their health history with their siblings, children, or other relatives.

There is a faith tradition that also silences perceived negative talk about illness. From a faith perspective, one does not give power to the disease by talking about it. A cultural norm of silence and a public view that breast cancer survivors are heroic and stoic do not leave much room for Black women's voices. There is no room to voice agreement or disagreement with popular opinions on how one is to react to and live through a health crisis. For a Black woman to express publicly the pain associated with living with breast cancer contradicts the expectation of both pink ribbon rhetoric and traditional Black faithtalk about disease and illness.

During interviews for The Pink and The Black Project© four specific survivors talked of having a negative view of the pink ribbon hype but felt it necessary to keep that opinion to herself. One woman bristled that when she spoke about not liking the pink ribbon and what it signified to her "People think you don't support your own cause." The other three women agreed and maintained "All that pink ribbon stuff is for white women" and "not really for us." One woman who did not comment earlier during this topic of conversation added, "We wear the ribbon, so we are not forgotten." There was a poignant pause as we all took time to reflect on her statement.

IT WASN'T ALWAYS PINK

As the story about the origination of the pink ribbon goes,[1] the original breast cancer ribbons were peach colored and were created in the early 1990s by Charlotte Haley while sitting at her dining table. Haley was a breast cancer survivor, one of four generations of women in her family who had battled with the disease. Haley's maternal grandmother died of metastatic breast cancer and her sister and daughter had breast cancer. In an effort to bring awareness and political action to the issue she distributed the peach ribbons in sets of five at her local grocery stores. Haley asked people to wear the ribbon and write to their legislators. Along with the ribbons, she gave each person a card that read, "The National Cancer Institute annual budget is $1.8 billion, only 5 percent goes for cancer prevention. Help us wake up our legislators and America by wearing this ribbon." Haley was not interested in creating an organization or accepting money for the peach-colored ribbons. Instead she encouraged others to spread the word to family, friends, and politicians. Her aim was to encourage women to become politically active.

It was also during the early 1990s that Alexandra Penney, then the editor in chief of *Self*, and Evelyn Lauder, a breast cancer survivor and senior corporate vice president of Estée Lauder, teamed up to create a pink ribbon. This followed a consultation with their attorneys who advised them to choose another color as Charlotte Haley, not wanting to commercialize breast cancer, refused the offer to work with them. The Estée Lauder Company used its makeup counters as marketing outlets and distributed millions of ribbons while also making millions of dollars in the process. In addition to the pink ribbons, each woman was given a breast self-exam card and was asked to sign a petition to increase government funding of breast cancer research.

One cannot forget about Susan G. Komen (Komen.org) and the organization's influence on breast cancer culture. The history of the pink ribbon is chronicled on the organization's website and reads:

> Susan G. Komen for the Cure® has used the color pink since its inception in 1982. The first Komen Race for the Cure® logo design was an abstract female runner outlined with a pink ribbon and was used during the mid 1980s through early 1990s.
>
> In 1990, the first breast cancer survivor program was launched at the Komen National Race for the Cure® in Washington, D.C. The survivors wore buttons that were printed in Black and white. Later that year, the survivor program developed, and pink was used as the designated

color for Komen to promote awareness and its programs. Pink visors were launched for survivor recognition.

In 1991, pink ribbons were distributed to all breast cancer survivors and participants of the Komen New York City Race for the Cure®. Then in 1992, Alexandra Penney, editor-in-chief of *Self* magazine, wanted to put the magazine's second annual Breast Cancer Awareness Month issue over the top. She did this by creating a ribbon and enlisting the cosmetics giants to distribute them in New York City stores. And thus, the birth of the pink ribbon! (Susan G. Komen Pink Ribbon Story, Komen.org, 2014)

The pink ribbon has resulted in a perfect storm of marketing, commercialization, and commodification of illness and women's bodies. This is a long way from the grassroots effort Charlotte Haley had in mind and a total acceptance of the corporate strategy of the Estée Lauder Company, which has been emulated by thousands of companies large and small.

Pink Backlash

Over the past several years there is now a pink ribbon backlash. This is a phenomenon that has been documented extensively in the United States, Canada, and the United Kingdom (King, 2006; Sulik, 2010). This backlash is a result of women openly voicing their concern and at times, disgust, at how breast cancer and personal tragedy has been marketed for commercial consumption. A new word has been added to our lexicon stemming from the pink backlash—*pinkwashing*. Pinkwashing is "a term used to describe the activities of companies and groups that position themselves as leaders in the struggle to eradicate breast cancer while engaging in practices that may be contributing to rising rates of the disease" (bcaction.org).[2]

In the current climate, it is somewhat safer to express contrary opinions about pink ribbons, the commodification of women's illness, and the commercialization of breast cancer. I recall a time when this was not the case. If you were a known breast cancer survivor and declined to wear a pink ribbon odd looks and accusatory statements would follow (Madlock Gatison, 2015d). There is an episode of the TV show *Seinfeld* in which the character Kramer refuses to wear a red ribbon at an AIDS walk. The other participants in the walk demand that he wear the ribbon while he tries to explain that it is not necessary for him to wear the ribbon to show his support. The other walkers disagree and challenge his decision by continuing to demand he do so and then physically attack him. The Internet and social media have provided a space for survivors, advocates, and any concerned party to voice contrary thoughts and opinions about pink ribbon culture. This virtual space provides a visibility that was once veiled and completely mediated by mainstream media gatekeepers. In reviewing the narratives of Black women who shared their experience with breast cancer, the Internet was most helpful as women used personal blogs and YouTube to document their own stories. These were stories that diverged from the pro-pink rhetoric.

The resulting pink backlash against the pinkwashing is a remedy to the weakness brought about by the focus on fund-raising for awareness and corporate profits. I have heard it said and seen it in print that too much pink can make one sick . . . as one blogger Nzingha opined, ". . . too much pink makes my stomach turn." There are those in the color therapy world that believe too much of any color can be overdone, but too much of the color pink can actually create physical weakness. There is weakness in the color pink when it comes to women's health. This is especially so for Black women as the research and data regarding health disparities show Black women have the highest breast cancer death rates (http://www.cdc.gov/vitalsigns/breast cancer/) of all racial and ethnic groups and are 40 percent more likely to die of breast cancer than white women. The Centers for Disease Control and Prevention (2015) has conducted several studies[3] to find out the reasons why certain populations, including Black women, have not benefitted equally from recent improvements in health care. Currently, there is no data that show a correlation between the dollars spent on pink ribbon advertising and the dollar amount donated for research on decreasing the mortality rate for Black women.

Pinkwashing calls attention to the use of carcinogens and toxins in the very products branded with the pink ribbon logo. The very companies that have capitalized on stamping their products with the pink ribbon may be using toxins and carcinogens that medical research has shown exacerbates cancer in our society. This is significant for Black women's health and for the health of our communities, especially given the problems of environmental racism and the lack of affordable health care to address emerging health issues.

The intersection of race, class, and gender is reflected in how Black women are disproportionately impacted by toxins in our environment, including lead paint in homes and old schools; soil, air, and water contamination; and landfills and toxic waste dumps in urban and rural neighborhoods. As a breast cancer survivor who struggled with the loss of hair due to "chemo induced alopecia" we cannot forget the chemicals we use to straighten and process our hair. The "kink factor" metaphor as defined by Spellers (2003) reminds Black women of the many times where their own hair played a pivotal role in their identity and how others defined them. It is a representation of the tension between the "interlocking structure of race, class and gender oppression" (Spellers, 2003, p. 228). More specifically, a Black woman's hair is important (Spellers & Moffitt, 2010) as it represents her halo of womanhood, her pride and glory, that very thing that most Black women lose during chemotherapy. Yet, the very products that we use on our hair may be contributing to our overall health issues.

For those who advocate the use of skin bleaching, it is important to note that some of those lotions and potions are banned in the Unites States because they contain known carcinogens. Yet, these products are widely available in Africa, the Caribbean, Latin America, and other developing world communities where Blacks try to lighten and brighten their skin buying into the white beauty ideal (Madlock Gatison, 2011b; 2015a; 2015c; 2015e; 2015f). These are also some of the same places where breast cancer is epidemic and the pink ribbon is used to signify awareness (Edge, 2014a; 2014b; Edge et al., 2014). Trying to conform to an unattainable standard of beauty is killing us from the inside out (Stiel et al., 2016).

NOT FORGOTTEN

While most narratives about breast cancer told from the mainstream perspective hold resonance they nonetheless exclude those outside the circle who have experienced this disease through an alternative cultural lens or standpoint. Organizations such as the Cancer Treatment Centers of America try to create an image of breast cancer that is not just about fund-raising and wearing pink ribbons. They do so by strategically featuring two Black women, Dawn Jones[4] and Phyllis Ellis.[5] Jones (who was also mentioned in chapter three as it relates to her family missing in the advertisement) is featured as she goes through various stages of treatment highlighting her meetings with doctors and other health care professionals, featuring rooms which display high-tech medical equipment while Ellis is shown talking about the care she received with pictures of the center locations flashing during the advertisements. I would agree that providing a more realistic view in the life of women with breast cancer is a move in the right direction, however we still must proceed with caution. A caution that reminds us that we cannot be reduced to a niche market in our quest to be recognized and remembered as the narrative does not include rest.

Issues of race, class, and gender are clearly evident in pink ribbon culture and the "battle" to raise awareness and end breast cancer. As Black women embrace the pink ribbon and breast cancer culture we are striving for the cure. We must also be cognizant of the probable causes of cancer in our communities as we purchase products in support of breast cancer research. The environmental and psychosocial factors as systemic issues are real and must be addressed, but unfortunately, environmental factors are difficult to overcome as they demand large-scale attention by local, state, and federal governments. Color theory and gender studies contend the body can be weakened in seeing too much of the color pink. Metaphorically speaking, perhaps this can account for the way in which grassroots action to end breast cancer was temporarily weakened.

I began the introduction of this work with a quote from Audre Lorde: "Caring for myself is not self-indulgence, it is self-preservation and that is an act of political warfare (Lorde, 1988). I close with it here to reaffirm that some of us embrace the pink ribbon to resist the oppression brought by breast cancer culture and its warrior metaphors with a full understanding of what it means to move from survivor to political advocate. Moving beyond the rhetorical trifecta of strength narratives that runs like fiber optic cable through the lives of breast cancer survivors is not an easy proposition. Those closest to survivors are also impacted by the rhetorical images of the Pink and Black Superwoman. These perceptions affect how Black women work outside the home in addition to taking care of their families and other obligations. The following chapter provides some insight into how friends and family perceive strength in breast cancer survivors.

NOTES

1. The original history of the peach and pink ribbon as it relates to Charlotte Haley, Estée Lauder Company, and *Self* magazine is well documented and publicized on numerous websites and media sources.

2. Breast Cancer Action is an organization that calls for women to "Think Before They Pink." Briefly, this organization calls attention to the contradictory nature of pink branded items that are toxic to women's health. http://www.bcaction.org/.

3. The studies listed here are only representative of the research that the CDC is currently doing: Socioeconomic disparities in breast cancer treatment among older women; Public health national approach to reducing breast and cervical cancer; Breast cancer screening of underserved women in the USA: results from the National Breast and Cervical Cancer Early Detection Program, 1998–2012.

4. Dawn Jones continues to document her health struggles and triumphs using her Facebook page. https://www.facebook.com/dawninrealtime and original Cancer Treatment Centers of America commercial retrieved http://www.youtube.com/watch?v=J5L9PZ3Li4U.

5. Phyllis Ellis breast cancer survivor featured in an advertisement for Cancer Treatment Centers of America retrieved from www.youtube.com/watch?v=cwqYOaQbqWU.

FIVE
Work and Family

"If I don't do it who will? There is no one to take care of me; there is no one to take care of my children. I have to pay to keep a roof over our heads and food on the table." —Nzingha

"Family and friends are great. We need them, but they get tired too . . . this thing never really goes away." —Tiye

Black women experience work differently than other populations and have a unique standpoint on what it means to work, the value placed on our work, and the ability to *get* work—in the form of finding a job or having a career. Like other indicators of social and economic well-being, glaring differences in employment and unemployment rates exist along lines of race and gender. African Americans have traditionally experienced much higher rates of unemployment than their white counterparts (Bureau of Labor Statistics, 2014; Center for Family Policy and Practice 2014).[1] In the United States, the primary source of income for the majority of all Americans is paid employment. From low, middle, to high, the economic well-being of the family is tied to earnings (Ell, Xie, Wells, Nedjat-Haiem et al., 2008). This includes most Black women diagnosed with breast cancer (Bureau of Labor Statistics; US Census, 2012). The women who participated in The Pink and The Black Project© were fully employed during their first occurrence of breast cancer. As time has progressed, their employment status has changed with one woman now fully retired; three who are now semi-retired, and the remaining 13 employed full-time.

During individual interviews and focus group discussions about perceptions of breast cancer survivors, faithtalk, being a strong Black woman, and work or employment issues the following themes emerged: how much time to take off, sick leave and when to use it; insurance benefits, financial support, how much to tell/privacy at work; and working as a way to cope with having breast cancer.

As Black women, we work to provide for our families and ourselves, and for some the role of provider goes beyond our immediate family, by including our extended family. For some of us, we are the sole breadwinner, while others of us are the primary earner even when two or more incomes are in the household. This is a responsibility that is not deterred by any illness which can range from the common cold to breast cancer. The sad reality is that Black women work in spite of failing health. Our backgrounds range from high school dropouts to college graduates with advanced degrees. Yet, breast cancer has no regard for persons who vary by their social class and having it does not obliterate the fact that obligations to employer and family remain.

Conversations with the survivors I spoke with reminded me of Patricia Hill-Collins' first point regarding our legacy of labor in the United States. She observes,

> First, Black women's political and economic status provides them with a distinct set of experiences that offers a different view of material reality than that available to other groups. The unpaid and paid work that Black women perform, the types of communities in which they live, and the kinds of relationships they have with others suggests that Black women as a group, experience a different world than those who are not Black and female. (pp. 45–48)

That experience of being in a different world when it comes to work is one that participants of The Pink and The Black Project© acknowledged.

> Yea, . . . I will admit it, I am a mule if you want to call it that. I am a work horse. I am fighting against a stereotype. You know the one - that lazy negro. You know what I mean. People think you are just trying to get a sick day. Who in their right mind would pretend they have cancer for a sick day? People who think that are sick. Then they see your hair fall out. Nobody believes you until you go bald.—Andromeda

> Well it is true what they say. We start out working twice as hard to get the same thing. Now it's harder, 'cause I'm sick. We always have to prove ourselves.—Mary

> I am tired. Tired of working two or three times as hard and I'm just keeping my head above water. Tired of explaining why I have a doctor's appointment. There was another woman in our section who had breast cancer. She never had to explain anything. They offered her time off. . . . I had to explain everything. . . . That wasn't fair to me.—Diana

> I really do believe that I would be much better now if I had taken time off. Time off without worry, worrying about who is going to pay the bills, worrying about insurance, worrying about do I have too many

doctors' appointments and will I get fired for taking time to go. . . . and you are right. We have to explain everything.—Andromeda

When you are the financial lifeblood for your family, you cannot quit, you cannot take time off. Girl, you have to keep it moving. You have to put on a brave face, smile and act like this is nothing. You have to keep working even . . . even if it is killing you . . . you can feel it in your bones . . . even if you are married, even if you have someone trying to help. They can't do it alone. You just keep going. You have to keep going. You can do it, girl. You can do it. You're a strong Black woman.—*Writings of an Insomniac*

We are well aware for some women, breast cancer can impose economic hardship whether one leaves her job or not. I did not find it unusual that a majority of the women spoke of not taking much time away from work for financial reasons. Those who took longer periods of time off from work than they wanted indicated that it was due to additional health complications related to radiation and or chemotherapy treatment, severe lymphedema, or other breast cancer–related issues. Yet others stated that they *"never really stopped working"* and requested a reduced workload to avoid loss of health insurance benefits and prolonged economic hardship. I include myself in the latter. A chorus of voices during this discussion asked, in unison, "What other choice did we have?" At the same time, I silently wondered, "And at what cost to our overall health?" In consideration of the sad shape we were in physically due to the multiple occurrences of breast cancer, the lingering side effects that survivors do not really want to discuss following treatment, knowing that some in the medical profession do not want to elaborate on the side effects, and the mental and emotional challenges that are tucked away inside each of us.

The women also agreed that it was their faithtalk—prayers, meditations, scripture reading—and the idea of being a strong Black woman that pushed them or "provided the necessary strength" to go to work and do what needed to be done. *Circe,* one of the interviewees, shared that the women on her job gathered around and prayed for her which provided some emotional support. She also indicated that this enabled her to take some time off without feeling guilty.

In the Black community the luxury of taking time off from work is not an option for most women (Satariano & DeLorenze, 1996) particularly for those with lengthy illnesses such as breast cancer. Variables such as type and level of job often dictate accrual and use of sick and vacation time and access to short-term or long-term disability benefits. These are significant factors in decisions regarding taking time to heal or receive treatment. In cases with employer-sponsored disability benefits, rules regarding how employees can use benefits make them attainable for those who could benefit from them the most. Even while available through the workplace, the requirements to receive them keep them out of reach. As Blinder and colleagues report a respondent as saying in their work, "I feel the majority of the African-American community cannot afford to stay off work for an extended period of time. They may be able to stay off of work, but not for an extended period of time. [Moderator: so if they needed to take more time . . .] I don't think they would be able to afford to take more time. I just feel that they would be forced to go back because of economics" (2012).

Trying to identify the experience of breast cancer survivors and work is not new, but few studies exist that specifically explore the unique experiences of Black women, breast cancer, and work-life balance. Those that do exist address issues related to returning to work and although they include women of color breast cancer survivors, a very small number were African American or Black women (Blinder, Murphy, Vahdat et al., 2012; Bradley, Oberst, & Schenk, 2006; Mujahid, Janz, Hawley, Griggs, Hamilton, & Katz, 2010). In spite of this, the concerns that were brought to light during my conversations with survivors confirmed that work-related issues such as those discussed below were on the minds of other breast cancer survivors of color of varying income levels.

NORMALCY

Working creates a sense of normalcy and served as a distraction from medical issues. Flexibility at work in terms of medical/sick leave or part-time schedule also plays a factor in determining how work can positively or negatively impact the treatment process. Additionally, but not surprisingly, the level or lack of support from employers and coworkers are also contributing factors in making the women feel that their lives were back to normal.

ECONOMIC/FINANCIAL STRESS

Breast cancer patients who choose to continue to work have a variety of issues that must be considered. The exorbitant costs associated with treatment can often result in breast cancer survivors (and their families) developing anxiety around the uncertainty of a steady income. The fear of losing their job because of taking time off, being forced out of a job, or forced into retirement can subsequently lead to being unable to pay rent/bills and the potential loss of health benefits. This is especially distressing for those who are the primary breadwinners in their households. Fear of financial disruption may extend their ability to heal or to heal thoroughly. Thus, they have the added burden of facing the potential loss of steady employment and access to benefits when they do exist.

DEPRESSION AND ANXIETY

Although the stress around keeping secure employment and thereby financial stability can result in anxiety in the treatment process, it is not the only factor that leads to anxiety or depression. I have already pointed out the importance of faith and faithtalk for the Black breast cancer patient. Nonetheless, it remains important to note that the level of self-disclosure deemed appropriate in a professional setting and ability to openly discuss what is needed can be a hindrance to the use of faith or faithtalk in a professional or work environment. Many places regard religious or expressions of faith offensive. In addition, there are anxieties associated with self-identifying as an employed person and not as a breast cancer survivor. The culture of silence is oftentimes self-imposed such that survivors limit discussion in the workplace about their illness. Resulting in survivors appearing to be fine when in reality, they are not.

The anxiety related to breast cancer can plague one but because they are suffering in silence, they seem to be handling their illness well. As such, coworkers and supervisors may treat them as though they *are not* ill. This can result in additional stress because they *are* ill. Their appearance and cancer treatment indicators such as hair loss or, not looking sick enough to take time off from work may cause undue stress because of the toll the cancer and treatments may be taking while they give the impression of being well. Conversely, looking sickly due to excessive weight loss or gain, loss of hair, and an overall appearance of frailty can be perceived as having an impact on customers and overall staff morale. Thus, there is a cycle of anxiety that can be felt by others who are around the woman who has breast cancer which can then result in increasing her levels of anxiety or depression.

PRIVACY

The last issue of concern is how much information about their illness needs to be shared. For many breast cancer survivors, there is anxiety surrounding how much of their private medical information needs to be shared with colleagues and employers. While it may appear necessary to share this information, there are risks involved. Individuals did not want to be the object of gossip, pity, and discrimination. In certain occupations where being strong (and not just appearing to be so) or working with vulnerable populations who may have difficulty understanding the transformation the breast cancer survivor is undergoing, this can be especially difficult.

Gender roles and societal expectations significantly influence the decision-making process regarding work during illness. Acknowledgment of this must be included in any future studies in order to impart a remedy to the psychosocial factors that contribute to the high rates of breast cancer in the Black community and the unwillingness of Black women to share this information when it might be beneficial to them health-wise and economically. As one respondent, Nzingha, stated, "Strong Black women do what they have to do. That means going to work when you don't feel like it."

To date, the research regarding the ways in which racial disparities influence Black women at work, stopping work, or returning to work after a breast cancer diagnosis is inadequate. Some studies address returning to work (Satariano & DeLorenze, 1996; Feuerstein, 2009), however, not much consideration is given to issues of race or class and returning to work (Hill-Collins, 2000; hooks, 1988). There is little available on the impact of a prolonged interruption of work and women who do not have the opportunity to stop working during treatment for breast cancer (with the exception of surgical procedures).

Studies concerned with the economic impact of lost productivity to employers in the guise of creating better therapies to minimize lost workdays are available. Yet much of the available research investigating the relationship between breast cancer survivorship, work, and quality of life are from countries other than the United States (Tiedtke, de Rijk, Dierckx de Casterlé, Christiaens, & Donceel, 2010; Roelen, Koopmans, De Graaf, Balak, & Groothoff, 2009; Roelen, Koopmans, van Rhenen, Groothoff, van der Klink et al., 2011; Banning, 2011). European health organizations and universities have completed a number of studies in an attempt to address these important issues. In one such study, researchers searched for studies using the following databases: The Cochrane Controlled Trials Register, Medline, Ovid, EMBASE and Psychinfo for intervention studies from 1970–2007 that focused on female breast cancer survivors and return to work. Of the 5,219 studies identified only four studies fit my research parameters. They include the following criteria:

1. Randomized controlled studies, cohort studies, and observational studies.
2. Women who were diagnosed and had survived breast cancer with or without adjuvant therapy (i.e., chemotherapy or radiation) during the intervention period.
3. Non-drug intervention studies.
4. Studies that measured work-related outcomes such as: return to work, absenteeism, work disability, sick leave, or employment status (Hoving, Broekhuizen, & Frings-Dresen, 2009).

Of the four studies, only two were completed in the United States, one in 1977 and the other in 1980. Work-life issues that specifically addressed Black women were in one study (Mujahid, Janz, Hawley, Griggs, Hamilton, & Katz, 2010) but the numbers of Black women are too small for the data to be meaningful. What this tells us is that there is room for more work on Black women and the factors that impact them in their day-to-day lieves as breast cancer survivors in the workplace.

FAMILY

A breast cancer diagnosis can have a profound impact on significant others and close family members as it is one of the many health problems that Black families[2] suffer from disproportionately. As Black women, we work long and hard because we care about family and most of the time we put their care before our own. This is representative of womanist theology—Black women keep going without mentioning that they need the help or support of others.

When trying to understand the imposed silence of the Pink and Black Superwoman[3] it is imperative to consider how this manifests in family communication (Harris, Bowden, Bader, Hannon, Hay, & Sterba, 2009). How do family members perceive a loved one who has completed treatment and has entered the realm of survivorship? As survivors how do we express our needs to family when the expectations of faith, hope, and strength influence what we say, when we say it, to whom we say it, and that is if we say it at all? Sharing and talking about one's experiences, thoughts, ideas, and emotions related to a traumatic life event such as breast cancer is considered healthy and produces positive results. The Black Women's Health Imperative asserts in their Breast Cancer Health Survey that "lack of emotional and family support" was one of the main factors associated with breast cancer disparities among Black women. Survivors I spoke with generally had a positive and optimistic view on family life and shared concerns in the following areas:

1. When and what to tell children, school aged,[4] or adult (Davey, Tubbs, Kissil, & Niño, 2011).
2. Death and dying.
3. Sharing the genetic information regarding BRCA1 and BRCA2.
4. Financial Assistance.
5. Stress, depression, and anxiety.
6. Relationships with significant others (Eaker, Wigertz, Lambert, Bergkvist, Ahlgren, & Lambe, 2011).

They confided how these areas concerned them and their families. I share some of their statements here.

> I have two daughters. One was open and wanted to be near me and talked with me all the time. The other, she just stays away.—Judith

> I really didn't want to have that conversation about dying but it needed to happen. You have to plan for certain things.—Candace

> My son was eight years old and he told me I was ugly and wanted to know why I shaved all my hair off like a man. . . . I didn't know what to say. That was five years ago. I still never told him I had cancer.—Medea
>
> My husband couldn't handle it. He just tuned out. But my in-laws picked up where he couldn't. I was emotionally abandoned.—Charlotte-Sopia
>
> We talked about this but it is important to repeat. Families need our income. I don't know too many people that can take sick days. I pray that I make it every day. Hmmph, strong Black woman.—Hypatia

The process of talking during the focus groups and individual interviews about breast cancer and the disharmony it brought not only on our mind, body, and soul, but also the disharmony that it brought to our families was very emotional. Louise-Marie confessed "This is the first time I have sat still long enough to think about these things all at the same time." Our conversations highlighted the fact that we are inextricably attached to our families and are concerned for them and most breast cancer survivors are aware that our families are also seriously concerned about us. We must understand how they see us as we transform into a life of survivorship (Kantsiper, McDonald, Geller, Shockney, Snyder, & Wolff, 2009).

Family Perceptions of Pink and Black Superwoman

In the preparation for writing this book I interviewed 11 individuals: three males and eight females who had a parent, family member(s), or close friends who had been diagnosed with breast cancer. They were eager to share their viewpoints on breast cancer culture, faithtalk, and most of all the idea of being a strong Black woman. I had not initially thought of including this group in my study. However, I realized that although they were not diagnosed with breast cancer or were survivors themselves, they knew those who had been. I found it informative to hear their points of view and the things they thought I should know. I share these areas and provide vignettes of my conversations with these individuals.

"They need to talk more":

> Black women cover their emotions. They cannot show what they really feel out in the open. Otherwise, they have a stereotype against them. That is how society is. At home, sometimes Black women show emotion but not on the outside . . . at home they can break down and cry. Sometimes they have headaches trying to deal with the stress. Sometimes it will lead to other ailment. But when they have to go to work,

someone calls them, or someone shows up at the door, it is totally different. They have to put on a front. —Joseph

[S]ometimes they try to keep things to themselves when the support at home starts to get a little weak. If they talk their supporters will know and then they can get stronger or better support instead of just keeping it covered up. . . . [S]ometimes they are afraid . . . if they say something . . . they won't be believed, it might lead to something else like arguments, or being afraid to talk to each other. —Makayla

It is different. Black women can't show their anger their frustration in today's society. White women can show things. They can be red [show anger, be angry, frustrated] at work or home. —Daniel

Needing more information about breast cancer and the side effects:

We are aware of breast cancer, ribbons and walks and things, but what does that really mean? —David

I worked with my mom and her doctors; they need to do a better job of explaining palliative[5] care, I know what it means, but I don't think she did. —Daniel

Fear of "catching cancer," family heredity, and genetics:

Television gives us an the idea that cancer can be cured if they catch it in time. I don't understand that. . . . My mom caught it in time, she caught hers, and caught it again. . . . I have to say this . . . I was a young teen when my mom was first diagnosed with breast cancer. I really didn't know what to say. I stayed away. I am ashamed and regret that now. But I was afraid she would die. I'm still afraid. She apologized to me for being defective, having bad genes. I have to take better care of myself. —Madison

Stress and mental health, everyone is impacted:

Education is important. How do you talk about the situation? How do you make things better for them? Black families lack education. Even though information is spreading worldwide, families don't know how to cope. Families need more information. They need more education. —Joseph

Death and dying:

There is something wrong with society when sickness is labeled normal—a new normal. Who came up with that? . . . It is not normal for Black women or any woman to be constantly sick. We are dying. —Margaret

Ribbon culture is encouraging . . . when you get a chance to talk about it . . . it just encourages other people to be stronger instead of thinking

> about dying. Recognition throughout the world to solve the problem; knock out cancer. But it all starts with talking first. —London

> Faithtalk—it does not influence my perceptions, it all goes down to the person's personal faith. . . . It just helps them stay positive. Otherwise they start thinking about death and dying or not making any strides to go forward. Everyone has ups and downs and if they say they don't feel well, that does not indicate to me that they are lacking faith. . . . [A]s a home supporter you just want to keep them positive. —Rachel

Although I could not link the comments from the family and friends interviewees to the survivors that were interviewed, I found value in the narratives that these family and friends provided.

Their statements show their concerns and can perhaps provide insight into how survivors might understand how their families and friends are impacted by what is happening to them. It is instructive to point out that the men in the family and friends interviews were the most vocal about their concerns for their wives and mothers when it came to the need for increased communication and information. They were perturbed by the lack of information they thought would be most useful in helping them or their loved one cope with breast cancer. At the end of this chapter you will find an *Interlude* (an extended narrative statement) written by Yvette Toko.[6] Ms. Toko writes as part of her *coping* strategy having had many women in her life diagnosed with breast cancer.

For Black breast cancer survivors it is family that is most important in our day-to-day lives, as they are our main support system. They assist us at doctor's appointments, sit with us through chemotherapy, remind us to eat right, exercise, relax, and to follow doctor's orders when at home (Turner, Adams, Boulton, Harrison, Khan, Rose et al., 2013; Ashing-Giwa, Padilla, Tejero, Kraemer, Wrights, Coscarelli, Clayton, Williams, & Hills, 2004). While our families are supportive, over time they can begin to tire or show signs of fatigue (Oktay, Bellin, Scarvalone, Appling, & Helzlsouer, 2011). The novelty of the diagnosis and treatment has worn off and when they do old expectations return. Artemis, a survivor, explained that "They expect you to do what you used to do before. They don't understand you can't go back" to which Minerva added "But we try, don't we?" The information gap experienced by some family members is evidence that the outcome of breast cancer treatment as not curative but with prolonged, even lifelong, side effects is not adequately understood by those closest to those with breast cancer.

Studies that include family communication dynamics that incorporate Black cultural patterns and focus on breast cancer survivors and their families are extremely scarce. Having this type of information would be beneficial to health care professionals, survivorship clinics, and support groups that can work to assist survivors in articulating what they need from family members and address what support their family member might need. Currently, studies on breast cancer survivors and family communication focus on white, middle-class families and emphasize spousal relationships. Black breast cancer survivors are minimally represented in these studies if included at all. There must be a concerted effort to improve the overall health outcomes for Black women. In order to reduce breast cancer and other health disparities there must be holistic approaches that address not only the socioeconomic issues but also the psychosocial context of the individual survivor, their family, and community.

INTERLUDE
A Friend and Family Member's Story in their Own Words: My Friends Victors Not Victims

Yvette Toko

I was invited by my longtime friend Annette Madlock Gatison to contribute to this wonderful writing project and participate in The Pink and The Black Project©. I met Annette at a church we both attended in 2000 and became close to her during remission of her cancer. It is a pleasure to write about the Black women in my life that battled with cancer. I want to tell their stories because they battled as victors and not victims. And I want to tell their stories as therapy for me to cope with their loss.

Cancer is devastating on the lives of those that have it and the lives of their family and friends. It can destroy overnight or take years and that is the painful part because loved ones never know when it will spread rapidly or if it will go into remission. Maybe one day there will be a cure that is simple as taking a pill for the common headache, until then I remain inspired by telling the stories of the great women who are now with the ancestors. Two were family members and the other two were close friends who were more like family. This piece is in honor of four amazing women by the names of Mae, Marie, Cynthia, and Gloria (their names have been changed to respect their privacy). I tell their stories because they inspired me to live the best life possible in spite of challenges.

Cancer is no stranger to me. I first was introduced to this ravaging disease when my grandmother said she had "bone" cancer. I was a teenager and thought the pronouncement meant immediate death and my cousins and I cried a river of tears. She reassured us that she could live a normal life with it. And she did. Grandma Mae lived ten more years. Her cancer was suspected to be caused by asbestos that was blowing in the air from old paint chips after a renovation of the building facility. We watched my grandmother bravely take chemo treatments and then decide to stop them because she felt they were making her more ill. Her hair grew back but her frail body from the weight loss remained. She was dropped in the hospital and suffered a permanently broken arm because of the bone cancer and it not healing. But that did not stop her from cooking and doing all the things she loved. She stayed strong until her last breath, which she took at home in her bed.

My aunt Marie had colon cancer. She may have had cancer but it didn't have her. She retired at age 55 and enjoyed life. She was an inspiration to me because she continued in so many of her normal activities such as traveling, shopping and sorority meetings even through the cancer until she could not get around anymore. She was one of my favorite aunts because she always encouraged anyone to do their best and go after their dreams. I stand on her shoulders today as I remember all the sound advice she gave me.

My friend Cynthia was like a big sister to me. She was a small frame woman with a big spirit and big heart. She was a nurse by profession and loved helping *others and shared the love of Africa, which I also share. I knew she was getting close to passing away so we cherished the time with prayer points and weekly talks every Tuesday at 7pm. From her hospital bed she thought enough of me on my birthday and sent me a wonderful gift. I later on wrote a speech about that gift as it completely reflected her as a person. She was truly a gem. I miss her.*

My friend Gloria was another amazing woman. She was a mother, aunt, big sister, and friend to me. She was a strong woman in stature and personality. She was always the life of the party. She would joke and say she didn't understand the symptoms of cancer concerning her weight because she continued to keep her weight on even after the chemo treatments. She traveled to the Caribbean and to her childhood place of birth in Nigeria during her illness on evangelical missions and was not deterred at all. I was amazed at her tenacity. I along with countless others celebrated life with Gloria, and it is a pleasure to call her friend.

What I learned from my friends and family members is that even though they were battling an illness that had no cure, they endured and withstood the medical treatments and continued with life. I am forever inspired and have become interested in how cancer affects Black women on a variety of levels. A few points they all had in common were to keep a positive attitude, have a wide support system, continue with a beauty regimen, continue with as much of normal activities as possible, and remain confident.

NOTES

1. Bureau of Labor Statistics, table A-2 Employment Status of the Civilian Population by race, sex, and age.

2. Family is defined here to include *immediate family*—two-parent or single-parent households, with and without children; *extended family*—grandparents, aunts, uncles, cousins, in-laws; *fictive kin*—individuals who are not blood relatives but have close ties to the family and have been adopted into the family and given titles such as "play uncle, play auntie, play cousin, play sister, play brother." This is representative of the support system of those interviewed for The Pink and The Black Project©.

3. Embraced identity that combines the idea of the mythic strong Black woman, faithtalk, and the warrior metaphors of breast cancer culture.

4. Consider for future research. Davey, M. P., Tubbs, C. Y., Kissil, K., & Niño, A. (2011). "We are survivors too': African-American youths" experiences of coping with parental breast cancer. *Psycho-Oncology*, 20(1), 77–87. doi:10.1002/pon.1712.

5. Palliative means alleviating pain and symptoms without eliminating the cause. Encarta Dictionary.

6. This is her real name used with permission.

Conclusion

Body Politics, Coping, and Reframing the Narrative

As I reflect on how I began this work I come back to Audre Lorde's statement: "Caring for myself is not self-indulgence, it is self-preservation and that is an act of political warfare" and the decades of work by women who worked in the women's health movement. Like anything it has its highs and lows, organizations come and go, individuals move in and out, but as problems persist there will be women who work towards and effect change. Change that encompasses the legislation and policies that have influence on women's health from quality of care, access to quality care, and research that moves beyond treatment of breast cancer but to cure breast cancer.

Participants of The Pink and The Black Project© have willingly taken on the fight against breast cancer. They embrace the warrior metaphors of breast cancer culture and the pink ribbon. These survivors recognize and understand that strength is a double-edged sword. They find encouragement and hope in faithtalk and reinforce the ideal of the strong Black woman. For these women, they appear to have found the trifecta of strength as mechanisms for coping. Strategies for coping can take on many forms from the personal to the political. Black women breast cancer survivors can benefit immensely from strategies that include a narrative of self-care, active agency, and personal value (Gaston-Johansson, Haisfield-Wolfe, Reddick, Goldstein, & Lawal, 2013; Sulik & Deane, 2008).

REFRAMING THE NARRATIVE

Messages targeted toward Black women need to include a narrative that includes a call to self-care. Everyone must question the narratives or language that we as a society present to those experiencing disease. This includes the sociocultural narratives of strength found in breast cancer culture and faithtalk that permeate the lives of Black women. These messages need to be reframed to include self-care and employ language that demilitarizes disease (Garrison, 2007; Khalid, 2008).

> If I believe that my body is engaged in contact rather than combat, I might be getting a step closer to the nurturance which [Audre] Lorde promotes. Such a shift might well be crucial in allowing us to bridge

the chasm between an ill body and its perceived war with the mind. (Khalid, 2008)

Shanesha Brooks Tatum (2012) in an article for the *Feminist Wire* states that "It's subversive to take care of ourselves because for centuries Black women worldwide have been taking care of others, from the children of slave masters to those of business executives, and often serving today as primary caregivers for the elderly as home health workers and nursing home employees. Black women's self-care is also subversive because to take care of ourselves means that we disrupt societal and political paradigms that say that Black women are disposable, unvalued. Indeed, people and things that aren't cared for are considered expendable. So when we don't take care of ourselves, we are affirming the social order that says Black women are disposable." Tatum also goes on to discuss the personal agency of moving from simply talking about actually engaging in self-care and doing self-care.

Those women in a position to begin this narrative shift come from a variety of backgrounds that include, but are not limited to, health communication, medical professions, public health, sociologists, theologians, and social workers, but also extend to friends, family, employers, and breast cancer survivors. We all share in spreading the message of strength but we need to also share in changing the paradigm that uses language of self-care.

THEORIES FOR HEALTH COMMUNICATION

There are many strategies and theoretical frames for health communication scholars, public health and medical professionals, researchers, and others interested in reshaping and reframing messages that encourage self-care for not only Black women but also other ethnic communities of color where women are silenced about their health (Madlock Gatison, 2015a). Table C.1 presents theories from the NIH handbook *Theory at a Glance: A Guide for Health Promotion* (2005) that provides basic communication theories that consider intrapersonal, interpersonal, and community models. Additional resources that should be considered when seeking to address communication come from the U.S. Department of Health and Human Services publication *Making Health Communication Programs That Work* (n.d.), which provides additional insights through the use of social science to assist in creating messages that influence health behavior. All of the information in these publications has been vetted and compiled by various researchers, scholars, practitioners, and advocates.

If we are to truly create a quality life that goes beyond just fighting and surviving breast cancer and the myriad sociocultural disparities that burden Black women and their communities we must heed the words of Audre Lorde[1] and the work of Bylley Avery, founder of the Black Wom-

Table C.1. Presents Theories used by the National Institutes of Health

	Theory	Focus	Key Concepts
Intrapersonal/ Individual Level	Health Belief Model	Individuals' perceptions of the threat posed by a health problem, the benefits of avoiding the threat, and factors influencing the decision to act	Perceived susceptibility Perceived severity Perceived benefits Perceived barriers Cues to action Self-efficacy
	Stages of Change Model	Individuals' motivation and readiness to change a problem behavior	Precontemplation Contemplation Decision Action Maintenance
	Theory of Planned Behavior	Individuals' attitudes toward a behavior, perceptions of norms, and beliefs about the ease or difficulty of changing	Behavioral intention Attitude Subjective norm Perceived behavioral control
	Precaution Adoption Process Model	Individuals' journey from lack of awareness to action and maintenance	Unaware of issue Unengaged by issue Deciding about acting Deciding not to act Deciding to act Acting Maintenance
Interpersonal Level	Social Cognitive Theory	Personal factors, environmental factors, and human behavior exert influence on each other	Reciprocal determinism Behavioral capability Expectations Self-efficacy Observational learning Reinforcements
Community Level	Community Organization	Community-driven approaches to assessing and solving health and social problems	Empowerment Community capacity Participation Relevance Issue selection Critical consciousness
	Diffusion of Innovations	How new ideas, products, and practices spread within a society or from one society to another	Relative advantage Compatibility Complexity Trialability Observability

Communication Theory	How different types of communication affect health behavior	Example: *Agenda Setting* Media agenda setting Public agenda setting Policy agenda setting Problem identification and definition Framing

Summary of theories as presented by the NIH *Theory at a Glance: A Guide for Health Promotion Handbook*, Second Edition, 2005.

en's Health Imperative, two among many Black women who call for both a political stand and practical application when it comes to advocating for women's health (Fisher Collins, 2006; Morgen, 2002; Seaman & Eldridge, 2012). Every community has local organizations and individuals that challenge the status quo seeking health equity.

Black women cannot afford to be complacent consumers of pink products and settle for just being aware. We are dying and must remember that most of the stressors that cause illness in the bodies of Black women are not the same for our nonblack counterparts. We have to be politically active when it comes to our health. There are other organizations that have a positive political agenda when it comes to Black women's health. However, we sometimes must look a little harder for the hidden messages of action as they are often co-mingled with so many other messages. The very health disparities that add to the stressors linked to breast cancer in the twenty-first century remain intersected along age, race, class, and gender lines. Mediated messages are often contradictory and from a variety of sources that influence perceptions held of Black women and illness and how these women learn to perceive themselves.

Black women have not only had to stand up and be counted as consumers of pink products, walkers, marchers, and runners, but counted politically when it comes to our health. Our voice and our vote reflect our way of knowing; our lived experiences are an important component in the mission to end breast cancer. We have to be diligent about ensuring that the interests of Black women are being served. Being counted should mean that we are seeing our mortality rates decrease and a reduction in the number of new cases of breast cancer. In other words, it should not just be about the role in the purchasing power of pink products the number.

Womanist Theology and faithtalk place the breast cancer patient at a crossroads. In order to endure the illness, one must do it alone and keep a strong face for the outside world. One must learn to challenge societal notions of how one should "be" as a breast cancer survivor. The culture of silence has left too many voices unheard. These unheard voices as Neumann asserts, have only perpetuated the myths associated not only with breast cancer but also with Black women and health. During the period in which Audre Lorde was diagnosed with breast cancer followed by a mastectomy, the National Cancer Institute reported that:

- In 1975, the incidence rate for female breast cancer in the United States was 105 new cases diagnosed for every 100,000 women in the population; the mortality rate was 31 deaths for every 100,000 women.
- Among women diagnosed with breast cancer during the period from 1975 through 1977, about 75 percent survived their disease at least five years. Among white women, the five-year relative survival rate[2] was 76 percent; among Black women, it was 62 percent.
- Mastectomy was the only accepted surgical option for breast cancer treatment.
- Only one randomized trial of mammography for breast cancer screening had been completed. Several other trials and the joint National Institutes of Health (NIH) and American Cancer Society (ACS) Breast Cancer Detection Demonstration Projects were just beginning.
- Clinical investigation of combination chemotherapy, using multiple drugs with different mechanisms of action, and of hormonal therapy as postsurgical (adjuvant[3]) treatment for breast cancer was in its earliest stages.
- In the mid-1970s, clinical evaluation of the drug tamoxifen, a selective estrogen receptor modulator (SERM), as a hormonal treatment for breast cancer was just beginning.

No gene associated with an increased risk of breast cancer had yet been identified during the 1970s. But, since then there have been advances in the research on breast cancer. Strides have also been made in treating breast cancer as a disease. Yet, it is necessary to consider the steps necessary to approach the health of breast cancer patients holistically. What are we doing to specifically address the needs and concerns of Black women breast cancer patients? Black women must use Black Feminist Thought and the other arguments in womanist theology to take agency over their health, in particular, with regard to breast cancer. When it comes to our health we are taking a stand and putting ourselves first. When one gets on a plane, the flight attendants explain when the oxygen masks should release. They tell us that we put the mask on and then help those around us. We are learning to put our oxygen mask on first as women who are diagnosed with, going through treatment for, and/or have survived breast cancer.

The women interviewed were adamant that the strong Black woman myth got in the way of their seeking enough help or asking for what they needed. Rebecca shared one of the most heart-wrenching experiences with me. She confided, "I hate that nonsense about being a strong Black woman. My cousin died of breast cancer at 26 years old. Her own mother told her: 'STOP all the crying. You are a strong Black woman. We don't do all that...' She was going to have her breast removed... [sobbing... tears... moderator: you do not have to continue.] I can go on just to say that it didn't matter. She died anyway." [Both of us were crying]. This is indicative of the stress that can come from internalizing the myth of needing to be the strong Black woman. She has been wreaking havoc on our lives. It is time to let her go.

As I bring this book to a close, I realize that sometimes as Black women we believe we have to wear the superwoman cape. We believe we must embrace the imagery of the pink and Black warrior woman, the super-shero who not only fights for her own life but also fights for the life of her contemporaries and the generations to follow. But she can be a danger to us. She can prevent us from taking the necessary steps to save ourselves from the power she has over us and society at large. We can, however, take the superwoman and use her strength to suit our own needs. Strong and silent need not be our mantra but strong and action-oriented can.

Throughout this book, I have used pseudonyms for each participant as a way to shield their privacy, while also giving them a sense of power. The pseudonyms were inspired by the edited collection of work *Black Women of Antiquity* compiled by Ivan Van Sertima, and is a compliment to the womanist theology understanding that Black women of antiquity were strong and powerful women. My use of names such as Andromeda, Nzingha, Makeda, and Neferteri pay homage to these women of antiquity but also work to strengthen each of the study participants. Their words speak to this strength:

> We cannot allow ourselves to be forgotten. — Andromeda

> I agree with Andromeda, we have to be remembered and I wear the pink ribbon as a way to let other women know that they are not alone.... Sometimes a woman will see you with that ribbon and there is just a way of knowing that you both went through the same thing without saying a word. — Makeda

There has been a shift in the silence since I first began this project several years ago. Black women are no longer as silent as they once were. Many more Black women breast cancer survivors have found voice and active agency. These women take on the fight and embrace the warrior metaphors and rhetoric of strong Black womanhood and breast cancer culture. As such the words of Audre Lorde, the work of Bylley Avery, and many other women named and unnamed in the social justice and activism of women's health can serve as a starting point for many. They can also serve as a middle point for others when it comes to taking a political stance when advocating for Black women's health. Black women cannot afford to be complacent consumers of pink products and settle for just being aware. Black women are dying. It is important to bear in mind that most of the societal stressors that cause illness in the bodies of Black women are not the same for nonblack women (Kaiser, Cameron, Curry, & Stolley, 2013; McCarthy, Jianing, & Armstrong, 2015; Woods-Giscombé, 2010) as discussed in the introduction of this work. Political action is no longer recommended, but required, when it comes to our health.

There are many organizations from the grassroots to the international level in which one can become involved. A number of them encompass a positive political agenda when it comes to Black women's health. These organizations can be community based and may not have a significant media presence. But they are there and one must be vigilant about finding them.

The twenty-first century is an era where age, race, class, and gender influence media messages. Black women not only have to stand up and be counted as consumers of pink products but must be counted politically. Our voice, our vote, it counts our way of knowing; our lived experiences are an important component to the mission of ending breast cancer. We have to be diligent about ensuring that the interests of Black women are being served.

Health Communication and Breast Cancer among Black Women: Identity, Spirituality, and Strength encourages a change in the strength narrative as it relates to Black women illness and survivorship. In the words of Audre Lord, "I write for those women who do not speak, for those who do not have a voice because they were so terrified, because we are taught to respect fear more than ourselves. We've been taught that silence would save us, but it won't." So we must write a narrative that includes rest as a place of strength.

NOTES

1. Lorde, A. (1980, 1997). *The cancer journals: Special edition.* San Francisco, CA: Aunt Lute Books.

2. This is a way of comparing the survival of people who have a specific disease with those who don't, over a certain period of time. This is usually five years from the date of diagnosis or the start of treatment for those with the disease. It is calculated by dividing the percentage of patients with the disease who are still alive at the end of the period of time by the percentage of people in the general population of the same sex and age who are alive at the end of the same time period. The relative survival rate shows whether the disease shortens life.

3. Additional cancer treatment given after the primary treatment to lower the risk that the cancer will come back. Adjuvant therapy may include chemotherapy, radiation therapy, hormone therapy, targeted therapy, or biological therapy.

Appendix

The Pink and The Black Project©: Breast Cancer Culture and Black Women

RESEARCH QUESTIONS AND DISCUSSION QUESTIONS

Research Questions

RQ1	How does faithtalk, breast cancer culture, and the myth of the strong Black woman influence the lives of Black women living with breast cancer?
RQ2	Does breast cancer culture influence the expectations others have of breast cancer survivors?
RQ3	What role does breast cancer culture have on self-expectations?
RQ4	What role does faithtalk have on one's ability to openly discuss health concerns?
RQ5	What role does faithtalk have on self-expectations?
RQ6	Does faithtalk influence the expectations others have of breast cancer survivors?
RQ7	Does the mythology of the strong Black women influence self-expectations?
RQ8	Does the mythology of the strong Black women influence the expectations others have of breast cancer survivors?

Definitions

Breast Cancer Culture/Pink Ribbon Culture for the purposes of this study refers to the commercialization of breast cancer (pink ribbon brand everywhere) and the warrior metaphors (fighter, survivor, she-ro) used to describe those being treated for or living with breast cancer.

Extended discussion of Breast Cancer Culture will utilize the following excerpts from *Pink Ribbon Blues* by Gayle Sulik, 2010:

Breast cancer culture, or pink ribbon culture, is the set of activities, attitudes, and values that surround and shape breast cancer in public. The dominant values are selflessness, cheerfulness, unity, and optimism. The she-ro uses the emotional trauma of being diagnosed with breast cancer and the suffering of extended treatment to transform herself into a stronger, happier and more sensitive person who is grateful for the opportunity to become a better person. In particular, she sees breast cancer as an opportunity to give herself permission for necessary personal growth—permission that she felt unable to give herself before, because of the restraints of her gender role (Sulik, 2010, p. 236). Breast cancer thereby becomes a rite of passage rather than a disease. (Ehrenreich, 2001; Sulik, 2010, p. 3)

The "she-ro" of breast cancer is the woman who publicly maintains a pleasant personal appearance and optimism while aggressively fighting breast cancer through compliance with mainstream medical advice. The ideal survivor is always diagnosed early because of her unswerving obedience to the aggressive screening mammography standards put forward by American (but not European or Asian) breast cancer organizations. She is educated as a medical consumer and firmly believes that modern science can cure breast cancer. She is always brave, always victorious, and never dies. (Sulik, 2010, pp. 158, 243)

Faithtalk for the purposes of this study is any reference to the belief in a higher power for healing and strength or the Christian tradition or belief of having faith in God or Jesus as a healing power based on biblical passages[1] such as:

- "While the sun was setting, all those who had any who were sick with various diseases brought them to Him; and laying His hands on each one of them, He was healing them." Luke 4:40
- "And He was not able to do even one work of power there, except that He laid His hands on a few sickly people [and] cured them." Mark 6:5
- "Let us all come forward and draw near with true (honest and sincere) hearts in unqualified assurance and absolute conviction engendered by faith by that leaning of the entire human personality on God in absolute trust and confidence in His power, wisdom, and goodness), having our hearts sprinkled and purified from a guilty (evil) conscience and our bodies cleansed with pure water." Hebrews 10:22

Or Christian slogans such as: "Too blessed to be stressed" or "God will never give you more than you can bear."

Strong Black Woman (SBW) archetype is a salient cultural symbol that may be relevant to Black women's breast cancer recovery and long-term survivorship. Historically, the symbol originated as a rationalization or justification for slavery, because Black women were touted as physically and psychologically stronger and more resilient than white women (Harris-Lacewell, 2001). This mythical image was appropriated within Black communities in response to other derogatory images of Black womanhood. The SBW image presents a picture to the world that Black women are inherently strong and resilient, self-reliant, have the ability to confront challenges, and provide encouragement to self and others during adversity. This same image fosters a belief that Black women can withstand all challenges and signs of vulnerability or weakness are tantamount to failing oneself, family, and community. The SBW ideology does not allow space for Black women to express their feelings related to traumatic experiences and has become a barometer of how Black women's behavior should be evaluated in adverse situations (Harrington, Crowther, & Shipherd 2010).

OPEN-ENDED DISCUSSION QUESTIONS FOR INDIVIDUAL INTERVIEWS, FOCUS GROUP, AND ONLINE DISCUSSION FORUM

Breast Cancer Culture Questions

1. What impact does breast cancer culture have on your ability to openly discuss your health concerns with your significant other?
2. If you have children, how old are they? (under ten, pre-teen, teens, young adult, adult)
3. What impact does breast cancer culture have on your ability to openly discuss your health concerns with your children?
4. What impact does breast cancer culture have on your ability to openly discuss your health concerns with your extended family?
5. What impact does breast cancer culture have on your ability to openly discuss your health concerns with a close friend?
6. What impact does breast cancer culture have on your ability to openly discuss your health concerns with your employer?
7. What impact does breast cancer culture have on your ability to openly discuss your health concerns with a coworker?
8. What other areas of breast cancer culture influence your ability to openly discuss your health issues?

Faithtalk Questions

1. What impact does faithtalk have on your ability to openly discuss your health concerns with your significant other?
2. If you have children, how old are they?
3. What impact does faithtalk have on your ability to openly discuss your health concerns with your children?

4. What impact does faithtalk have on your ability to openly discuss your health concerns with your extended family?
5. What impact does faithtalk have on your ability to openly discuss your health concerns with a close friend?
6. What impact does faithtalk have on your ability to openly discuss your health concerns with your employer?
7. What impact does faithtalk have on your ability to openly discuss your health concerns with a coworker?
8. What other areas of spirituality/religion influence your ability to openly discuss your health issues?
9. If you are not Christian, does spirituality or religion influence your communication with family, friends, coworkers, or employers?

Strong Black Woman Questions

1. What impact does SBW mythology have on your ability to openly discuss your health concerns with your significant other?
2. If you have children, how old are they?
3. What impact does SBW mythology have on your ability to openly discuss your health concerns with your children?
4. What impact does SBW mythology have on your ability to openly discuss your health concerns with your extended family?
5. What impact does SBW mythology have on your ability to openly discuss your health concerns with a close friend?
6. What impact does SBW mythology have on your ability to openly discuss your health concerns with your employer?
7. What impact does SBW mythology have on your ability to openly discuss your health concerns with a coworker?
8. What other areas of SBW mythology influence your ability to openly discuss your health issues?

Names of women from The Journal of African Civilizations book *Black Women in Antiquity* (Van Sertima, 1995) *were* used as pseudonyms for Black female breast cancer survivors.

1. Andromeda
2. Artemis
3. Candace
4. Circe
5. Diana
6. Hatshepsut
7. Hypatia
8. Judith
9. Louise-Marie
10. Makeda
11. Mary

12. Medea
13. Minerva
14. Nefertere
15. Nzingha
16. Tiye
17. Charlotte-Sophia

This is a generic description of family and friends who were part of a preliminary study to assess the perceptions that friends and family have of Black female breast cancer survivors. All names are pseudonyms.

1. RACHEL: Elder-religious leader who had a daughter diagnosed with breast cancer
2. MARGARET: Pastor—who had friends and relatives diagnosed with breast cancer
3. DAVID: Male in his 20s—mother in her late 30s at the time of diagnosis
4. DANIEL: Male in his 40s whose mother in her 60s was a cancer patient
5. JOSEPH: Male whose wife was diagnosed twice once in her thirties and again in her forties.
6. REBECCA: Female whose cousin died of breast cancer in her twenties.
7. LONDON: Female with several friends diagnosed with breast cancer of varying ages.
8. PARIS: Female with several friends diagnosed with breast cancer of varying ages
9. MADISON: Female whose mother was diagnosed with breast cancer twice
10. MACKENZIE: mother whose daughter had breast cancer twice
11. MAKAYLA: Sister of a breast cancer survivor

NOTE

1. Bible passages from http://www.biblegateway.com/New American Standard Bible or Amplified translations.

Bibliography

Abel, E., & Subramanian, S. (2008). *After the cure: The untold stories of breast cancer survivors*. New York: NYU Press.

American Cancer Society (2016). *Cancer facts and figures for African Americans 2013–2014*. Retrieved from http://www.cancer.org/acs/groups/content/@epidemiologysurveilance/documents/document/acspc-036921.pdf.

Anderson, C. A., & Whitehouse, D. G. (2003). *New Thought: A Practical American Spirituality* (Revised). Bloomington, IN: AuthorHouse.

Anderson, L. (2006). Analytic Autoethnography. *Journal Of Contemporary Ethnography*, 35(4), 373–395.

Ashing-Giwa, K. T., Padilla, G., Tejero, J., Kraemer, J., Wrights, K., Coscarelli, A., Clayton, S., Williams, I., & Hill, D. (2004). Understanding the breast cancer experience of women: A qualitative study of African American, Asian American, Latina and Caucasian cancer survivors. *Psycho-Oncology*, 13: 408–428. doi:10.1002/pon.750.

Baird, K. L., Davis, D., & Christensen, K. (2009). *Beyond Reproduction: Women's Health, Activisim, and Public Policy*. Madison, NJ: Fairleigh Dickinson University Press.

Banning, M. M. (2011). Employment and breast cancer: a meta-ethnography. *European Journal Of Cancer Care*, 20(6), 708–719. doi:10.1111/j.1365-2354.2011.01291.x.

Beauboeuf-Lafontant, T. (2009). *Behind the Mask of the Strong Black Women: Voice and the Embodiment of a Costly Performance*. Philadelphia, PA: Temple University Press.

Bibb, S. (2001). The relationship between access and stage at diagnosis of breast cancer in African American and Caucasian women. *Oncology Nursing Forum*, 28(4), 711–719.

Black, A. R., & Woods-Giscombé, C. (2012). Applying the stress and strength hypothesis to black women's breast cancer screening delays. *Stress Health*, December, 28(5): 389–396.

Black Breast Cancer Alliance. (2011). *Facts to Know*. Retrieved from http://aabcainc.org/facts-to-know/.

Black Women's Health. (2013). *Moving Beyond Pink to End Breast Cancer Disparities*. Retrieved from http://www.Blackwomenshealth.org/news/2013/04/06/breast-cancer/breast-cancer-death-rates-higher-for-black-women-study/.

Black Women's Health Imperative. (2014). Things you should know about breast cancer. Retrieved from http://www.bwhi.org/issues/breast-cancer/breast-cancer/.

Blinder, V. S., Murphy, M. M., Vahdat, L. T., Gold, H. T., de Melo-Martin, I., Hayes, M. K., Scheff, R. J., et al. (2012). Employment after a breast cancer diagnosis: A qualitative study on the ethnically diverse urban women. *Journal of Community Health*, 37: 763–772. doi 10.1007/s10900-11-9509-9.

Bourjolly, J. N., & Hirschman, K. B. (2001). Similarities in coping strategies but differences in sources of social support among Black and white women coping with breast cancer. *Journal of Psychosocial Oncology*, 19(2), 17–38.

Bradley, C. J., Oberst, K., & Schenk, M. (2006). Absenteeism from work: the experience of employed breast and prostate cancer patients in the months following diagnosis. *Psycho-Oncology*, 15(8), 739–747. doi:10.1002/pon.1016.

Breast Cancer Deadline. (2014). Facts and Statistics about Breast Cancer in the United States and Progress Report. Retrieved from http://www.breastcancerdeadline2020.org/breast-cancer-information/.

Breast Cancer.Org. (2009, 2016). U.S. Breast Cancer Statistics. http://www.breastcancer.org/symptoms/understand_bc/statistics.

Breast Cancer Survivors Network. (2014). *Breast Cancer Health Survey*. Retreived from http://sistersbreastcancersurvivorsnetwork.org/downloads/Breast%20Cancer%20Leadership%20Development%20Initiative%20Survey%20Powerpoint-%20percentages.pdf.

Brooks Tatum, S. (2012). Subversive self-care: Centering Black women's wellness. The Feminist Wire. Retrieved from http://www.thefeministwire.com/2012/11/subversive-self-care-centering-black-womens-wellness/.

Bureau of Labor Statistics. (2014). Table A-2 Employment Status of the Civilian Population by race, sex, and age. Retrieved from http://www.bls.gov/news.release/empsit.t02.htm.

Buzard, J. (2003). On Auto-ethnographic authority. *The Yale Journal of Criticism* 16(1): 61–91.

Campesino, M., Saenz, D. S., Choi, M., & Krouse, R. S. (2012). Perceived discrimination and ethnic identity among breast cancer survivors. *Oncology Nursing Forum*, 39(2), E91–E100.

Campo, S. & Mastin, T. (2007). Placing the burden on the individual: Overweight and obesity in African American and mainstream women's magazines. *Health Communication*, 22(3): 229–240.

Cannon, K. G. (1988). *Black womanist ethics*. Atlanta, GA: Scholars Press.

———. (1995). *Katie's Cannon: Womanism and the soul of the Black community*. New York: Continuum.

Carey, M. A., & Asbury, J. (2012). Focus group research. Walnut Creek, CA: Left Coast Press.

Carter, T. (2003). Body Count: Autobiographies by Women Living with Breast Cancer. *Journal Of Popular Culture*, 36(4), 653.

Center for Family Policy and Practice. (2013). Employment Statistics. Retrieved from http://www.cfpp.org/.

Centers for Disease Control. (2009). *Power of prevention: Chronic disease the public health challenge of the 21st century*. Retrieved from http://www.cdc.gov/chronicdisease/pdf/2009-Power-of-Prevention.pdf.

Centers for Disease Control and Prevention. (2012, November). *Vital Signs*. Retrieved from http://www.cdc.gov/vitalsigns/breastcancer/.

———. (2015, March). *Health disparities in cancer*. Retrieved from http://www.cdc.gov/cancer/dcpc/resources/features/CancerHealthDisparities/.

Chisholm, J. F. (1996). Mental health issues in African-American women. In J. A. Sechzer, S. M. Pfafflin, F. L. Denmark, A. Griffin, & S. J. Blumenthal (Eds.), *Women and mental health: Annals of the New York Academy of Sciences* (Vol. 789, pp. 161–179). New York: New York Academy of Sciences.

Circle of Promise. (2011). Breast Cancer Statistics for Black women. Retrieved from http://www.circleofpromise.org/africanamericanstatistics.html.

Clayton, J. A., Brooks, C. E., & Kornstein, S. G. (2014). Toward more individualized medicine: Introducing the Women of Color Health Data Book, Fourth Edition. In W. A. Leigh & Ying Li (Eds.), *Women of Color Health Data Book*. National Institutes of Health Office of Research on Women's Health, NIH Publication No. 14–4247.

Coggin, C., & Shaw-Perry, M. (2006). Breast Cancer Survivorship: Expressed needs of Black Women. *Journal of Psychococial Oncology*. Volume 24 (4).

Cone, J. H. (1969, 1989, 1997). *Black theology and black power*. Maryknoll, NY: Orbis Books.

———. (1970, 1986, 1990). *A Black theology of liberation*. Maryknoll, NY: Orbis Books.

———. (1975, 1997). *God of the oppressed*. Maryknoll, NY: Orbis Books.

Conway-Phillips, R., & Janusek, L. (2014). Influence of Sense of Coherence, Spirituality, Social Support and Health Perception on Breast Cancer Screening Motivation and Behaviors in African American Women. *ABNF Journal*, 25(3), 72–79.

Couser, G. T. (1997). *Recovering bodies: Illness, disability, and life writing*. Madison, WI: University of Wisconsin Press.

Davey, M. P., Tubbs, C. Y., Kissil, K., & Niño, A. (2011). "We are survivors too": African-American youths' experiences of coping with parental breast cancer. *Psycho-Oncology, 20*(1), 77–87. doi:10.1002/pon.1712.

Davis, C. S., Gallardo, H. P., & Lachlan, K. A. (2010). *Straight talk about communication research methods*. Dubuque, IA: Kendall Hunt Publishing.

Davis, S. (2015). The "Strong Black Woman Collective": A developing theoretical framework for understanding collective communication practices of Black women. In *Women's Studies in Communication, 38*: 20–35.

Davis-Carroll, H. (2011). An Ethic of Resistance: Choosing Life in Health Messages for African American Women. *Journal Of Religion & Health, 50*(2), 219–231. doi:10.1007/s10943-010-9434-8.

Eaker, S., Wigertz, A., Lambert, P. C., Bergkvist, L., Ahlgren, J., & Lambe, M. (2011). Breast Cancer, Sickness Absence, Income and Marital Status. A Study on Life Situation 1 Year Prior Diagnosis Compared to 3 and 5 Years after Diagnosis. *Plos ONE, 6*(3), 1–9.

Edge, J. (2014a). Breast cancer. *South African Medical Journal, 104*(5): 376.

———. (2014b). Pink ribbons for breast cancer awareness – a perspective. *South African Medical Journal, 104*(5): 321. doi: 10.7196/samj.8300.

Edge, J., Buccimazza, I., Cubasch, H., & Panieri, E. (2014). The challenges of managing breast cancer in the developing world – a perspective from Sub-Saharan Africa. 104(5): 377–379.

Ell, K., Xie, B., Wells, A., Nedjat-Haiem, F., Lee, P.-J., and Vourlekis, B. (2008). Economic stress among low-income women with cancer. *Cancer*, 112: 616–625. doi: 10.1002/cncr.23203.

Fernandez, L. (1998). Retrieved from http://thinkbeforeyoupink.org/?page_id=26.

Feuerstein, M. (2009). *Work and cancer survivors*. New York: Springer.

Fisher Collins, C. (2006). *African American women's health and social issues*. Westport, CT: Praeger.

———. (2013). *African American women's life issues today: Vital health and social matters*. Westport, CT: Praeger.

Friedman, L., Barber, C., Chang, J., Tham, Y., Kalidas, M., Rimawi, M., . . . Elledge, R. (2010). Self-blame, self-forgiveness, and spirituality in breast cancer survivors in a public sector setting. *Journal Of Cancer Education, 25*(3), 343–348 6p. doi:10.1007/s13187-010-0048-3.

Gallia, K., & Pines, E. (2009). Narrative identity and spirituality of African American churchwomen surviving breast cancer survivors. *Journal Of Cultural Diversity, 16*(2), 50–55.

Garrison, K. (2007). The Persona Is Rhetorical: War, Protest, and Peace in Breast Cancer Narratives. *Disability Studies Quarterly, 27*(4).

Gaston-Johansson, F., Haisfield-Wolfe, M. E., Reddick, B., Goldstein, N., & Lawal, T. A. (2013). The Relationships Among Coping Strategies, Religious Coping, and Spirituality in African American Women With Breast Cancer Receiving Chemotherapy. *Oncology Nursing Forum, 40*(2), 120–131 12p. doi:10.1188/13.ONF.120-131.

Gibson, L. M., & Hendricks, C. S. (2006). Integrative review of Spirituality in Black Breast Cancer Survivors. *The ABNF Journal, Spring*, 67–72.

Gillespie, M. A. (1984). The myth of the strong Black woman. In Jaggar, A. M. & Rothenberg, P. S. (Eds.), *Feminist Frameworks: Alternative theoretical accounts of the relations between women and men*, pp. 32–35. New York: McGraw-Hill.

Grant, J. (1989). *White women's Christ and Black women's Jesus: Feminist Christology and womanist response*. Atlanta, GA: Scholars Press.

Gregg, G. (2011). I'm A Jesus Girl: Coping Stories of Black American Women Diagnosed with Breast Cancer. *Journal Of Religion & Health, 50*(4), 1040–1053. doi:10.1007/s10943-010-9395-y.

Grimes, T. and Hou, S. (2013). "'A Breast Ain't Nothing but a Sandwich': Narratives of Ella, a Black Social Worker Breast Cancer Survivor." *Social Work in Public Health, 28*, 44–53.

Gullatte, M., Brawley, O., Kinney, A., Powe, B., & Mooney, K. (2010). Religiosity, Spirituality, and Cancer Fatalism Beliefs on Delay in Breast Cancer Diagnosis in African American Women. *Journal Of Religion & Health, 49*(1), 62–72. doi:10.1007/s10943-008-9232-8.

Happe, K. E. (2006). The rhetoric of race in breast cancer research. *Patterns Of Prejudice, 40*(4/5), 461–480. doi:10.1080/00313220601020171.

———. (2013). The Body of Race: Toward a Rhetorical Understanding of Racial Ideology. *Quarterly Journal Of Speech, 99*(2), 131–155. doi:10.1080/00335630.2013.775700.

Harrington, E. F., Crowther, J. H., & Shipherd, J. C. (2010). Trauma, binge eating, and the "Strong Black Woman." *Journal of Consulting & Clinical Psychology, 78(4)*, 469–479.

Harris, D., & Gibson, L. (2011). Breast cancer fear, fatalism and spirituality in African American women. *University of South Carolina Upstate Undergrad Research Journal.* Fall, pp. 40–42.

Harris, J., Bowen, D. J., Bader, H., Hannon, P., Hay, J., & Sterba, K. R. (2009). Family communication during the cancer experience. *Journal of Health Communication, 14*: 76-84. doi: 10.1080/10810730902806844.

Harris-Lacewell, M. (2001). No place to rest: Black political attitudes and the myth of Black women's strength. *Women and Politics, 23*, 1–33.

Henderson, P. D., Gore, S. V., Davies, B. L., & Condon, E. H. (2003). Black women coping with breast cancer: a qualitative analysis. *Oncology Nursing Forum, 30*(4), 641–647.

Herndl, D. P. (2006). Our Breasts, Our Selves: Identity, Community, and Ethics in Cancer Autobiographies. *Signs: Journal Of Women In Culture & Society, 32*(1), 221–245.

Hill, S. A. (2009). Cultural images and the health of Black women. *Gender and Society, 23*(6), 733–746.

Hill-Collins, P. (1995). A Black women's standpoint: The foundation of feminist thought. In B. Guy-Sheftall (Ed.), *Words of fire: An anthology of Black Feminist Thought.* New York: The New Press.

———. (2000). *Black feminist thought: Knowledge, consciousness, and the politics of empowerment.* New York: Routledge.

Hoffman, R. M. (2006). Gender Self-Definition and Gender Self-Acceptance in Women: Intersections with Feminist, Womanist, and Ethnic Identities. *Journal Of Counseling & Development, 84*(3), 358–372.

Holzner, B., Kemmler, G., Kopp, M., Moschen, R., Schweigkofler, H., & Dunser, M., et al. (2001). Quality of life in breast cancer patients: not enough attention for long-term survivors? *Psychosomatics, 42*, 117–123.

hooks, b. (1993). *Sisters of the yam: Black women and self-recovery.* Boston: South End Press.

———. (2000). *Where we stand: Class matters.* New York: Routledge.

Hooks-Anderson, D., & Anderson, R. (2015). The culture of medicine: A critical autoethnography of my encounter with the healthcare system. In A. Madlock Gatison (Ed.), *Communicating women's health: Social and cultural norms that influence health decisions.* New York: Routledge.

Hoving, J. L., Broekhuizen, M. A., & Frings-Dresen, M. W. (2009). Return to work of breast cancer survivors: a systematic review of intervention studies. *BMC Cancer,* 91-10. doi:10.1186/1471-2407-9-117.

Hurston, Z. N. (1969). *Their eyes were watching God.* Greenwich, CT: Fawcett Publications.

Johansen, V. F., Andrews, T. M., Haukanes, H., & Lilleaas, U. (2013). Symbols and Meanings in Breast Cancer Awareness Campaigns. *NORA: Nordic Journal Of Women's Studies, 21*(2), 140–155. doi:10.1080/08038740.2013.797024.

Jones, C., & Shorter-Gooden, K. (2003). *Shifting: The double lives of Black women in America.* New York: HarperCollins.

Kaiser, K., Cameron, K., Curry, G., & Stolley, M. (2013). Black Women's Awareness of Breast Cancer Disparity and Perceptions of the Causes of Disparity. *Journal Of Community Health, 38*(4), 766–772 7p. doi:10.1007/s10900-013-9677-x.

Kantsiper, M., McDonald, E., Geller, G., Shockney, L., Snyder, C., & Wolff, A. (2009). Transitioning to breast cancer survivorship: perspectives of patients, cancer specialists, and primary care providers. *Journal Of General Internal Medicine, 24* Suppl 2S459-S466. doi:10.1007/s11606-009-1000-2.

Khalid, R. J. (2008). Demilitarizing disease: ambivalent warfare and Audre Lorde's cancer journals. *African American Review,* 42.3–4 (Fall/Winter 2008): 697–714.

King, S. (2006). *Pink ribbons, Inc.: Breast cancer and the politics of philanthropy.* Minneapolis, MN: University of Minnesota Press.

Koffman, J., Morgan, M., Edmonds, P., Speck, P., & Higginson, I. J. (2008). "I know he controls cancer": The meanings of religion among Black Caribbean and White British patients with advanced cancer. *Social Science & Medicine, 67,* 780–789.

Komen.org. (2014). *Susan G. Komen Pink Ribbon Story.* Retrieved from http://ww5.komen.org/uploadedFiles/Content_Binaries/The_Pink_Ribbon_Story.pdf.

———. (2014). Susan G. Komen for the Cure. *Understanding Breast Cancer.* Retrieved from http://ww5.komen.org/BreastCancer/Statistics.html.

Kutz, M. R. (2004). Observations on prayer as a viable treatment intervention: A brief review for healthcare providers. *The Internet Journal of Allied Health Sciences and Practice, 2*(1).

Leigh, W. A. & Li, Y. (Eds.) (2014). *Women of Color Health Data Book.* National Institutes of Health Office of Research on Women's Health, NIH Publication No. 14-4247.

Lorde, A. (1980, 1997). *The cancer journals: Special edition.* San Francisco, CA: Aunt Lute Books.

———. (1988). *A burst of light essays by Audre Lorde.* Ithica, NY: Firebrand Books.

Lynn, B., Yoo, G., & Levine, E. (2014). "Trust in the Lord": Religious and Spiritual Practices of African American Breast Cancer Survivors. *Journal Of Religion & Health, 53*(6), 1706–1716 11p. doi:10.1007/s10943-013-9750-x.

Madlock Gatison, A. D. (2011a). Playing the game communicative practices for negotiating politics and preparing for tenure. In M. Niles & N. Gordon (Eds.), *Still Searching for Our Mother's Garden.* Lanham, MD: University Press of America. (pp. 109–120).

———. (2011b). Skin Bleaching. In M.Z. Strange and C. K. Oyster (Eds.), *Multimedia Encyclopedia of Women in Today's World.* Los Angeles, CA: Sage Publications.

———. (2015a). Cameroon. In C. A. Colditz & J. G. Golson (Eds.), *Encyclopedia of Cancer and Society, 2nd Edition.* Los Angeles, CA: Sage Publications.

———. (Ed.) (2015b). *Communicating women's health: Social and cultural norms that influence health decisions.* New York: Routledge.

———. (2015c). South Africa. In C. A. Colditz & J. G. Golson (Eds.), *Encyclopedia of Cancer and Society, 2nd Edition.* Los Angeles, CA: Sage Publications.

———. (2015d). The pink and black experience: Lies that make us suffer in silence and cost us our lives. *Women's Studies in Communication,* 38:2, 135–140, doi:10.1080/07491409.2015.1034628.

———. (2015e). Zambia. In C. A. Colditz & J. G. Golson (Eds.), *Encyclopedia of Cancer and Society, 2nd Edition.* Los Angeles, CA: Sage Publications.

———. (2015f). Zimbabwe. In C. A. Colditz & J. G. Golson (Eds.), *Encyclopedia of Cancer and Society, 2nd Edition.* Los Angeles, CA: Sage Publications.

———. (2016). Body Politics-Strategies for Inclusiveness: A Case Study of the National Breast Cancer Coalition. In E. Gilchrist & S. Long (Eds.), *Contexts of the Dark Side of Communication.* Lanham, MD: Peter Lang Publishing.

———. (In Press). African American communication and culture. In M. Allen (Ed.), *The Sage Encyclopedia of Research Methods.* Thousand Oaks, CA: Sage.

Mandal, A. (2014). What is life expectancy? Retrieved from http://www.news-medical.net/health/What-is-Life-Expectancy.aspx.

Mastin, T., Campo, S., & Askelson, N. M. (2012). African American women and weight loss: disregarding environmental challenges. *Journal of Transcultural Nursing.* 23(1): 38–45. doi: 10.1177/1043659611414140.

McCarthy, A. M., Jianing, Y., & Armstrong, K. (2015). Increasing Disparities in Breast Cancer Mortality From 1979 to 2010 for US Black Women Aged 20 to 49 Years. *American Journal Of Public Health, 105*S446-S448.

McLaughlin, B., Yoo, W., D'Angelo, J., Tsang, S., Shaw, B., Shah, D., Baker T., & Gustafson, D. (2013). It is out of my hands: how deferring control to God can decrease quality of life for breast cancer patients. *Psycho-Oncology, 22*(12), 2747–2754. doi:10.1002/pon.3356.

Mellon, S., Gold, R., Janisse, J., Cichon, M., Tainsky, M. A., Simon, M. S., & Korczak, J. (2008). Risk perception and cancer worries in families at increased risk of familial breast/ovarian cancer. *Psycho-Oncology, 17*(8), 756–766. doi:10.1002/pon.1370.

Metastatic Breast Cancer Network. (2014). *Thirteen facts about metastatic breast cancer everyone should know.* http://www.mbcn.org. Retreived from http://mbcn.org/images/uploads/13_Facts_about_Metastatic_Breast_Cancer2014.pdf.

Mitchell, A., & Herring, K. (1998). *What the blues is all about: Black women overcoming stress and depression.* New York: Berkley.

Moadel, A., Morgan, C., Fatone, A., Grennan, J., Carter, J., Laruffa, G., et al. (1999). Seeking meaning and hope: self-reported spiritual and existential needs among ethnically-diverse cancer patient population. *Psycho-Oncology, 8*(5), 378–385.

Moore, S. E. (2008, 2010). *Ribbon culture charity, compassion, and public awareness.* New York: Palgrave MacMillian.

Morgan, J. (1999). *When chickenheads come home to roost: My life as a hip-hop feminist.* New York: Simon & Schuster.

Morgen, S. (2002). *Into our own hands: The women's health movement in the United States, 1969–1990.* New Brunswick, NJ: Rutgers University Press.

Mujahid, M., Janz, N., Hawley, S., Griggs, J., Hamilton, A., & Katz, S. (2010). The impact of sociodemographic, treatment, and work support on missed work after breast cancer diagnosis. *Breast Cancer Research And Treatment, 119*(1), 213–220. doi:10.1007/s10549-009-0389-y.

Mukherjee, S. (2010). *The emperor of all maladies: A history of cancer.* New York: Scribner Simon and Schuster.

Mullins, N. (2015). "Insidious Influence of Gender Socialization on Females' Physical Activity: Rethink Pink." *The Physical Educator, 72,* 20–43.

National Cancer Institute at the National Institutes of Health. (2009a). *Managing chemotherapy side effects – Memory changes.* NIH Publication No. 09-6510.

———. (2009b). *Managing chemotherapy side effects – Nerve Changes.* NIH Publication No. 09-6506.

———. (2011). *Cancer Health Disparities Fact Sheet.* Retrieved from http://www.cancer.gov/cancertopics/factsheet/disparities/cancer-health-disparities.

Noelle-Neumann, E. (1984). *The Spiral of Silence: Public Opinion—Our Social Skin.* Chicago: Chicago University Press.

———. (1991). The Theory of Public Opinion: The Concept of the Spiral of Silence. In J. A. Anderson Newbury, *Communication Yearbook* 14 ed. Park, CA: Sage, pp. 256–287.

Northhouse, L. L., Caffey, M., Deichelbohrer, L., Schmidt, L., Guziatek-Trojniak, L., West, S., et al. (1999). The quality of life of Black women with breast cancer. *Research in Nursing & Health.22,* 449–460.

Oktay, J. S., Bellin, M. H., Scarvalone, S., Appling, S., & Helzlsouer, K. J. (2011). Managing the impact of posttreatment fatigue on the family: Breast cancer survivors share their experiences. *Families, Systems, & Health, 29*(2), 127–137. doi:10.1037/a0023947.

Olson, K. (2011). *Essentials of qualitative interviewing.* Walnut Creek, CA: Left Coast Press.

Park, C. L., Zlateva, L., & Blank, T. O. (2009). Self-Identity after cancer: survivor, victim, patient, and person with cancer. *Journal of General Medicine*, 24(2), 430–435. doi:10.1007/s11606-009-0993-x.

Phillips, J. M., Cohen, M. Z., & Moses, G. (1999). Breast cancer screening and African American women: Fear, fatalism, and silence. *Oncology of Nursing Forum*. 26(3): 561–571.

Pitts, V. (2004). Illness and internet empowerment: writing and reading breast cancer in cyberspace. *Health: An Interdisciplinary Journal for the Social Study of Health, Illness and Medicine*. 8(1): 33–59.

Potts, R. G. (1996). Spirituality and the experience of cancer in an African American community: implications for psychosocial oncology. *Journal of Psychosocial Oncology*, 14(1), 1–19.

Price, B. R. (1998). *Through the fire and through the water: My triumph over cancer*. Dr. Fredrick K. C. Price Ministries Publisher.

Roelen, C. M., Koopmans, P. C., De Graaf, J. H., Balak, F., & Groothoff, J. W. (2009). Sickness absence and return to work rates in women with breast cancer. *International Archives Of Occupational & Environmental Health*, 82(4), 543–546. doi:10.1007/s00420-008-0359-4.

Roelen, C., Koopmans, P., van Rhenen, W., Groothoff, J., van der Klink, J., & Bültmann, U. (2011). Trends in return to work of breast cancer survivors. *Breast Cancer Research And Treatment*, 128(1), 237–242. doi:10.1007/s10549-010-1330-0.

Romero, R. E. (2000). The icon of the strong Black woman: The paradox of strength. In L. C. Jackson & B. Greene (Eds.), *Psychotherapy with Black women: Innovations in psychodynamic perspective and practice* (pp. 225–238). New York: Guilford Press.

Rubin, R. B., Rubin, A. M., & Piele, L. J. (1996). *Communication research: Strategies and sources* (4th ed.). Belmont, CA: Wadsworth.

Satariano, W., & DeLorenze, G. (1996). The likelihood of returning to work after breast cancer. *Public Health Reports*, 111(3), 236–243.

Saunders, C. M., & Jassal, S. (2009). *Breast cancer facts all the information you need straight from the experts*. New York: Oxford University Press.

Schiavo, R. (2007). *Health communication from theory to practice*. San Francisco, CA: Jossey-Bass.

Schneider, M. (2007). Broadening our perspective on spirituality and coping among women with breast cancer and their families: implications for practice. *Indian Journal Of Palliative Care*, 13(2), 25–31 7p.

Seale, C., Charteris-Black, J., MacFarlane, A., & McPherson, A. (2010). Interviews and internet forums: A comparison of two sources of qualitative data. *Qualitative Health Research*, 20(5): 595–606.

Seaman, B., & Eldridge, L. (2012). *Voices of the women's health movement, volume one and volume two*. New York: Seven Stories Press.

Sisters Network, Inc. (2011). http://www.sistersnetworkinc.org/.

Skloot, R. (2010). *The immortal life of Henrietta Lacks*. New York: Random House.

Spellers, R. E. (2003). The kink factor: A womanist discourse analysis of African American mother/daughter perspectives on negotiating black hair/body politics. In R. L. Jackson & E. Richardson (Eds.), *Understanding African American rhetoric: Classical origins to contemporary innovation*. New York: Routledge.

Spellers, R. E., & Moffitt, K. R. (Eds.). (2010). *Blackberries and Redbones: Critical Articulations of Black Hair/Body Politics in Africana Communities*. Creskill, NJ: Hampton Press.

Stacks, D. W., & Salwen, M. B. (2009). *An integrated approach to communication theory and research*. New York: Routledge.

Stead, L. A., Lash, T. L., Sobieraj, J. E., Chi, D. D., Westrup, J. L., Charlot, M., . . . Rosenberg, C. L. (2009). Triple-negative breast cancers are increased in black women regardless of age or body mass index. *Breast Cancer Research* 11(2): R18. doi: 10.1186/bcr2242.

Sterba, K., Burris, J., Heiney, S., Ruppel, M., Ford, M., & Zapka, J. (2014). "We both just trusted and leaned on the Lord": a qualitative study of religiousness and spirituality among African American breast cancer survivors and their caregivers. *Quality Of Life Research, 23*(7), 1909–1920. doi:10.1007/s11136-014-0654-3.

Stiel, L., Adkins-Jackson, P. B., Clark, P., Mitchell, E., & Montgomery, S. (2016). A review of hair product use on breast cancer risk in African American women. *Cancer Medicine.* Accessed http://onlinelibrary.wiley.com/doi/10.1002/cam4.613/epdf.

Sulik, G. A. (2010). *Pink ribbon blues: How breast cancer culture undermines women's health.* New York: Oxford University Press.

Sulik, G., & Deane, A. (2008). Coping in Pink: Representations of Breast Cancer Support and Survivorship in Women's Magazines. *Conference Papers -- American Sociological Association,* 1.

Sumi, C., Crenshaw, K. W., & McCall, L. (2013). Toward a Field of Intersectionality Studies: Theory, Applications, and Praxis. *Signs: Journal Of Women In Culture & Society, 38*(4), 785–810.

Surveillance Epidemiology and End Results – SEER. (2011). Cancer of the Breast SEER Stat Fact Sheet. Retrieved from http://seer.cancer.gov/statfacts/html/breast.html.

Taylor, T. R., Williams, C. D., Makambi, K. H., Mouton, C., Harrell, J. P., Cozier, Y. . . . & Adams-Campbell, L. L. (2007). Racial discrimination and breast cancer incidence in US Black women. *American Journal of Epidemiology* 166(1): 46–54.

The Reiki Center. (2016). *What is reiki?* Retrieved from http://www.thereikicenter.net/what-is-reiki.html.

Thomas, A. J., Witherspoon, K. M., & Speight, S. L. (2004). Toward the development of the Stereotypic Roles for Black Women Scale. *Journal of Black Psychology, 30,* 426–442.

Tiedtke, C., de Rijk, A., Dierckx de Casterlé, B., Christiaens, M., & Donceel, P. (2010). Experiences and concerns about "returning to work" for women breast cancer survivors: a literature review. *Psycho-Oncology, 19*(7), 677–683. doi:10.1002/pon.1633.

Turner, D., Adams, E., Boulton, M., Harrison, S., Khan, N., Rose, P., & ... Watson, E. (2013). Partners and close family members of long-term cancer survivors: health status, psychosocial well-being and unmet supportive care needs. *Psycho-Oncology, 22*(1), 12–19. doi:10.1002/pon.2050.

Tuskegee University (2015). *U.S. Public Health Service Syphilis Study.* Retrieved from http://www.tuskegee.edu/about_us/centers_of_excellence/bioethics_center/about_the_usphs_syphilis_study.aspx.

United States Breast Cancer Statistics. (2016). Retrieved from http://www.breastcancer.org/symptoms/understand_bc/statistics.

Unites States Census Bureau. *2012 Statistical Abstract.* Retrieved from https://www.census.gov/compendia/statab/cats/labor_force_employment_earnings.html.

United States Department of Health and Human Services, Public Health Service, National Institutes of Health, National Cancer Institute (n.d.). *Making Health Communication Programs That Work (The Pink Book).* Retrieved from http://www.cancer.gov/publications/health-communication/pink-book.pdf.

United States Department of Health and Human Services. (2011). *Obesity and African Americans.* Retrieved from http://minorityhealth.hhs.gov/templates/content.aspx?lvl=3&lvlID=537&ID=6456.

United States Department of Health and Human Services. (2013). *Cancer and African Americans.* Retrieved from http://minorityhealth.hhs.gov/omh/browse.aspx?lvl=4&lvlid=16.

United States Department of Health and Human Services. (2005). *Theory at a glance.* National Institutes of Health. Retrieved from https://www.k4health.org/sites/default/files/NCI%20Theory%20at%20a%20Glance.pdf.

United States Department of Health and Human Services Office on Women's Health. (2015). *Minority women.* Retrieved from http://womenshealth.gov/minority-health/african-americans/.

Van Sertima, I. (1995). *Black women in antiquity.* The Journal of African Civilizations, LTD, Inc.

Villagran, M. M., Fox, L. J., O'Hair, D. H. (2007). Patient communication processes: An agency-identity model for cancer care. In H. D. O'Hair, G. L. Kreps, & L. Sparks

(Eds.), *The handbook of communication and cancer care.* Cresskill, NJ: Hampton Press, Inc.

Walker, A. (1983). *In search of our mother's gardens: Womanist prose.* San Diego, CA: Harcourt Brace Jovanovich.

Wallace, M. (1990). *Black macho and the myth of the superwoman.* London: Verso.

Washington, H. (2006). *Medical apartheid: The dark history of medical experimentation on Black Americans from colonial times to the present.* New York: Doubleday.

Watts, J. (2010). bell hooks on self-esteem. *Essence Magazine.* Retrieved from http://www.essence.com/2010/03/03/bell-hooks-self-esteem.

Wesley, Y. (2009). *Black Women's Health: Challenges and Opportunities.* New York: Nova Science Publishers, Inc.

White, M. L., Peters, R., & Meyers-Schim, S. (2011). Spirituality and Spiritual Self-care: Expanding self-care deficit nursing theory. *Nursing Science Quarterly, 24 (1), 46–48.*

Williams, D. (1993). *Sisters in the wilderness: The challenge of womanist God talk.* Maryknoll, NY: Orbis Books.

Williams, T. (2008). *Black Pain: It only looks like we're not hurting.* New York: Simon & Schuster, Inc.

Winterich, J. (2007). "Aging, Femininity, and the Body: What Appearance Changes Mean to Women with Age." *Gender Issues,* 24, 51–69.

Woods-Giscombé, C. L. (2010). Superwoman Schema: African American Women's Views on Stress, Strength, and Health. *Qualitative Health Research,* 20(5), 668–683. http://doi.org/10.1177/1049732310361892.

Wyatt, G. E. (1997). *Stolen women: Reclaiming our sexuality, taking back our lives.* New York: John Wiley & Sons, Inc.

Index

Abel, Emily, 16
adjuvant therapy, 65n3
African American (AA) defined, xi
American Cancer Society Cancer Facts and Figures for African Americans, 16
Asante, Molefi Kete, 23, 35n3
audience analysis. *See* communication
autobiographical/autoethnography, xxi, 8–10. *See also* qualitative methodology and research design
Avery, Bylley, 60

background and theoretical framing, xix, 1–4. *See also* Black feminist thought; health communication; standpoint theory interlocking components; womanist, theology
Beauboef-LaFontant,Tamara, 16
Behind the Mask of the Strong Black Woman: Voice and the Embodiment of a Costly Performance, 16
Black defined, xi. *See also* African American (AA) defined
Black feminist thought, 4
Black Women of Antiquity, 64, 70
Black women's health: chronic health issues defined, xv; disparities, 42; list of conditions common in African American women, 6; optimal standards, xiv; state of, xiii. *See also* body politics
Blackwomenshealth.org, 1
The Black Women's Health Imperative, 51, 60
Black Women's Health Study from 1997–2003, 16
body politics, 59
breast cancer: culture research questions, 69; five year survival rates, 1; health survey, 51; historical data, 63; triple negative, 1. *See also* mortality; pink ribbon culture; survivor
Brooks Tatum, Shanesha, 60
Bureau of Labor Statistics, 45

Cannon, Katie G., 26
caregiver fatigue, 54
Centers for Disease Control, xv
Center for Family Policy and Practice, 45
centric, 4
Coggin, Claudia, 2
commercialization/commodification, 38; pink products, 62; women's illness, 41
communication, 5; audience analysis, 23, 26; Black family, 54; communal, 11, 18; conversation monitoring, 18; conversation patterns, xxi
coping strategies, 59; decision making, 5; faithtalk, 29; long-term wellness, 3; passive coping, 21; self-help, xviii; writing, 54
Cummings, Melbourne S., 23, 35n4

Davis, Shardé, 18

environmental stress, 42
Essence magazine, xiii
ethnography, 6

faithtalk: Christian slogans, 28, 68; defined, 18, 24, 27; healing scriptures, 24; renegotiated faithtalk, 26; research questions, 68, 69; work, 47
faith tradition, Black, 22; silence, 39

family perceptions, 52–53. *See also* work and family
Fisher Collins, Catherine, xxii

Galloway, Alika P., 26
gender roles, 49
Grant, Jacquelyn, 26

hair, 42
Handbook of Communication and Cancer Care, 5
health communication: agency-identity model, 5; message construction, 5; theories for, 60, 61
Hill Collins, Patricia, 13, 37
holistic treatments, 22
hooks, bell: interview, xiii
Hurston, Zora Neale, 13

identity: four cancer identities, xvii; negotiate, 4; three aspects of identity, 5, 6. *See also* health communication
illness as punishment, 26

Judeo-Christian, 23

labor, 46. *See also* work and family
Lacks, Henrietta, 9
leisure and literacy, 38
Lorde, Audre: *The Cancer Journals*, xvii, xix–xx; quote, xvi

media representation, 29, 38; Cancer Treatment Centers of America, 43. *See also* stereotypes; survivors
Medical Apartheid the Dark History of Medical Experimentation on Black Americans from Colonial Times to the Present, 9
mental health: affects, 2; depression anxiety, 49; environmental and psychosocial, 43, 47; family impact, 53; societal stressors, xvi; stress factors/psyche, 16–17
mortality: breast cancer mortality rates, 1; chronic illness and mortality rates, xiii, 21; expectancy defined, xiv; leading causes of death by age, 6; life and death, xiv, 53

narrative: of self-care, 59; of strength, 2–3; of survivorship, 2. *See also* reframing the narrative
Neumann, Noelle, 62
nommo, 23
normalcy, 48

palliative care, 58n5
The Pink and the Black Project©, xx; Pink and Black superwoman, xxi, 51; research questions, 67, 70
pink ribbon culture: defined, xix, 38, 67; history of, 40–41; pinkwashing/backlash, 41
Pinn, Vivian W., xvi
political action, 64
Price, Betty R., 25
privacy, 49

qualitative methodology and research design, 5–8

reframing the narrative, 59–60; *See also* narrative
reiki laying on of hands, 22
religious practice, 21; faith movement, prosperity gospel, 24, 35n5; healing school, 25
rest, xx

self-care, 5; is subversive, 60
Shaw-Perry, Mary, 2
silence, xvii, xviii; culture of, 62; family medical history, 39; self-imposed, 49; spiral of silence, 38. *See also* privacy; voice
skin bleaching, 43
Smith, Vernell, 31. *See also* leisure and literacy; narrative; voice
social issues, xvi, xxii
social media. *See* voice
social support network, 3
spirituality. *See* faithtalk; religious practice
standpoint theory interlocking components, 37

stereotypes, 11; "isms", age, race, class, gender, 11, 65; matriarch/welfare mother/Jezebel, 13–15; mule/workhorse, 13, 46. *See also* identity; strong Black woman

strength, resiliency, survival imagery, and metaphors, xviii

stress. *See* mental health

strong Black woman: collective, 18; cost of strength, 16; defined/discussed, xviii, 11, 68; historical context, 12; superwoman/super-shero, 64

Subramanian, Saskia, 16

Sulik, Gayle, xxii, 38

Superwoman Schema, 17; conceptual framework, 19

support groups, 25

survivor: counting survivorship in years, xxiii, 65n2; long-term survivor, xxi, 2; survivorship meaning of, xxii. *See also* breast cancer

televangelists, 24

Toko, Yvette, 54. *See also* leisure and literacy; narrative; voice

trifecta of strength, xxi, 7

Tuskegee Syphilis Experiments, 9

US Census, 45

US Department of Health and Human Services: Minority Health Report, 16; Office on Women's Health, xv

visibility of Black women's health, xvi

voice: in research, xvi; virtual spaces, 41; vote, 65. *See also* leisure and literacy

Walker, Alice, 4

Washington, Harriet, 9

Watts, Jenisha, xiii

Williams, Delores, 26

Williams, Terri, 17. *See also* mental health

womanist: theologians, 26, 35n11; theology, 1, 4

Women of Color Health Data Book, xv

women's health movement and Black women, xiii

Woods-Giscombé, Cheryl, 17

work and family, 45; family, 51, 58n2; financial stress, 48; time off/sick leave, 47; work life balance, 48; youth, 58n4

Wyatt, Gail, 13

About the Author

Dr. **Annette D. Madlock Gatison** is an associate professor in the Department of Communication at Southern Connecticut State University. She completed her doctoral work in Communication at Howard University. Her primary research interests explore social activism, health, and media as it relates to Black women's health both globally and domestically. Issues of identity, family, and work-life balance and policy and socioeconomic factors are explored through content, discourse, and thematic analysis as well as focus groups, interviews, and survey methods. Other significant areas of scholarship include the intersection of communication within S.T.E.M. careers.

To ground and inform her research and applied approach, Dr. Madlock Gatison serves on Breast Cancer Consortium Advisory Board, an international partnership committed to the scientific and public discourse about breast cancer that promotes collaborative initiatives among researchers, advocates, health professionals, educators, and others who focus on the systemic factors that impact breast cancer as an individual experience, a social problem, and a health epidemic. She is also a graduate of the National Breast Cancer Coalition's Project L.E.A.D. which is an intensive science institute taught by renowned research faculty covering the basics of cancer biology, genetics, epidemiology, research design, and advocacy.

Dr. Madlock Gatison has presented over 35 papers at various professional conferences and has been a featured speaker at various community education and women's conferences. She has also published selections in the following SAGE References: *Encyclopedia of Communication Research Methods*, 2016; *Encyclopedia of Cancer and Society, 2nd Edition*, 2015; *Multimedia Encyclopedia of Women in Today's World*, 2012; among others. Her most recent publication, *Communicating Women's Health: Social Norms That Influence Health Decisions* (Routledge, 2015), is an edited volume that explores the sociocultural dynamics of women's health from diverse ethnic and racial backgrounds.